CURRICULUM
DEVELOPMENT
IN NONGRADED
SCHOOLS

Bold New Venture

ALREADY PUBLISHED IN THE

Bold New Venture *Series*

TEAM TEACHING
INDEPENDENT STUDY
FLEXIBLE SCHEDULING
PROGRAMMED INSTRUCTION
TEACHING FOR CREATIVE ENDEAVOR
EDUCATIONAL MANPOWER
INSTRUCTIONAL TELEVISION
INSTRUCTIONAL MEDIA CENTER

CURRICULUM DEVELOPMENT IN NONGRADED SCHOOLS

Bold New Venture

EDITED BY

EDWARD G. BUFFIE

AND

JOHN M. JENKINS

INDIANA UNIVERSITY PRESS

BLOOMINGTON AND LONDON

To Dave, who affected the lives of people,
an educator who made a difference. Our friend—
gone but not forgotten.

Preface

Bold New Venture Series

AMERICAN EDUCATION is emerging as a new frontier. Staggering challenges brought about by the contemporary demand for quality education for a bulging and diverse student population must be met. Old solutions for new problems will not suffice.

Pioneer educators are testing promising new programs and practices to effect fundamental improvement in the schools. Healthy dissatisfactions have led to the belief that if the schools are to be significantly better, they will have to be substantially different. Both the substance and the form of instruction are undergoing searching reappraisal. Exciting innovations have been instituted in schools scattered throughout the country. The *Bold New Venture* series is designed to inform educators and the interested public about these new developments and to assist in their evaluation.

The books in this series differ from much of the professional literature in education. The contributors, for the most part, are practitioners. Admittedly they are partial to their topics. Nevertheless, pitfalls are exposed and candid treatment is given to the issues. Emphasis has been put on reporting *how* as well as *why* new practices and programs were inaugurated. The volumes in this series are intended to be a stimulus to the conversation which must take place if fresh methods of teaching are to find their way into the schools.

Topics included in the *Bold New Venture* series include team teaching, flexible scheduling, independent study, the nongraded school, instructional materials centers, data processing, small group instruction, and technological aids.

While journalists criticize, scholars theorize about, and philosophers analyze education, the teachers of America must act. Educators must leap from theory to practice in individualizing instruction. More responsibility must be given and accepted by youngsters for their own learning. Intellectual inquiry must become full-time, leisure-time, and life-time pursuits.

Progress in education does not always come by the process of addition with more teachers, more books, more courses, and more money. Real improvement can come from original uses of scarce human talent, precious time, and new methods.

Because it is intended primarily for teachers and administrators, the *Bold New Venture* series focuses on the practical problems of teaching. What has been operationally successful for some teachers may have application for other teachers. If new practices or programs result from these books, then the series will have fulfilled its aim, for the *Bold New Venture* books are calls and guides to action.

BLOOMINGTON, INDIANA   Edward G. Buffie

Contents

Introduction   xi

PART I THE DISCUSSION

IN RETROSPECT
1 A Historical Perspective   *Edward G. Buffie*   3
ELEMENTARY SCHOOL EDUCATION
2 The Nongraded School: A Dynamic Concept
                                       Maurie Hillson   28
3 Establishing Nongraded Reading Programs
                                       Carl Bernard Smith   54
4 Science: Focus on Process   *Roger Cunningham*   76
5 Social Studies: Dynamics of Change *Dorothy J. Skeel*   102
MIDDLE SCHOOL EDUCATION
6 Nongrading the Middle Years   *Ann Grooms*   113
SECONDARY SCHOOL EDUCATION
7 The Nongraded High School   *John M. Jenkins*   135
8 The Curriculum in the Nongraded High School:
   Restoration of Curiosity   *John M. Jenkins*   152

PART II A LOOK TO THE FUTURE

9 Research Has a Word: Some Generalizations
                                       Henry J. Otto   171
10 A Strategy for the Development of Nongraded Schools
                                       Roy A. Larmee   188

PART III THE PROCESS OF BECOMING

11 Exemplary Centers for Continuous Progress Education
    Title III Project in the State of Utah   *Edwin A. Read*   207

12   The Development Research Center
     The Nova Schools, Broward County, Fla.
                                   Warren G. Smith   243

13   The House Plan
     The Fox Lane Middle School, Bedford, N.Y.
                                   Peter Telfer, Jr.   252

14   Student Responsibility for Learning
     Meadowbrook Junior High School, Newton, Mass.
                                   Maurice Blum   257

15   Secondary Continuous Advancement Program
     Binford Junior High School, Bloomington, Ind.
                                   Martha A. Lee   268

16   The Frontier of Change
     Ridgewood High School, Norridge, Ill.
                                   Scott G. Richardson   284

17   New Dimensions
     Archbishop Ryan Memorial High School, Omaha, Neb.
                                   Sister M. Pacis Roth, o.s.f.   295

18   A School That Cares
     Miami Springs Senior High School, Miami Springs, Fla.
                                   Kenneth D. Jenkins   300

     Selected Bibliography and Addendum   307
     Index   327

Introduction

SOME IMPORTANT CHANGES have been brought about in education. But *some* changes are not enough. If the elementary and secondary schools of the United States are to be improved significantly, they must be substantially different.

The schools must provide quality education for every youngster. To do so the instructional program must be personal, flexible, and without artificial limits. Personal intellectual needs and interests must be accounted for in designing instruction on an individual basis for each learner. Standards, policies, and programs must be flexible to be appropriate for the individual requirements of a widely diverse school population. Administrative policies and organizational arrangements must not set limits that will restrict the maximum development of the able and ambitious learner or frustrate the slow and disadvantaged learner. The schools of today must leap from theory to practice in individualizing instruction. New methods must replace old traditions of school organization. The nongraded school concept is proposed as a practical means of improving teaching and learning.

Monumental effort has been expended to bring about improvements in the programs of studies in both elementary and secondary schools. Scholars of the highest stature have given attention to the content of science, mathematics, and modern foreign language courses. English and social studies are undergoing searching reappraisals. Curriculum reform is in the air. But as valuable as improved course content is, it alone is not enough to provide quality education for all youth. There is a need for a new organization for learning to make individual methods of instruction a standard mode of operation.

The Teacher's Role

Teaching is more than talking. Learning is more than listening. The teaching–learning process requires a diagnosis of the individual student by the teacher and a high degree of personal involvement by the learner. Effective teaching requires close observation of the student by the teacher. Ample time must be provided for students to work individually, sometimes with and other times without the teacher at hand. Careful prescriptions by the teacher of appropriate learning activities need to be given to every child. The school's organization should make it possible for teachers to meet with students on an individual basis to make particular recommendations for study. Students need to be able to work at their own rate on subjects they are best able to handle.

Even when instruction is given in groups, learning is an individual enterprise. Group membership often puts a burden on the learner. Group progress is sometimes too rapid, other times too slow. In either case, the individual is disadvantaged. The focus of the group will nearly always be only in the shadows of interest or understanding for some individuals. The school's organization for instruction must therefore be reformed so that personal attention takes the place of group teaching practices.

The nongraded school is a promise for progress in education. Such an organization for learning values highly and places profound faith in the professional competence of its teachers and implies that each student has unique instructional needs.

Individual Not Group Focus

The nongraded school ignores group classifications, with their attendant individual transgressions, and focuses instead on nurturing each human being, regardless of how his accomplishments compare with those of others of his age. The establishment of the nongraded school does not imply a radical departure from the accepted educational objectives of American schools. The nongraded organization helps teachers and students meet those objectives more easily and with new and personal advantage. The nongraded school gives considered attention to human variability. The goal of quality education for every student is the foundation of such a school. However, for some teachers, nongrad-
vastly different mind-set about how the schools are to be ordered, as
edness does demand new approaches to instruction and requires a
the program descriptions in this book show.

The nongraded school offers advantages to teachers as well as to students. For students, the nongraded school offers freedom from the un-reasonable assumption that one lesson, one course, and one set of re-quirements suit all. For teachers, the nongraded school organization offers the opportunity to exercise personal judgment, give skillful ser-vice, and receive increased professional satisfaction. In the nongraded school, the teacher makes a diagnosis, gives a prescription, and some-times even works as a therapist while learning takes place. Teaching takes on a new meaning as an intimate, strong relationship is built be-tween student and teacher.

The Rate of Adoption

The spread of nongraded schools has been both alarmingly slow and surprisingly rapid. Contrasted with the increased introduction of new programs in science, mathematics, and foreign languages, the non-graded movement has been slow in development. But there are no fed-eral funds to sponsor institutes, prepare guides, and concentrate on development for the nongraded school, as there have been for content revisions. The introduction of the nongraded concept requires wide-spread faculty participation in the innovation, while in changes of course content, only the teachers in a particular subject are called upon to alter their programs. In spite of these factors, the nongraded organi-zation has increased in use in recent years at an unusual rate, consider-ing that adoption of this concept implies the rejection of the traditional way teachers were taught to teach.

National study groups can develop grand statements of purpose, and scholars can follow scholars in developing new materials, but in the end the teachers and administrators are the ones who must decide how and what youngsters will be taught. The faculty in every school has a great potential for improving instruction. Some ignore this potential by refusing to search for more effective ways to teach, but others—and happily the number is increasing—are actively seeking better solutions for educational problems.

This Book

The organization of this book comprises three major components. Part I presents a discussion of the nongraded concept. The rationale and the historical development of school organization are discussed in Chapter 1. Further elaboration of the concept with particular emphasis on implication for curriculum follows in Chapters 2–8.

Part II is concerned with the process of curriculum change and development, and the procedures and problems related to the establishment of nongraded schools.

In Part III, Chapters 11–18 provide in-depth descriptions of schools in the "process of becoming" nongraded models. The scope of these programs ranges from individual schools to a school cluster in Florida and a statewide program in Utah. All these efforts to institute nongraded programs are indeed *bold new ventures*. While the ultimate is yet to be achieved, each effort in its own way is truly in the "process of becoming."

If this book helps teachers to examine critically the instructional arrangements in their schools, it will have satisfied one of its purposes. If this book is any help to schools in introducing a nongraded program, it will have achieved its ultimate purpose.

Acknowledgments

WITHOUT THE GENEROUS cooperation and interest of countless educators this book would not have been possible. Some helped by discussing informally the need for a book on the nongraded school. Others assisted by recommending contributors and by evaluating the raw manuscript. Still others interrupted their busy schedules to write chapters for this book.

A single author would be hard pressed to present the range of ideas expressed here. This book is intended as a guide to action as well as a discussion of certain educational theories. Much of it represents the experience the contributors have had in their own schools.

Special mention must be given to our colleagues in the public schools and in the universities. With their questions and assertions, and through our association with them, our convictions about the nongraded school were formulated and cemented. We are particularly indebted to Dr. Robert H. Anderson, Professor, Graduate School of Education, Harvard University; Dr. B. Frank Brown, former principal of Melbourne (Florida) High School; and Dr. J. Lloyd Trump, Associate Executive Secretary of the National Association of Secondary School Principals Association, for their professional inspiration.

BLOOMINGTON, IND.   Edward G. Buffie
CLARKSVILLE, MD.   John M. Jenkins

CURRICULUM DEVELOPMENT IN NONGRADED SCHOOLS

Bold New Venture

PART I

THE DISCUSSION

CHAPTER 1

A Historical Perspective

by

EDWARD G. BUFFIE

*Throughout his professional career, Dr. Buffie has been asso-
ciated with innovations in education. He was an elementary
school teacher and later an administrator in the nongraded
primary schools in Park Forest, Illinois—one of the first communities to use a nongraded organization. He has served as
curriculum coordinator, principal, and consultant to the Indiana University Laboratory School.*

*Dr. Buffie is chairman of the Department of Elementary
Education at Indiana University, and co-author of* Nongraded
Schools in Action *(with Beggs) and* Educational Manpower:
From Aides to Differentiated Staff Patterns *(with Olivero).*

THE MOST WIDELY ACCEPTED PLAN of school organization today is the
graded school plan in which each grade level represents a pre-determined year of work and the subject content for all the pupils is approximately the same. Despite numerous attempts to change this basic organizational structure, the schools in our country, with few exceptions,
have maintained this traditional graded structure for well over a century. The time has come to reconsider and revise the school's organization to make it serve the educational demands of these times. Today,
there is little consolation in Alexander Pope's comment: "Not to go back
is somewhat to advance."

Historical Development of Elementary School Organization

This nation has every right to be proud of its public education. The
United States was one of the first countries to develop an educational

system designed to provide free public education for all its people. Although it evolved from a combination of social and economic factors present in the early development of our democracy, the system also owed much of its organization and philosophy to the European countries from which the colonists emigrated.

As each wave of colonization brought people from different countries to the New World, a variety of European traditions were transplanted. The dame school, the district school, the writing school, the Latin grammar school, and the college were based almost completely on counterparts in England, France, and Spain. The greatest scholastic influence, however, came from England.

The schools were not always graded in the colonies; the seventeenth-century dame schools and the eighteenth-century district schools disregarded grade classification. In the dame school children ranging in age from three to ten met together for instruction and youngsters usually received twenty minutes or so of individualized help twice a day. The rest of the time they either worked on written lessons or listened to the older students.

Children attended the district schools only when the teacher and school came to their particular district. The teacher simply picked up where he had left off at the end of the last trip. Each district school was organized for a specific academic purpose and followed similar practices in accepting children of various ages and abilities. The pupils met together in a single room and worked under the direction of a single teacher, primarily on an individual basis. Identification of pupils by grade levels was generally unknown and promotion came only after students had mastered enough of the fundamentals to succeed at the Latin school or in college.

By the beginning of the eighteenth century, the dame schools were well established. Together, the writing school and the dame school provided all the reading and writing instruction considered essential in that era. These lower schools were terminal for the masses, and promotion to higher schools, especially for girls, was rare indeed. But in those times, for most people, to be educated was to be able to read and handle simple arithmetic processes.

Soon, however, educational leaders began to envision a unified system of education, publicly controlled and supported, and open to all in order to meet the needs of the emerging democratic society. Long before the beginning of the national period, elementary education began to assume the character of the one-room schoolhouse, long to be a familiar part of the American scene. This type of district school achieved a certain permanency, and accepted pupils of any age. Small, one-room schools soon dotted the landscape. Mostly because of their small enrollments, these schools were ungraded.

Samuel Hall, in 1823, and James G. Carter, in 1827, opened the first normal schools in the United States, fashioning them after German examples. Thus, the teacher-training institution in this country was on its way. The last half of the nineteenth century saw these institutions contribute to the spread of the graded structure. As they trained teachers, they instilled in them a belief in a precise order for instruction and promoted a common educational practice based on the graded school system.

Another development that had considerable impact on the movement toward the graded structure was the appearance of the graded textbook. The phenomenal acceptance of the 1836 edition of the *McGuffey Eclectic Reader*, which was graded through six levels, was enough to encourage others to produce graded textbooks. Textbook series—available first in reading and arithmetic—were soon on the market for all areas of the curriculum.

Finally, the influence of European educational thought and policy was once again felt as leading American educators who had traveled to Europe returned to extol the virtues of foreign schools. Horace Mann was particularly impressed with his visit to the graded schools in Prussia, and he returned to urge the adoption of a similar system in this country during the 1840's.

All these developments, together with the tremendous increase in the number of children flocking to the schools and the new state laws lengthening school terms and extending the number of years of schooling led to a system of classifying pupils according to a predetermined criterion based solely on age. Goodlad and Anderson[1] give a good description of the major developments that ultimately resulted in the creation of the graded school.

As early as 1799, in Middlesex County, Conn., and 1800, in Providence, R.I., school districts had been calling for some kind of pupil classification. (The desire of educators to classify pupils in instructional groups is deep in the professional grain.) While there is disagreement as to the exact origin of the graded school, the Quincy Grammar School, established in 1848, is generally recognized as the first graded structure in the United States. The merits of the graded plan, particularly its administrative convenience, caused it to take hold quickly, and wherever applicable, the system spread. It came to be expected that arithmetic would be learned at a certain age, writing at another, and that each grade would have as its goal some particular set of accomplishments. By 1870, our present system of graded schools, graded textbooks, and grade-oriented teachers was firmly established.

The development of the graded elementary school in the nineteenth century was a significant creative effort appropriate for its time. Goodlad and Anderson state:

> It permitted the convenient classification of unprecedented numbers of pupils pouring into the schools during the second half of the century. It encouraged the division of knowledge into segments to be taught at the various grade levels. Consequently, it simplified the task of preparing needed teachers quickly; teachers were simply taught what they were themselves to teach in a given grade. Man's zeal for efficiency was challenged and he met the challenge vigorously. Soon an enterprise of gigantic proportions was functioning with amazing efficiency while continuing to expand at an astonishing rate. That so many people agreed so quickly and so generally on distinct learning tasks for each grade level is truly amazing.[2]

After the graded system came the monitorial system, which put the older and, hopefully, the more able student in the role of teacher's helper. The schoolmaster would teach a lesson to the more apt of his students, and they, in turn, would attempt to teach what they had learned to their immediate subordinates. The responsibility of these monitors extended even to examining and promoting the pupils for whom they were responsible.

Early Innovations

Within a period of approximately twenty years the graded elementary school organization spanned the nation. Soon a few rumblings were heard, and it became clear that not all educators agreed completely on its merits. The same educational system that gloried in its new-found efficiency also gave rise to an inhibiting form of regimentation. The pendulum had swung from no system to nothing but system. Heavy pupil dropout, resulting from too much rigidity in teaching methods and an unbending method of annual promotion, was viewed by some educators with dismay. Educators began to speak out against the graded system as one that demanded mass conformity. To the critics, it seemed as if the uniqueness of each individual was being overlooked in the schools' organization. Consequently, innovations designed to correct some of the more obvious defects of the early graded schools began to appear.

Early attempts to modify the basic, rigid pattern (as well as those that followed throughout the remainder of the nineteenth and into the early twentieth century) usually tried to vary the instructional program within the framework of the graded school, rather than trying to break down the existing graded structure. Thus, the interest of the post-Sputnik days in special classes for gifted students was not new.

The galaxy of plans and approaches that emerged were all variations on the graded regimentation. Some attempted to temper the adverse effects of grading, particularly failing; others tried to provide more realistically for the differences in groups of children progressing through school; others were designed to provide opportunities for individuals to progress at varying rates through the curriculum. Still another plan examined the teacher's position and how his strengths might best be employed.

The graded structure has long been a concern of thoughtful educators, but variations of the graded structure, rather than departures from it, were the means used to compensate for its weaknesses.

Problems of Failure

Not too many years after the graded movement became popular, one of its less fortunate by-products—pupil failure—became apparent. "I failed first grade" became a horrendous phrase heard much too often. Failing reached its awesome peak in the 1920's, when some of our large eastern cities were reporting failure rates for first grade pupils as high as 40 percent.[3]

Several school systems created plans with more frequent promotion in the hopes that they would offset failure. In the Elizabeth (New Jersey) Plan, for example, there was promotion three times a year. If a student failed in this plan, it was not quite as bad as failing in a community that had only annual promotion. The best-known of these attempts was the St. Louis (Missouri) Plan. Even though St. Louis had formally adopted the graded plan of organization in 1857, by 1862 a new course of study was in operation in which some of the recognized disadvantages of graded organization, particularly with regard to promotion and retention, could be lessened if not eliminated. The year's work was divided into four ten-week units, and promotions were made every ten weeks. Quarterly promotion was a unique variation in comparison to what was then in vogue. Reports are not clear as to how successful this experiment was within its own sphere, but the quarterly plan had very little impact on the national level and was not generally adopted.

Focus on Groups

Most of the early innovations based on the first graded schools were concerned with the lock-step pace in which all children proceeded through the schools. Although grade programs did not vary, the children did vary widely in many ways, and educators began to vary the curriculum to cope with these extreme differences. However, the programs were changed very little except for placing the children in ability groups so that the length of time each group spent on any particular phase of the curriculum could vary. Still, individuals were treated as members of a group of 30 students or more most of the time.

The Cambridge (Massachusetts) Plan and the Portland (Oregon) Plan are good examples of attempts to provide for individual differences within the group organization. In Cambridge, in 1895, a plan was devised wherein all pupils would take the same work during the first three years of a nine-year elementary course. The work of the last six years was arranged in two parallel courses, with the regular course for average students taking the full six years to complete, while a special advanced course for brighter pupils required only four years. By 1910, in Cambridge, the elementary curriculum had been reduced to eight years, and the double-track system extended down to the first grade.

In Portland, Oregon, in 1900, a nine-grade course of study was divided into 54 units. The average children covered six units each year; the bright children were placed in a separate division and permitted to take eight units each year, thus completing elementary school in seven years. Elements of this plan have been found in various other plans, but inadequate data make it difficult to determine the extent to which it was adopted by other schools.

At Batavia, New York, special provision was made for slow-learning pupils. Interestingly, the emphasis here was on the slow student rather than on the average or bright student. At this time, classes were large, consisting of 80 or more students, and two teachers worked with each class—the direct instruction teacher and an assistant. The slow children received special instruction from the assistant teacher in the back of the room, and this extra work was expected to help them come up to standard. This plan was in effect for approximately 30 years in Batavia and elsewhere in various forms. Certain phases of the plan can be recognized in the various special classes in existence today, such as remedial reading, which are designed specifically to bolster achievement of particular youngsters.

Other attempts were made to vary not only the rate of progress but also the content. The North Denver (Colorado) Plan was just the reverse of the Batavia Plan. Here the bright children were singled out for additional instruction. Classroom organization remained the same with all pupils covering certain minimum requirements or assignments. However, enriched work was provided for the brighter students, and each classroom was provided with 50 to 75 carefully selected library books for their use.

The Santa Barbara (California) Concentric Plan, devised by Frederick Burk, called for the division of pupils into three groups designated A, B, and C. The C group did the basic work; B did a little more; and the A group did the most work. This plan also provided for promotion three times a year. After it had been in effect only a short time, it was reported that the plan had been discontinued because it was too impractical and difficult to administer. It can be assumed the benefits to the students were less telling than the work involved for the educators.

Undaunted, Frederick Burk moved to the San Francisco Normal School and extended the Pueblo Plan, which had been developed earlier by Preston W. Search. Grades were still retained, but the curriculum was organized into various units. Successful test performance completed the work of a given unit in a subject. There were no grade failures and children simply moved forward on an irregular front, subject by subject, according to the number of units completed.

Focus on Individuals

Even as interest in providing challenge within the curriculum for groups of varying abilities continued to grow and gain impetus, another interest posed a new question: What about the development of the individual?

Preston W. Search, superintendent of schools in Pueblo, Colorado, from 1888 to 1894, has been given credit for being the first American educator to protest loudly against the class lock-step method of teaching and to argue for complete individual progress for each pupil. His idea was put into practical application during his tenure in Pueblo, and later in Los Angeles, where he was superintendent in 1895. This was one of the first attempts to bring about a radical change at the high school level.

Each high school subject was outlined in such a way that each child could progress at his own rate in each subject. All the units in each course were studied by every student but at varying rates. No marks were given, the concept of nonpromotion was eliminated, and teachers' records simply indicated the number of units completed satisfactorily. Emphasis was on individual work and progress as opposed to group work and group progress. While this plan was applied most extensively in high school, Search believed that it could be used in the elementary school.

Again, how extensively the basic principles of this plan were utilized and adopted in other cities is difficult to assess. Although the term Pueblo Plan has been obscured through the years, there is evidence that its influence was strongly felt and that it had considerable impact on the programs and thinking found in subsequent deviations from group-centered educational practices. In his own writings, Search gives many illustrations of school practices that embodied certain elements of his Pueblo Plan. The work done a little later by Morrison at the University of Chicago High School, the programs developed under the name of the Dalton Plan, and the elementary plans developed by Frederick Burk in San Francisco and Carleton Washburne at Winnetka, Illinois, have many interesting parallels to the pioneer enterprise of Preston Search.

Although both the Dalton Plan and the Pueblo Plan place great emphasis on the individual, the former was mostly concerned with the individual's performance in group situations. The Dalton Plan was first introduced in 1919 by Helen Parkhurst in an ungraded school for crippled children. The next year it was adopted by a high school in Dalton, Massachusetts, from which it took its name.

In the Dalton Plan the subjects were divided into academic and vocational groups. The academic subjects were organized sequentially, and students worked and progressed on an individual basis. The individual job-sheet-unit conference technique was employed. The work of each academic subject was laid out in a series of related jobs or contracts, each consisting of a number of smaller units. The learning tasks were thus identified for each child, and he was permitted to progress to the completion of his requirements, which were determined through a checking conference with his teacher. The nonacademic part of the curriculum was taught by class or group methods. There were specialized teachers and facilities, and students were grouped on a nongraded basis. Pupils had considerable freedom of choice regarding the units of work they undertook. While each pupil was free to determine his own pace, each was required to complete the corresponding grade-level units for a subject before moving on to advanced work in a single subject matter area.

The Winnetka Plan was very closely related to the Dalton Plan and perhaps better known. It derived its name from the work of Carleton Washburne in Winnetka, Illinois, where he carried on the ideas introduced by Frederick Burk in California. As in the Dalton Plan, the individualized task approach was emphasized. This idea was also developed extensively in Chicago, Illinois, by James E. McDade and in Bronxville, New York, by Willard W. Beatty.

In Winnetka the course of study was divided into two parts, one in the morning and one in the afternoon, each devoted to a different type of activity. First came "common essentials," which consisted of the so-called basic subjects—knowledge and skills that everyone, presumably, was expected to master. In this phase of the program, pupils worked on individual assignments, each at his own rate. Tests were administered at appropriate times to measure academic achievement. Established standards had to be met before successive units of work could be undertaken. The second part of the program dealt with "group and creative activities"—literature, music, art, physical education, and manual arts. Self-expression and the individual development of interests and abilities were stressed, and there were no specific standards to be met.

The quality of the Winnetka program has been recognized for several decades. However, the program has undergone several modifications since its original introduction, and for an up-to-date treatment of the program as it exists today, the reader is referred to Washburne's recent writings.[4]

Innovation and Role Change

Some innovations have had a much greater impact on the role of the teacher than have others. The plans described previously, while changing the composition of the group and the time spans, did not greatly alter the one teacher–one class relationship. However, modifications of this arrangement had also been considered.

The earliest plan for changing the one-class-per-teacher arrangement was the Platoon System. It was first established in Bluffton, Indiana, in 1900, by William A. Wirt, when he was superintendent in that small midwestern community. In 1908 Wirt moved to Gary, Indiana, and put the plan into operation there. Sometimes referred to as the "work-study-play" program, it called for the division of students into two groups. Instruction in the fundamental subjects was provided by the homeroom teacher for one group, while opportunities for activity were available to the other group. The activities included such things as manual arts, physical education, art, music, auditorium, library, nature study, and home economics, most of which required special facilities or laboratories. These areas were taught by specialists on a departmental basis. Often, some sort of special grouping by ability or I.Q. was made. Except for auditorium and gymnasium periods, the grade-level structure was maintained. By limiting the number of areas in which a teacher would give instruction, it was assumed that his proficiency in his areas of concentration would grow, and consequently, the educational program would be improved.

Departmentalization, an outgrowth of the Platoon System, gained widespread acceptance during the 1920's and 1930's, particularly at the high school level. To date, departmentalization has had a more lasting impact on education than any other organizational innovation except for the basic graded plan. Departmentalization in junior and senior high school is often taken for granted. Today, there is a trend in the direction of departmentalization at the intermediate level (grades four, five, and six).

In 1930, along with the growth of departmentalization, there was an early attempt at team teaching. The Cooperative Group Plan, as it was named, was simply an attempt to have groups of teachers, each a specialist with a classroom designed for his subject, coordinate their efforts in planning and evaluating the work of students. The primary purpose was to provide for the individual differences of both the pupils and the teachers.

Pupils in a given group usually ranged across several grade levels, so that multi-age group instruction and some degree of continuous education were possible. Children often stayed with the same group of teachers for two or three years, and each teacher in a group (there were usually three to six in a group) was expected to relate his work to the work of the others, so that the picture was one of general cooperation and unity of purpose, in which each teacher sought to capitalize on the strengths of the others. Too advanced for its time, the Cooperative Group Plan quickly disappeared and remained under cover until its vestiges were brought to life in the mid-1950's in the form of team teaching.

One of the most comprehensive and carefully designed grouping plans, the Dual Progress Plan, was developed by George D. Stoddard and his associates at New York University, in cooperation with the Long Beach, and Ossining, New York, school systems. Based on an elaborate cultural and learning-theory analysis, it represents a highly specialized and well-designed synthesis of many of the important features of earlier programs. The plan is creatively and sensitively handled and is an exciting approach to the fundamental question in education today: How can we best provide for individual differences?

In the Dual Progress plan a distinction is made between what the authors designate as cultural imperatives—English, social studies, health, and physical education—and cultural electives—mathematics, science, art, music, and foreign languages. The school day is divided into two halves: One half is devoted to the cultural imperatives under a single teacher, who generally has an academic background in English and social studies, and who functions as a homeroom teacher responsible for registration, counseling, and so forth. The other half of the day is devoted to the cultural electives, taught by teachers who are specialists and offer their subjects on a longitudinal basis.

The cultural imperatives are offered in grade units, and the students are divided into sections at each grade level according to their ability.

The electives are nongraded and organized into systematic subject sequences. The students are placed within each continuum according to their interests, ability, and performance. Scheduling is handled on a platoon basis. However, the specialist teachers must work together like a team in order to develop sequences and schedule pupils to provide best for their interests and abilities.*

Many Attempts over Many Years

The programs described above do not tell the entire story; many attempts at improving school grading systems have been made throughout the century over the decades. Those mentioned are among the better-known examples and represent a good cross section of the plans that have been described in the literature. It is evident that from 1900 to the present considerable discussion and action relating to the inadequacies of the graded pattern resulted in little agreement regarding an improved structural framework for teaching and learning. Because all the attempts to cope with the situation had been made from the point of view of a graded organization, they were off to a wrong start. The evils of the graded approach cannot be taken away if any form of the graded structure is preserved.

The graded school then, as now, is simply not in harmony with the basic purpose of American education; namely, that every child should have an opportunity to develop his talents to the fullest extent possible. If one recognizes that children vary tremendously in past achievement, potential, interest, and socioeconomic background, and if one believes what many decades of painstaking study have taught regarding learning theory and child development, it is obvious that graded schools, graded classrooms, graded textbooks, graded expectations, and graded instructors are all out of step with the goal of individualized teaching. With programs geared to the mythical average student, graded-school organization has, for the most part, simply ignored the variety in human capabilities by the very nature of its lock-step pattern and rigidity of structure.

* In a demonstration test of the Dual Progress Plan results were not very favorable due primarily to the homogeneous grouping aspects of the design. For a complete description of the results see *Organizing Schools Through the Dual Progress Plan* (Danville, Ill.: Interstate, 1967).

Like several of the innovations described in this chapter, the non-graded school is designed to implement a theory of continuous school progress. However, the nongraded plan differs very dramatically in one important aspect: It makes a complete break with the traditional graded-school organization of the past; it is not just a modification of that organizational structure. The organizational form thus complements, rather than hinders, the educational purpose of continuous progress for all pupils, who vary in all aspects of their development. Some pupil differences are great and cannot be substantially modified; therefore, it is the school structure that must be pliable enough to bend with the child. Nongrading works for, rather than against, the basic premise that each child is different. It encourages the efforts of all involved to treat this difference as a challenge, rather than as an inconvenience to be sidestepped, and it does so by its very nature.

This is not to say that the philosophy that undergirds nongraded organization could not be implemented within a graded pattern of organization, but this simply does not happen. Admittedly, there are fine schools that are not nongraded that are doing an outstanding job in curriculum planning and program development, but, unfortunately, year after year, they remain the exceptions not the rule. Similarly, there is no guarantee that a smashing curricular success will grow out of every organizational shake-up, but the likelihood of success is much improved when the organization for education that is adopted is consistent with the philosophy to which the plan's supporters subscribe.

Emergence of the Nongraded School

None of the plans described in the preceding pages, with the exception of departmentalization, withstood the test of time. Although traces of certain plans were to be found in one form or another, the search for better ways to organize schools continued.

The 1930's mark the emergence of the nongraded movement. Although it is difficult to identify the exact beginning of this organizational operation, a nongraded school at Western Springs, Illinois, seems to have been the first of its type. The method of organization was called the Flexible Progress Plan. It was initiated in 1934, and in September 1935, grades one, two, and three were abolished. In the 1936–37 school year, the program was extended to the intermediate grades. The only phase of the program in which there was actual differentiation in teaching procedures was in reading.

There were several other nongraded schools in the late 1930's. In 1936 a junior primary unit was first organized in Richmond, Virginia. This unit replaced kindergarten and first grade and is still utilized in many schools today. The College Avenue School in Athens, Georgia, has had a nongraded system called the Continuous Progress Plan in effect since 1939. At that time, a letter was sent to all the parents explaining why grade symbols were being abolished and replaced by the primary grade plan or organization. Some experimental work in the direction of nongrading was done in Fond du Lac, Wisconsin, during the late thirties under the leadership of Lowell P. Goodrich.

The development of nongraded schools in the early 1940's was reported in Petoski, Michigan, Glencoe, Illinois, and Cleveland, Ohio. However, the plan begun in 1942 in Milwaukee, Wisconsin, under Lowell P. Goodrich, is generally recognized as the oldest nongraded school plan still in existence. Certainly, this was the first large school district to initiate such a plan on a wide scale and it represented a milestone in the nongraded school movement. Today, all but two of the Milwaukee schools have ungraded primary units. Though the development of the Ungraded Primary School at Milwaukee did much to focus attention on this concept of elementary school organization, the movement remained more or less stagnant throughout the late forties.

The depression and World War II did not further the cause of educational change. In the 1950's and early 1960's the search was renewed and finally the break came. Early innovations had paved the way for a massive attack on the strict gradation of the elementary school. The nongraded school was born.

Proof that the modern nongraded school was born at the primary level came in the studies made by Goodlad in 1955.[5] Of sixteen nongraded centers identified by Goodlad at that time, ten were of the primary-unit pattern. Slater[6] identified 28 primary school organizations. Starting with a single nongraded school in 1942, Milwaukee had 78 primary schools functioning under this organization by 1955.

As late as 1955, then, the nongraded movement was still developing at a very slow pace, though beginning to pick up momentum. Anderson wrote:

> Although I should like very much to regale you with accounts of numerous successful examples of the ungraded primary school, the

distressing truth is that the movement is very young and has accelerated at the pace of the tortoise rather than the hare.[7]

By 1957 Austin[8] identified 31 centers with active nongraded units. Most of the centers identified by Goodlad and Austin were started between 1947 and 1950. Generally speaking, except for a few scattered efforts, the nongraded school has been in existence only since the end of World War II. There was a little flurry of action between the years 1947 and 1950, after which spread of the movement slowed down somewhat for a five-year period. From 1955 on, however, considerable momentum was gained as indicated in surveys compiled by Goodlad and Anderson in 1958 and 1960, by the United States Office of Education in 1960, and by the National Education Association Research Division in 1961. This interest is reflected in the frequency with which the professional journals and educational literature focused attention on nongraded schools.

Goodlad and Anderson[9] reported that as of 1957–58, 44 of the 180 communities contacted in a questionnaire survey operated one or more nongraded schools, according to the definition they had devised. They defined the nongraded school as one in which grade labels were entirely removed from two or more grades. Thirty other communities were reportedly studying the nongraded organization at that time. The number of schools actually involved ran into the hundreds. Two years later, another survey conducted by the same writers revealed that 89 communities or centers had nongraded schools and 550 were believed to be utilizing this method of organization.

In a very comprehensive and extensive survey carried on in 1958 and 1959 by the United States Office of Education, Stuart Dean reported that 18 percent of the elementary schools in this country were using the primary unit. Regarding the inclusion of this type of organization in a survey of national practices, Dean remarked:

> A third area of Early Elementary Education investigated was the "primary unit." Variously, this is known as the ungraded school, the ungraded primary, the nongraded elementary school, the primary department, a continuous growth plan, the primary group and the primary unit. It was felt that it was pertinent and essential to the purposes of this survey to discover national practices and trends in this new and timely aspect of elementary school organization and administration. Increasingly public schools have been reporting the adoption of this administrative and instructional practice and the

volume of educational literature has been building up markedly on this topic.[10]

A random sampling of cities of over 2,500 population was made (555 cities out of a possible total of 4,307). Projections indicated that 776 urban areas were using the primary unit at that time, and 473 others were considering adoption of this type of organization.

The findings reported by Dean are unusually high, particularly when compared with the 1960 Goodlad and Anderson survey and a 1961 National Education Association Research Division survey. This is understandable when one examines the definition used in Dean's study: "Primary unit means an administrative device by which children are grouped to permit continuous progress during a period of two or more consecutive years. The teacher may remain with the same group for more than one year."[11] Nevertheless, this survey provides some idea of the extent of influence of the continuous progress philosophy with which the nongraded school is most closely associated and identified.

In a survey made the following year, the National Education Association Research Division sent out questionnaires to 1,495 urban school districts regarding the extent to which nongraded plans were in use. Out of 819 replies, 71 reported the use of a nongraded plan. Using weighted estimates based on the sample of replies, it was determined that about 6.3 percent of all urban school districts (about 230 systems) were using an ungraded primary block plan either for the entire system or on an experimental basis in just a few schools.[12]

Most of the growth realized up to the late 1950's was at the elementary school level. The decade of the 60's found renewed interest in the junior high school movement and the introduction of the middle school organization. The latter frequently overlapped existing elementary school/junior high school organizational patterns.

National attention was first centered on the middle school in 1965 as a result of an article written by Paul Woodring.[13] From then on the number of middle schools grew considerably. Assuming that a middle school must house grades 6 and 7, and possibly grades 4, 5, and/or 8, there may be well over 1,500 such schools in operation today—Alexander reported 1,100 in 1967–68.[14] Though there are many reasons for developing the middle school—including dissatisfaction with the junior high school, concern for racial integration, and better utilization of facilities —nongraded philosophy frequently permeates the thinking and actions of its advocates. The movement toward middle school education, its development, and its frequent thrust toward nongradedness are very often attempts to provide more adequately for individual differences.[15]

The high schools have also been moving toward nongrading. The Staff Utilization Studies directed by J. Lloyd Trump and the emphasis on team teaching have given considerable push to the development of the nongraded high school. The interest with which B. Frank Brown's *The Nongraded High School,* the first full-length book describing in detail the inception and operation of a nongraded high school, was received gives strong indication of the educational climate in the 1960's.[16] Today, many nongraded high schools are in the blueprint stage, particularly in California.

It is evident from professional publications released since 1961 that interest continues to mount. The first of these papers is rather innocently entitled *Elementary School Organization: Purposes, Patterns, and Perspectives* (The National Elementary Principals Department, NEA, December 1961). This little book, which reveals the thinking of this normally conservative group, leaves little doubt that for them nongraded schools were very much in the future. The next year a study reported by another NEA group predicted that some sort of nongrading would appear in 26 percent of the schools by 1966. In 1963 the National Education Association Project on Instruction, through its *Planning and Organizing for Teaching* report, made firm recommendations regarding the exploration of nongrading and multi-grading, both of which are based on the concept of continuous progress.

One of the more interesting facets of the current literature on nongraded education is that the number of items published is on a steady upward trend. Articles and books are written and reviewed in a plethora of publications ranging from magazines for harried housewives to journals for professional scholars. Schools all over the country, both experimental and conventional, are making conscious efforts to implement part, if not all, of the nongraded philosophy. There seems to be little difficulty in convincing those involved that it is a worthy venture and is helping to improve instruction for their students. Both the programs and the literature produce positive effects on participants and readers. The nongraded approach is not considered just another temporary educational gambit, and the movement continues to gain support. Various writings reflect the fact that something new and exciting is evolving: Brossard (1965) mentions "school for the future"; Anderson (1966) "innovation characteristic of our time"; Anthonita (1967) calls it "an adventure in achievement"; Drake (1968) "the idea of novelty"; Casavis (1969) says "a formula for change"; and Weise (1970) "a revolution for relevance."[17]

Though nongraded programs at the middle school, junior high, and secondary school levels are relatively new, such programs have been in operation at the elementary school level for a number of years. Yet, there is an extraordinary paucity of research studies on nongrading. The few studies that have been conducted are inconclusive. Most of them suffer from weaknesses in research design. Acceptance of the nongraded school, as an organizational alternative, is based primarily on philosophical beliefs, not research findings.

The Nongraded Outlook at the Moment

Today the nongraded movement pervades the educational scene—from the nursery/primary schools through the secondary schools. Implementation of nongraded philosophy, if only in part, seems to be taking place in most parts of the country. It frequently occurs without any basic change in organizational structure. Hence, a "graded school" may, in fact, be an excellent example of the philosophy and educational stance advocated here. We once believed that modification in organizational structure was absolutely necessary to trigger other changes, but obviously this is no longer the case. Organization is a means to an end but an organization per se never "works." Only people work. Today many believe that changing the way people work is the real key to significant and lasting change; therefore they are concerned about new professional roles, roles which will enable teachers and administrators to be more effective and more productive.

Events in the last year or two have had the effect of "playing down" efforts to change patterns of organization—the middle school is a major exception—such as nongradedness, while at the same time placing great emphasis on the very philosophical foundations on which such an organizational plan rests. Extensive development of instructional materials, particularly programmed materials, has resulted in more effective individualization of instruction. Concern for accountability, as reflected in performance contracting and the advocacy of educational voucher plans, will undoubtedly have its impact. The British Primary Schools and open education are other contributing factors.

Perhaps the most important developments are the new professional and paraprofessional roles. Team teaching and differentiated staffing patterns offer promising alternatives to the more traditional self-contained and departmentalization roles so long associated with teaching. *These two movements*—team teaching/differentiated staffing and non-graded organization—*inevitably seem to lead to each other.* To be truly effective the nongraded philosophy requires new professional roles; otherwise the changes are superficial at best.

What Is a Nongraded School?

A nongraded school is a school that denies the limitations of grade structure and is organized so that the individual student may develop his academic and creative talents as rapidly or as slowly as his abilities permit. Instead of 16 grades, we might envision a program such as the one shown in Figure One.

	PRIMARY	INTER-	JUNIOR	SENIOR	
An educational continuum		MEDIATE	HIGH	HIGH	
	SCHOOL	SCHOOL	SCHOOL	SCHOOL	

FIGURE ONE

Ideally, before entering the primary school (which would be, roughly, the equivalent of work traditionally covered in grades one, two, and three) the pupil would have the opportunity to spend one, two, or three years in a pre-primary school. We already have kindergarten programs that represent the nucleus of such a program. As concern for the education of the culturally disadvantaged child grows, there is a good chance that a real pre-school (or pre-primary) movement may be on its way. Operation Head Start is a solid move in this direction.

Pupils would spend two, three, or four years in each school, three being the average. Progress in each academic area would be continuous, as illustrated in Figure Two.

THE NONGRADED PRIMARY SCHOOL

Progress of three pupils through an ungraded primary reading program

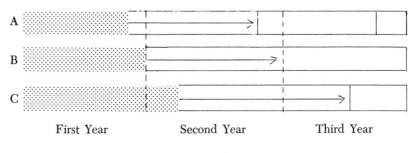

First Year   Second Year   Third Year

FIGURE TWO

The program for the various schools can overlap since a pupil may very well be considerably ahead in one area and not in another. This should not create a problem if the content program is set up on a continuum. Each teacher would simply continue the program of instruction for each child at the point where the pupil discontinued work in the previous school.

The pupil who is able to move ahead rapidly in all areas and whose overall maturity seems to indicate his readiness may move on to the next school block, of course. He is the pupil who would conceivably complete the average three-year program in only two years.

In the case of a youngster who is advanced academically but who shows other indications that his needs would be met better within his peer group, the accelerated move to the next school would probably not be wise. Here again, however, a flexible curricular program would allow him to pursue advanced academic work while remaining with his chronological peers. Advanced placement programs at the high school level are applications of this same idea.

The less able pupil, too, benefits from the flexibility nongrading provides. He might spend four years, for example (consider the very young six-year-old, who just makes the first-grade deadline), in primary school and, through this added year and a somewhat less intense approach to his early learning, find every ensuing year a welcome experience rather than a hurdle. The older, physically more mature primary student, still academically slow, might be moved on to the next (intermediate) level so that he remains with his peers, but every attention would be given to keeping his program at a level consistent with his abilities.

Let us be clear. One of the most unfortunate misconceptions about nongrading has been that it serves only the "gifted" child and that the other 99 percent of the pupils in the educable stream are left to paddle along in the same old way. This is not correct. The whole idea of nongrading is bastardized if only one segment of the student population is served.

For the skeptic who chides, "impossible," just stop for a moment and think. We all know that every primary teacher worth his or her salt already provides for the beginning readers' differences in ability, and, for years, pupils at the secondary level have been scheduled in band, orchestra, and art classes on the basis of ability and interest, rather than by chronology or years in school. Marching bands, orchestras, clubs, and athletic teams are excellent examples of nongraded, multi-age programs. A talented freshman or sophomore is not "excluded" from varsity competition. His placement is based on what he is able to do at a particular time. Almost every extracurricular activity cuts across grade lines. In the community, swimming lessons, tennis lessons, Little League, even summer school offerings pay little attention to anything but interest and ability. Why should there be any less effort put into the child's total academic program?

Nongraded Schools and Their Justification

The development of a nongraded school program is not a simple task. Any time people turn their attention and energy to innovations that represent a marked departure from the status quo, their reasons and justifications for doing so must be well grounded. The development of the nongraded school will be seen as a completely natural advance if one realistically examines the basic educational philosophy in our nation and the accumulated knowledge regarding child development and learning. The issues involved will be dealt with throughout this book.

It has been said time and time again that the role of the school is to help each child develop his potential to whatever degree his abilities permit. Few educators would argue that point, but the means selected to achieve this end are open to debate. Typically, graded schools simply are not designed to individualize instruction or they are not able to do so. A careful look at the programs in most schools seems to imply that all children should be subjected to the *same* content at the *same* time and at the *same* rate simply because they are in the *same* grade and are approximately the *same* chronological age. The focus is on the content to be covered rather than on the individual to be taught. Within such a rigid framework, it is virtually impossible to visualize how the pupil's personal potential is ever individually considered.

For hundreds of years, physical differences have been quite naturally accepted and understood. Not so academic differences. Only within the last thirty years have we had reliable data on the pupils we teach. In a typical first grade class, it is not unusual to find mental ages spanning as much as four years and I. Q. scores varying as much as 60 points. It does not take too many years before those differences in potential are reflected as differences in academic achievement, as can be seen in Table One. The data are taken from a typical fourth grade class in Bloomington, Indiana, in 1965.

TABLE ONE

TYPICAL ACHIEVEMENT DATA FROM
A FOURTH-GRADE CLASS

	Reading	Language	Arithmetic
High	8.7	7.9	4.9
75%	6.4	6.6	4.3
Median	4.7	4.6	3.9
25%	3.9	4.0	3.7
Low	2.9	2.7	2.8

These test scores are from a standardized test battery. For each area the average score would be 4.1. This class is slightly above average in reading and language but somewhat below average in arithmetic. Note the wide range of scores in every area.

Table Two shows the results of a diagnostic reading test administered in September to a group of six-, seven-, and eight-year-olds in a nongraded primary school in Bloomington, Indiana. These data are shown simply to reinforce the thesis that pupils vary greatly in terms of potential and achievement. Since there are these academic extremes, to say nothing of social and emotional differences, the implication is that not all pupils should begin or end their formal education at precisely the same place, nor will they progress in school at the same rate.

It all boils down to a need for two elements in the school: an organization for instruction that encourages flexibility and—this is a big need

TABLE TWO

READING TEST RESULTS OF 166 PUPILS IN A
NONGRADED PRIMARY SCHOOL

Level	Number of pupils	8 years old	7 years old	6 years old
8.5	2	1	1	—
7.5	7	6	1	—
6.5	10	7	2	1
5.5	8	5	2	1
4.5	18	8	10	—
3.8	10	4	4	—
3.3	12	5	1	—
2.8	11	3	6	1
2.3	16	5	10	1
1.8	4	—	4	—
1.6	9	1	5	3
1.3	1	—	1	—
Beginners	58	—	4	54
T =	166	47	58	61

Tests were administered in September. Most 6-year-olds had just completed one year of kindergarten.

—teachers with the training and ability to determine what their pupils' individual strengths and weaknesses are and plan a program of instruction accordingly. If the latter element seems to be the stumbling block, remember that no one said it would be easy, but teachers need to do these tasks. We will probably see a good deal more cooperative planning and teaching in the future than we have ever seen in the past, as the nongraded school continues to be developed.

"But," comes a cry of dismay, "how many teachers can boast of even the most minimal diagnostic skill?" Perhaps only a few today, but effective in-service programs, more research, and increased experience will furnish knowledge and guidance for the teacher's role in diagnosing individual students' learning problems and potentials. Years ago, few teachers could make claim to even a smattering of child psychology or philosophy, or, for that matter, to a four-year degree. But progress has been made. It is not fair to say that teachers cannot make changes in their instruction—look at the new science and modern mathematics programs.

We must have confidence not only in the teacher's ability to learn but also in his judgment of diagnostic data. Today's teacher is a professional with a minimum of four years of college, and many states require a master's degree for teacher certification. He is also expected to continue his education, formally or informally. We can surely rely on such a person to plan and implement programs of continuous instruction and optimum academic growth.

A Climate For Change

As is often true during periods of rapid expansion of new educational practices, there is little in the way of statistical or experiential descriptive data to support nongraded programs, and not all of the new programs are being researched or evaluated with much objective consistency. This is understandable as the program development calls for a staff's full attention. However, it must be realized that changing an organizational structure only provides the opportunity for bringing about significant educational improvement. The real heart of the educative process is to be found in the influences of curriculum and instruction of youngsters. In too many cases labels have been changed, but the basic school program has remained unaffected. To create the climate for change, to establish an organization that provides the means for a substantial breakthrough in program development, and then to fall short of individualizing instruction is to discredit the nongraded movement seriously.

Notes

1. John I. Goodlad and Robert H. Anderson, *The Nongraded Elementary School* (New York: Harcourt, Brace and World, 1959), pp. 44–60.

2. Ibid., p. 204.

3. Henry J. Otto and Dwain M. Estes, "Accelerated and Retarded Progress," *Encyclopedia of Educational Research*, ed. by Walter Scott Monroe (New York: Macmillan, 1960), p. 7.

4. Carleton W. Washburne and Sidney P. Marland, *Winnetka: The History and Significance of an Educational Experiment* (Englewood Cliffs, N.J.: Prentice-Hall, 1963).

5. John I. Goodlad, "More about the Ungraded Unit Plan," *N.E.A. Journal*, 44 (May 1955), 295–97.

6. Eva M. Slater, *The Primary Unit*, Curriculum Bulletin No. 3 (Storrs, Conn.: School of Education, University of Connecticut, 1955), pp. 1–33.

7. Robert H. Anderson, "The Ungraded School as a Contribution to Improved School Practices," *Frontiers of Elementary Education,* ed. by Vincent J. Glennon, II (Syracuse, N.Y.: Syracuse University Press, 1955), pp. 28–29.

8. Kent C. Austin, "The Ungraded Primary School," *Childhood Education* 33 (Feb. 1957), 260–63.

9. John I. Goodlad and Robert H. Anderson, "The Nongraded Elementary School," *N.E.A. Journal,* 47 (Dec. 1958), 642–43.

10. Stuart E. Dean, *Elementary School Administration and Organization,* Bulletin No. 11 (Washington, D.C.: U.S. Department of Health, Education, and Welfare, Office of Education, 1960), pp. 1–126.

11. Ibid., p. 23.

12. National Education Association Research Division, *Non-grading: A Modern Practice in Elementary School Organization,* NEA Research Memo (Washington, D.C., Oct. 1961), pp. 1–13.

13. Paul Woodring, "The New Intermediate School," *Saturday Review,* 48 (October 16, 1965), 77.

14. William A. Alexander, *The Emergent Middle School,* 2nd ed. (New York: Holt, Rinehart and Winston, 1969), p. 164.

15. For a most interesting and up-to-date report of the middle school movement see Morris Mellinger and Jack A. Rackauskas, *Quest for Identity: National Survey of the Middle School, 1969–70* (Chicago: Chicago State College, 1970), 32 pp.

16. B. Frank Brown, The Nongraded High School (Englewood Cliffs, N.J.: Prentice-Hall, 1963).

17. See Selected Bibliography and An Addendum at the end of this book.

CHAPTER 2

The Nongraded School:
A Dynamic Concept

by

MAURIE HILLSON

*A former elementary school teacher, Dr. Hillson is now a pro-
fessor of education at Rutgers University. He has been on the
faculties of Bucknell University, Harvard University, the State
University of New York, and Fairleigh Dickinson University.
He has directed and taught in-service programs for teachers,
and has served as a consultant to numerous school districts in
the United States and Canada.*

Among Dr. Hillson's publications are Change and Innovation in Elementary and Secondary School Organization *and*
Continuous Progress Education: A Practical Approach.

E̲ven a cursory glance at the history of graded and nongraded
education in America leads to the conclusion that circumventions of the
graded structure are attempts to eliminate the restrictions that such an
organization imposes on its users. The desire to deal more effectively
with individual differences is central to almost every attempt to eliminate the graded school structure.

At this moment in the short history of the nongraded movement,
limitations of another kind are seen in some plans. Frazier's observation on the problems of nongrading, the "criterion of progress combines
quantity and rate to carry the old conception of the curriculum to a new
point of impoverishment,"[1] is not very different from the protestations
of some enlightened educators in the late 1800's concerning the graded

school. But Robert Anderson's insights are well taken when he says, "The great majority of pilot programs have been deficient. Most of the efforts at nongrading between 1942 and the mid-1960's can be classified as follows: (1) serious efforts to give the idea full-scale development in a well-conceived form, (2) serious efforts to implement one or more aspects of the nongraded idea in a well-conceived form, (3) modest efforts to achieve nongrading within an inadequate theoretical frame of reference, and (4) fraudulent or naive use of the vocabulary of nongradedness to describe what is in fact a conventional graded program."[2]

Philosophy of Nongraded Schools

The philosophy of nongraded schools is one born in the heat of reaction. It is pragmatic and inextricably bound up in the great scientific and child-centered movements of the past three decades. It grew out of the wholesome desire to deal with the individual and his needs and the empirical scientific evidence indicating how to obtain better learning results.

Nongraded schools represent an attempt at organizational plans that embrace the scientific findings about the learner and how he learns. They are attempts to deal with the problem of inflexibility in the education of the child, for the nongraded school gears its administrative structure to the child's intellectual development. Nongraded schools (which are now being given various other names because the term "nongraded" is one that more or less describes what is to be eliminated, rather than the broad-based activities of continuous progress that are to replace it) are practical means of personalizing and individualizing instruction. Their teachers collaborate in both planning and teaching. These two components continue to support the scientific findings about learning and the learner. They greatly broaden the philosophy of the nongraded school and insist that new forms and models be established so that this philosophy can be turned into tangible behavioral situations.

Educational Tenets

Several basic educational tenets, drawn from a vast number of fragmented studies, suggest the essential need for rethinking and recasting the present educational-organizational scheme of the schools. These studies frequently repudiate the wisdom of the traditional graded school, and reject the features of teaching, grouping, and advancement that are indigenous to such an organization. By necessity these findings lead to a different organizational format and to the creation of a different type of school. The list of tenets given below is not exhaustive. A much more comprehensive treatment of the basic idea that these tenets propound was given by the late William H. Burton.[3] His perceptive analysis inescapably leads to the conclusion that what is needed is a new school organization, not just a tinkering with established, sacred practices. These six tenets drawn from the literature may serve to clarify the philosophy behind nongraded education:

1. In every group of learners there are wide differences in quality, desire, and intent. One of the better articles dealing with this tenet, by Edgar A. Doll, observed that, in reality, four I.Q.'s must be recognized as factors in achievement. "The intelligence quotient," "the inner quest," "the ideal qualities," and "the innate quirks"—any of which may be operative in any individual at any given time.[4] This concept alone could act as the impetus for finding an organziation that is completely different from the traditional graded school, where consideration is usually limited to the intelligence quotient.

2. Certain undesirable growth characteristics, unrealistic school programs, and poor progress in school are associated with nonpromoted children more frequently than with slow-learning promoted children. The slow-learning children who have been promoted usually make better progress and exhibit better mental health habits and adjustment than do their peers who have been retained. The fact that repeating a grade yields very slight, if any, advantage relegates nonpromotion as an academic practice to a vestigial position in educational growth and progress. Retention and failure, with all of the attendant frustrations and social stigma, are still widely practiced in graded schools. Yet of all the evidence for or against these tenets, the collection of empirical evidence indicating that nonpromotion is unequivocally indefensible is by far the most consistent and impressive. If progress through the graded school is primarily based on mastering certain subject matter in a given period of time, then failure, retention, or nonpromotion are clearly basic by-products of such a system. Conversely, acceptance of tenet two, which specifically rejects the concept of nonpromotion, must lead to a divergent type of school organization.

3. Every pupil in the elementary and secondary schools should be judged by the best that he can do. This tenet actually restates that bold philosophy of education that calls for instruction to meet the needs of all the children of all the people. If a child works to capacity, makes strides in learning according to his intellectual growth pattern, and becomes in essence an ultimate learner, he has accomplished a full measure in this area of his living.

4. No child should be judged by the median performance of a non-select group. This tenet moves sharply away from a graded-school philosophy. Ample evidence supports it; for instance, every book on the teaching of reading importunes its readers to group reflectively according to the various ranges that result from nonselective assignments and grouping. Goodlad "once found himself in a teaching situation which offered promise of considerable homogeneity. The institution was a specialized one in that it received only boys committed for delinquent acts. The pupils were relatively homogeneous on a criterion supposedly related to learning in that almost all of them fell in low I.Q. range of 70 to 110, with a mean of 85." It did not take long for the obvious to happen. In six weeks Goodlad reports that he "found himself wishing for a 'special' specialized school down the road that might receive those who deviated most markedly from the others on various significant traits."[5]

5. No child should be judged solely on the basis of his chronological age. This premise follows from the previous one. Unfortunately, chronological age plays a large part in many of the endeavors of our daily lives. Everyone knows people over the legal voting age who should never be allowed to exercise a franchise because they are too immature to make sound, rational judgments. Cronbach contends that "age-grading is inconsistent with the facts about pupil differences, and allocating pupils to grades according to their over-all ability in one subject does little to improve the situation."[6] Age-grading is inconsistent with the evidence amassed in the studies of educational psychologists.

6. No child should be judged on a grade standard that is clearly indefensible and that cannot be defined in realistic terms related to the research on child growth and development. This tenet is an adjunct to the concept that any assessment and placement based on chronological age only is invalid. Grade standards, as a matter of fact and as a measurement of educational progress, become very untenable in light of the studies of intuition, cognition, and mental age. Bruner hypothesized that "any subject can be taught effectively in some intellectually honest

form to any child at any stage of development. . . . No evidence exists to contradict it; considerable evidence is being amassed that supports it."[7] Thirty years ago, without the sophisticated techniques presently being used, Luella Cole observed that individual differences must be coped with even though these differences exist in every grade.[8]

For many years the literature of education has been replete with similar ideas. Some are based on the perceptions of day-to-day educational practitioners. Others are carefully documented by controlled studies. The late William S. Gray summed up the conclusions in the vast body of research in this area of education: "Research has shown conclusively that children differ widely in capacity to learn and other basic characteristics. The need is urgent, therefore, of organizing instruction to provide adequately for the needs of all."[9]

A New Position

Today these tenets lead to a philosophical position on the organization of the public school from the first through the twelfth year. It provides for varying levels of instruction to meet the needs of learners who differ widely in their rates of learning and capacities. It calls for an organization that takes into consideration the millions of retentions found every year in the primary and intermediate grades, and the host of failing grades given in secondary schools. At the same time, it is a plan that considers progress within the realm of reality, and replaces frustration, fear, and failure by continuous growth. It considers the variations in learning, the aspects of cognition, the timing for the presentation of materials, and the spurts and lags that typify the process of learning. Most importantly, it considers the factors of readiness and embraces the concept enunciated in Cronbach, that "under a nongraded plan, learning activities are determined by readiness, not by seniority."[10]

Since graded school education is inimical to learning, a different organizational scheme is necessary, one that is a dynamic structure, not a static form. The nongraded school may be that dynamic structure.

Nongraded is a reactive term. It means the absence of, or the reverse of grades. Armed with the scientific findings on learning, bolstered by the historical attempts to get around the grades, and encouraged by a Space-Age public's growing receptivity to change, the educational movement of nongraded schools is a bold new venture on the educational scene. Nongraded schools are no longer academic exercises. They exist throughout the country in all kinds of school districts; they are viewed as one of the valuable organizational ideas for education in slum areas and have vital use in affluent school areas. Nongraded schools are found more often at the elementary school level, but this kind of organization is just as valid in secondary schools. The tenets set forth above, and research on child growth, development, mental health, and learning find themselves in compatible balance in nongraded schools.

It should be remembered, however, that there is no one "model" nongraded school. What was considered as merely an organizational plan when it was first introduced has become a more pervasive concept in the educational world. Even though the mechanics of organization are employed (redeployment of pupils and teachers, alteration and modification of the self-contained classroom, teaming teachers for various areas of the curriculum, scheduling a large block of time for skills development programs), many other activities must take place. Organization alone does not answer all of the problems that confront the schools.

The Nongraded School Plan

Nongraded education is not just a simplistic method of teaching. It is not an administrative or teaching panacea. But it does create a framework in which better methods can be used and in which fluidity and flexibility allow exploitation of various activities that further learning. As Goodlad and Anderson point out, "the nongraded school is not for those who would stop with a little organizational reshuffling. It is for those educators who would use present-day insights into individual differences, curriculum, and theories of personality, and who would commit themselves to a comprehensive revision of education."[11]

Because of the very decentralized nature and self-determination of the American educational setup, various plans of nongrading exist. Before attempting to define precisely what a nongraded school is, let us contemplate what the ultimate nongraded situation could be. The ideal might be realized when each child is intrinsically motivated to work to his full capacity and is faced with problem-solving situations at his level of competence. But since it is necessary to deal with group situations in our heavily populated school systems, some framework for capitalizing on each child's commitment to his ultimate development must be thought out. The organization could be one in which collections of children, each of whom is a group unto himself, are taught at the same time. In a particular substantive area they would be at nearly the same problem-solving level with respect to ability, desire, intent, and skill in learning. Any teacher will agree that this situation is devoutly to be wished, and represents the ideal. It remains the ultimate nongrading ideal, however. Immediate nongrading of a different sort can be a practical reality, and can prepare the way for that ideal.

At present nongraded elementary schools, for the most part, rely on levels of accomplishment in reading as the bases for advancement and assignment in a six-year program of vertical progression. With some rare but exciting departures, these schemes could be characterized as nominal nongraded programs. To expand them into full-fledged, individualized programs of instruction underpinned by continuous progress is another thing. To do so in only one subject would be a contradiction of the concepts of individualized continuous progress education and of nongraded education.

Some thought has been given to groupings based on a total language arts constellation, and Weaver[12] has written about a nongraded sequence in elementary mathematics, but the most frequent practice is to make assignments to classrooms on the basis of reading accomplishment. Some school districts couple this practice with semi-departmentalized groupings based on arithmetic study.

Elementary school science still remains in an area of curricular heterogeneity. Whether this practice should continue is open to question. If the impressive evidence being built up in behalf of nongraded schools is correct, and since present controlled experimental studies indicate that nongrading significantly improves reading achievement, it seems plausible that under a different type of organization a significant advance could be made in the learning of science in the elementary school.[13]

As an educational movement, the nongraded schools developed as organizational attempts to deal with the problem of inflexibility in the education of the child. These schools have plans that call for continuous academic progress. As noted above, this progress is usually based on the accomplishment of reading levels, which replace the grades. The child or group of children moves through these levels at its own comfortable learning rate. Imprecise and unrealistic year-end norms are eliminated. Just because the winter snows have passed into the warmth of June, a first-grader does not by some magical experience turn into a second-grader.

Promotion and nonpromotion and their attendant fears are eliminated. How can there be failure if the child is working at his capacity? The fear of encroachment on material reserved for the next higher grade becomes a thing of the past. When the child is competent at a particular level he is ready for more difficult material; he moves ahead regardless of the number of stars, circles, or lines boldly imprinted on the binding of the books indicating a certain grade level. This movement realistically recognizes the various rates of learning that exist in a normal school population. Pupils of almost the same chronological age work at academically different levels at different rates, in keeping with their ability, desire, intent, and readiness to learn.

The nongraded elementary school allows for a concentration on the individual pupil, his needs, and the attendant skills and content areas that relate to his educational as well as to his affective concerns. The concentration should be based on a diagnostic workup of each individual child: the diagnostic inventory plus a learning development inventory that screens out the elements of the diagnosis. The concentration usually consists of a three-year program (primary nongraded) or a six-year program (elementary nongraded). During these years, the activities, grouping, teaching, and learning reflect the research on human growth and development. The collocation is one in which a fruitful educative experience is realized. This concept of grouping, based on reading or language factors, and its success, based on pupil growth in this area, assumes the existence of what could be called a pole of intellectuality. One such pole does exist for mathematics, and it would seem from the current discussions that a third pole exists in science. However, in present nongraded programs, levels of sequential reading content are most often the first organizational stepping-stones to nongradedness.

In nongraded programs that could be created, sequential science, mathematics, or any other desirable content area could be another organizational stepping stone. The present nongraded schemes based on reading levels may be attempting to achieve unlimited aims with limited means. A more precise assessment of the polarities that offer themselves as bases for various groupings, and a clearer and more concentrated research activity concerning these polarities (i.e., the content itself) are now in order. Add to this still other bases for grouping (teaming, collaboration, etc.), and one can begin to sense that the distance traveled so far is small.

When one realizes that nongrading offers limitless possibilities to the perceptive and enthusiastic educator, and that within the movement some amorphous non-graded plans exist, it is obvious that a traditional plan of nongrading just scratches the surface. Nongraded plans based on reading levels, and considerations about grouping, progress, and grade remotion should have a universal rather than an esoteric application.

If these plans can be expanded to seek certain other objectives, then they can serve as the great first step toward more flexible models that would insure greater educational opportunity for all youngsters. The objectives that must be sought are: (1) an educational program arranged so that every child is in an appropriate, pertinent place, which reflects his educational development; (2) a clearly written curriculum whose stated objectives and philosophy are clear, sequential, adaptable, and able to be defined operationally; (3) items to diagnose the pupil's competence in relation to the stated curriculum; (4) a developmental inventory that screens out the components of the diagnosis in order to establish a very precise, pertinent, and appropriate learning stage for the pupil; (5) learning stages (or learning levels, or reading levels, etc.) arranged longitudinally, and organized according to the essential educational concepts, ideas, and skills needed by the learner regardless of grade level and not applicable to the concept of grade level; (6) an appropriate reporting and record-keeping system that is consistent with this particular sequential development and the operationally defined and adaptable curriculum.[14]

A Nongraded Reading Plan

The nongraded reading levels plan is one in which continuous academic progress is based on the accomplishment of clearly described reading levels. The number of levels varies from plan to plan. One well-known nongraded elementary school program uses twenty levels. The children start at level one, which is an "extended readiness" level, and progress through to level twenty, which uses a traditional sixth-grade reading book. The even-numbered levels employ basic books of a basal reading series required of all children, and the odd-numbered levels employ supplementary books of a co-basal reading series. The odd-numbered levels sustain and reinforce the work of the immediately preceding even-numbered level.

The actual nongraded reading levels plan starts at level three because all the children are involved in the basic readiness levels of one and two. The child progresses upward through a series of small steps, each even level being bolstered by a lateral movement to the odd level. Schools that use programs of "individualized reading" lend themselves very neatly to this kind of progressive arrangement.

The child's own selection of trade books—children's books within the suggested guidelines of each level—allows for healthy progress. The child may be more intensely motivated because of his interest in the story, a quality sometimes absent in the usual basal reading series. Even though the basal and co-basal books represent the same level, most nongraded reading levels plans include other representative "back-up" books of the same level of difficulty, drawn from various other reading series. The back-up books are available for the child who needs reinforcing work over a longer period of time and of a more intense nature in order to achieve the essential competencies.

In this type of program I was able to do two things that seem to complement each other. After setting up the levels program using the basal and co-basal idea described above, I made a careful analysis of the trade books, and for each level I listed the core books, which are basic in terms of difficulty and content suggested for that level. These books sustain, bolster, or clinch the competencies called for in the description of the level. Skills acquisition and story enjoyment complemented one another in an expanding program of reading accomplishment, unhampered by grade-level promotion, retention, and pressure. Figure One might represent levels XII, XIII, XIV, and XV of such a program.

LEVEL XII   Basal Reader III[1]

   LEVEL XIII   Co-Basal Reader III[1] and Several Trade Core Books

      LEVEL XIV   Basal Reader III[2]

         LEVEL XV   Co-Basal Reader III[2] and Several Trade Core Books

FIGURE ONE

The amount of time it takes a child to accomplish these levels varies. The average child generally does it in one school year. The slower child, who needs more work at level XII, does not fail. He is advanced to the next level, level XIII, where he has materials of the same difficulty to reinforce or fix the competencies called for at that reading level. The odd level helps children who are having specific difficulties or gives support to the child who needs help in making the next step. If a child is absent or enters school from another district, this type of organization provides reinforcement or reorientation without going backwards. With several groupings operating at different levels, the child can come back and take up where he left off, albeit in another group. Thus, the nongraded elementary school could be defined as a school that groups children for instruction according to criteria other than academic attainment or chronological age. Many nongraded programs are based on a reading levels progression. Lest this statement seem to contradict the definition stated above, let us discuss some of the criteria for grouping in our definition of the reading levels program of the nongraded elementary schools. (The same principles apply in the secondary school, although the reading program would not be the content vehicle.)

There are relative short-comings to a basal reading plan. It has been pointed out by many that no two basal readers teach the same skills, develop the same vocabulary, or use a similar approach. My colleagues and I have been having marked success with a different format because we have expanded the levels concept into progressive stages without regard to basal readers. It is a concept in which sequences of learning are developed. The skills development material is stated in behavioral terms from readiness to mastery. Included in the guide are the suggested methods of procedure, the materials to be used, and the source of those materials. These suggested activities create a format for the teacher. The diagnosis of the pupil and his placement in the appropriate level allows the teacher to use several media to teach the skills. Using social studies or language arts content as the vehicle through which these skills are taught expands the program greatly. Programs of this nature are in operation in Fresno, Cal., Mountain Lakes, N.J., the seven inner-city schools of the Department of Education, Archdiocese of Baltimore, under the direction of Sister Alice Gillen, S.N.D., and in various other places throughout the United States.

Grouping Considerations in Elementary Schools*

The grouping of youngsters in a continuous progress nongraded program, whether one uses the basal reader approach or the learning

* For the most up-to-date research available on grouping practices see Glen Heathers' chapter in *Encyclopedia of Educational Research*, fourth edition (New York: Macmillan, 1970).

sequence stages approach (made up of skills development), still relies on many factors. Consideration must be given to the ways in which children learn, to a major diagnosis of their skills, or to a workup of their strengths and weaknesses. This does not mean that they are grouped according to I.Q. scores, or that they move in the same group forever. It means that for various reasons people learn, have the desire to learn, or are ready to learn at different times and at different rates, and the decisions that are made about their instructional prescriptions are consistent with these learning differences. To facilitate learning, the extremes of the ranges of a whole host of abilities in any given class-room need to be narrowed. Narrowing the range in any one area by careful grouping creates a better opportunity for a child with an able teacher to achieve up to his capacity. In many nongraded rooms, one can find a wide range of I.Q. scores; they are not the single determinant for success in learning. Desire, motivation, obstacles to learning, matur-ity, physical well-being, and social adaptation are all factors that are related to success in reading and are, therefore, necessarily considered in grouping, especially at the earliest reading levels. They should be considered in the later levels as well. The natural result of this kind of grouping would lead to a nongraded school running from at least the kindergarten through what is now the sixth grade.

Increased sophistication in grouping practices and the adoption of the obvious new approaches of team teaching, cooperative teaching, pupil-team learning, and various methods of nongrading cannot help but lead to programs of continuous growth in which realistic rates of learning are a prime consideration. It means that a child completing six years of elementary school, seven including kindergarten, does not need to move into the rigid departmentalization that exists in many junior and senior high schools. It could mean a closer and more realistic articulation between the elementary and junior and senior high schools. It could mean that eventually each child could become a group unto himself and the hoped-for genuine attention to individualized learning would be attained.

A Survey Report

A survey of 107 nongraded programs, to ascertain what criteria were employed in grouping, reveals that for the most part these programs rely on the nongraded reading levels plan. A few school systems established nongrading on a broader base, such as competency in language arts. In general, however, the responses can be grouped into eight basic categories. It seems safe to say that ideally the following items should be considered in grouping in the nongraded school. They are not ranked in order of importance, nor did the survey indicate the single most important criterion used in grouping. The categories are:

1. Chronological Age (with special note of behavioral activities)
2. Achievement Test Results (with special note of reading ability)
3. I.Q. Test Results (with special note of the Mental Age)
4. Social Maturity (with special note of relations with others)
5. Reading Ability (with special note of readiness at that stage)
6. Interest (with special note of desire or motivation to achieve)
7. Needs (with special note of school and family background)
8. Physical Set (with special note of physical maturation in terms of motor skills)

A recent bulletin of a nongraded school district, which has been in successful operation since September 1953, explains the way that district's initial grouping was done.[15] In the spring of the year a battery of tests was given to all students in grades one through six. Armed with the test results, the teachers, principal, school psychologist, and supervisors discussed the mental and emotional maturity, health, and family background of each child, and placed him in the level most suited to his particular needs and abilities, regardless of his chronological age. The ten-year evaluation of this nongraded program showed that there was a marked decrease in the behavior problems normally encountered under the old graded system, plus a marked increase in achievement in all areas of the curriculum—convincing evidence of the value of the nongraded school.

This all-at-once grouping is an atypical, rather than common, practice. For the most part, nongrading is done on an emerging basis; that is, after the kindergarten program the child moves into the first year of a nongraded program, and each successive year he moves upward through the levels.

There are recurring questions concerning how, when, and in what ways determinations are made about this succession from initial assignments through to progress, movement, and transfer of pupils in the nongraded schools. Any full definition of nongraded schools by necessity must attempt to answer these questions. It must be understood that they are not simply answered because of the basic commitment to individuality that characterizes nongrading. It is readily apparent that it is difficult to establish an operable yet consistent set of circumstances that apply to all aspects of pupil assignment. Some guidelines can be drawn from the experiences of others, but the particular situation will dictate how far they should be followed.

Initial assignments to nongraded levels are made on a tentative basis at the end of kindergarten by using a profile of each youngster. Reading readiness and an assessment of the characteristics that indicate readiness (emotional development, social readiness, and physical set for learning) are studied and evaluated so that a precise profile is ascertained. The youngsters are then assigned to "pools," from which assignments to more specific levels are drawn. Figure Two indicates a schematic picture of this procedure.

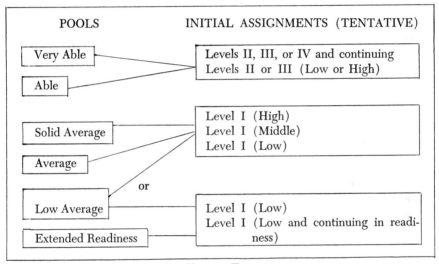

FIGURE TWO

In the first two or three weeks of the first year of the nongraded program, especially during the reading readiness program, careful assessments of each child's placement are made so as to catch over-estimations, under-estimations, or changes resulting from summer growth and experiences, any of which may indicate a need for a transfer or a different assignment. If the original or initial grouping was carefully done, these changes do not amount to more than one or two percent. As learning spurts and lags are noted throughout the year, additional changes may be made.

At the ends of the first and second years, levels assignments are made on the basis of the child's achievements, as well as on other factors necessary for fruitful learning. Growth spurts and lags, rate of learning, motivational aspects of growth, and the rate of the previous advancement are noted and studied. Teacher assessment, service tests allied with the basal reading series in use, and a selected set of standardized tests are used. Other criteria suggested by teachers' observations can also be established in order to arrive at a comprehensive inventory of the child. Assignments should become more sophisticated, resulting in a greater narrowing of the range or spread within each classroom.

Adjustments of Assignments for Various Types of Learners

The slow mover can benefit more from a nongraded than a graded school. An early prognosis of his educational advance is desirable. He may take four years to complete what others do in three. The first opportunity to notice his slower rate will occur in the extended readiness program. Preparation for this four-year program, barring a learning spurt that obviates the necessity for the extra year, is continuous and progressive. It is done through transfers to other rooms, where the child can exercise leadership in a level, and where his continuous progress, albeit slow, is studied, understood, and capitalized on.

The fast mover also benefits under this plan. The decision to enrich or to advance the child who finishes three years in two involves such variables as age, size, intellect, flexibility, and a host of other social and psychological considerations. If he had been held up because of a school entrance-date conflict, it may be wise to advance him. If he is immature, it may be wiser to place him in a level in another room for reading and enrichment in other areas, while he works with his own group.

Some General Thoughts Concerning Levels Assignments

When sufficient numbers of varying cases are dealt with, a heightened sophistication in the whole process in grouping will be achieved. A good rule of thumb is to under-assess the child's capabilities in assigning him to a level so as to assure making future assignments or transfers upward rather than downward.

The schematic design, Figure Three, which follows the progress of a levels plan and the movements through it, indicates some possibilities.

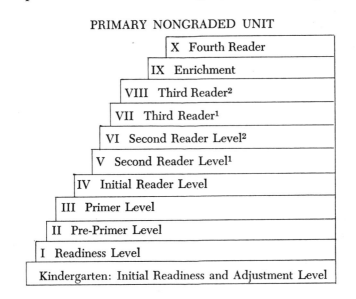

PRIMARY NONGRADED UNIT

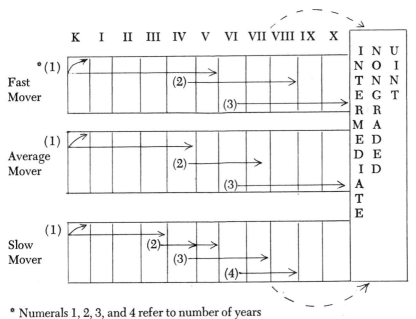

* Numerals 1, 2, 3, and 4 refer to number of years

FIGURE THREE

The figure is intended to represent a primary nongraded school with ten reading levels.

The nongraded reading levels program provides for various rates of growth and learning. The levels are not geared to any one kind of learner, but serve the fast, average, and slow learner. Because of the reduced ranges in reading levels, the teacher is able to deal more directly with individual differences. The first-year teacher will generally be teaching beginning learners. The second-year teacher will generally be teaching youngsters who are in their second year of school. The third-year teacher will generally be dealing with youngsters in their third year of school, and so on. Both teachers and youngsters will be working within a flexible framework in which youngsters of the same chronological age may be together but will still be challenged at levels commensurate with their academic ability, or inter-aged groups may emerge in a natural way.

These reading levels and the philosophy that supports both the operation and the spirit of teaching them allows for continuous growth. Teacher efficiency is improved if the child is taken when he is most ready to learn, carried by good teaching to a level that he can comfortably achieve, and then regrouped at each stage of his development with other youngsters and another teacher, who picks him up at that place and continues to carry him forward. When the program is organized into reading levels, the teacher can realistically do this. The slower child can move slowly, and the rapid learner can move rapidly. The grouping of the children and the narrowing of the ranges within the groupings allow the teacher to maximize his teaching impact, using the principles of child growth and development from which he derives his methodology.

Briefly, then, many of the present nongraded schools are ones in which grades are replaced by levels that a child accomplishes at his own speed. No grade designators are used. These levels of experience are clearly described and there is no fear of retention. Conversely, without fear of encroaching on material reserved for the next higher grade, the child progresses through them as competency is achieved. He is not pressed into achieving some prescribed year-end norm regardless of his ability. The rapid learner may accomplish a three-year nongraded program in two years. In the graded school, where he usually faced lassitude or boredom because of his rapid assimilation, he could become a problem. In the nongraded school he either moves into the intermediate nongraded unit or has his program enriched. He has the competency and skill to delve more deeply into the substantive areas as well as the skills areas of the curriculum. The slow learner may take four years to accomplish three. He does not have to repeat a whole year, as in the graded school. Instead, he takes up where he was when he left school for the summer. This is not retention, nor does it carry the stigma of retention.

The nongraded school is a realistic attempt to recognize the various ways and rates of learning that exist in any normal school population. It is an attempt to create a methodological approach to teaching and learning. Research to date indicates that pupil progress is better, tensions are lessened, attempts at unrealistic accomplishments are eliminated, individual adequacy replaces personal rivalry, and higher levels of general academic performance are achieved in nongraded schools.

A Nongraded Mathematics Program

Some schools are beginning to develop nongraded mathematics programs. As in reading, efforts have been made to identify a continuum in terms of skills or concepts to be mastered. As one might suspect, the initial attempts correlate closely with the levels approach used in reading. Again, as with reading, most of these early innovators have used a basal textbook series in the continuum planning. This is logical since most textbook series in mathematics move from the simple to the complex in skill development and concepts.

For elementary school, a mathematics levels plan might look like Figures Four and Five.

Level 1	Level 2	Level 3	Level 4
Readiness	Book 1	Book 2	Book 3

FIGURE FOUR

Level 1	Level 2	Level 3	Level 4	Level 5	Level 6	Level 7	Level 8
Readiness	Book I Ch 1–5	Book I Ch 6–10	Book II Ch 1–5	Book II Ch 6–10	Book III Ch 1–5	Book III Ch 6–10	Book III Ch 11–15

FIGURE FIVE

Using book tests (end-of-chapter and/or semester), and standardized tests, one can develop a fairly accurate picture of the computational skills possessed by any group of students, but at present we know of no standardized instruments that yield equivalent measures of mathematical understanding.

When the data is accumulated, a picture like Figure Six will probably unfold.

MATHEMATICS DATA (AND I.Q.) FROM A
TYPICAL FIFTH-GRADE CLASS

| | | Arithmetic Grade-Level Performance | |
	I.Q.	Computation	Problem Solving
High	130	7.5	7.9
75%	118	6.0	6.8
Medium	111	5.6	6.0
25%	104	5.4	5.5
Low	87	4.2	3.4

FIGURE SIX

From Figure Two we can see that there is a wide range in reading, not only within a single chronological age period but also over a span of several years. The same is true in mathematics. Once the data have defined the range of difference, the point of concern is again how to provide for those differences through a continuous or nongraded program.

There are several ways to plan curriculum for continuous education. One possibility is to provide for individual or group differences within a self-contained classroom. Another involves a change in class or group structure, and makes use of cooperative teacher planning (team teaching) and/or large- and small-group instruction.

Providing Differences Within the Classroom

Within a given group of students, all functioning at approximately the same level of performance, several alternatives are available. In Plan No. 1, which follows, the basic unit of study may be a chapter in a book or the development of a skill or an understanding. All the pupils have the same basic introduction to the new concept. As soon as differences in mastery or understanding become apparent, the better students move on to enrichment, which might involve group instruction of the same topic, skill in depth, exploration of new topics, or independent study using programmed materials. Other pupils are helped by further instruction based on their respective problems, so that they are assured of a firm grasp of the new concept before going on to more advanced work. Again, group or individual instruction plays a part, depending on the need (see Figure Seven).

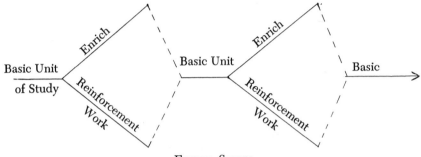

FIGURE SEVEN

In Plan No. 2, the design is a little different (see Figure Eight). Before moving into a basic unit of instruction, the pupils are tested to

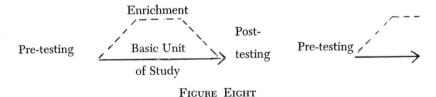

FIGURE EIGHT

find out what skills and concepts they already possess. After an introduction for all the pupils, the more able branch off and participate in enrichment work, which may be group- or individual-oriented. The class is brought together from time to time for various purposes: introduction of a unit, testing, or whenever the need dictates (as indicated by the converging dotted lines).

Depending on the organization of the continuum, a teacher may have more than one level in a classroom, and it may be necessary to work with two groups—as in reading—for basic instruction. Enrichment activities may be woven into the program at appropriate times. Some basic concepts, such as solving problems or measurement, which are fundamental to the many skill activities and do not necessarily fit into any special niche in a mathematics continuum, may be taught to all the pupils, regardless of their general level of achievement.

No matter which plan of action is chosen, the focus must be on the use of diagnostic tools, identification of a pupil's approximate position within the mathematics continuum, and then provision for group and/or individual differences. The emphasis will be on the individual's uninterrupted and secure growth in his math learning, rather than on an occasional stab at "catching up" activity for the slower learner or a "fill-in" enrichment activity, which is too often simply repeat practice for the student who is ready to study an already assimilated concept in depth or to move ahead to a more advanced area.

Providing for Differences Through Specialized Grouping Plans

For years, junior and senior high schools have attempted to provide for group differences by using track plans of various types. Based on mathematics tests, grades, and teacher recommendations, pupils are placed in one of several different courses. For example, practical mathematics or ninth grade algebra might comprise one division. Little attempt is made, however, to provide for the wide range of differences *within* these groups.

The nongraded school, which might possibly begin with a similar pattern, would go on to some valuable extensions. In these schools the mathematics continuum must be developed very carefully. After testing, the pupil should be placed at his level or in his position on the continuum. Provision should be made for individual differences and variety of instruction within each level. At any time of the year the pupil should be allowed to move from one level to the next as his growth in achievement permits.

With the growing emphasis on "modern mathematics" and its related drive for increased understanding of basic concepts, pupils' mathematical abilities will grow. The classroom teacher, armed with a better understanding of mathematics through in-service programs, institutes, and conferences, and a greater emphasis in his training on understanding, problem-solving, and technique, should be able to provide a much better program for students. However, increased mathematical under-standing, better materials, and more effective techniques may still be aimed at the same classes that were taught previously. The real break-through will not come until more effective organization for instruction is sought—an organization that recognizes the great differences in human abilities and makes its plan accordingly.

Whether the mathematics program is traditional or modern in con-tent, whether the basic design is the self-contained classroom or some type of special cross-class grouping, the emphasis must be on the in-dividual and his continuous learning.

Nongrading and Secondary Schools

Someone once observed that from grade four on, the number on the door indicating the grade level was also the minimum number of years of spread in the achievement levels of the pupils of that grade. If this is generally so, then junior and senior high school pupils are more likely to be irrationally grouped under a traditional plan than pupils in the traditional elementary school, which makes much more use of intra-class grouping. As a matter of fact, the literature clearly supports the fact that among children in the first grade the range in readiness to learn spans as much as five years, as indicated by the range of materials of a typical first-grade program. By the end of the sixth grade, the range in the ability to learn doubles. If these differences are added to the differ-ences in learning found in the various areas of the curriculum, it can be readily seen why Wiles and Patterson[16] and Grambs et al.[17] call for high school programs "planned individually" and nongraded junior high schools.

One of the spokesmen for nongrading at the high school level, B. Frank Brown, has set down in some detail what a nongraded high school is, and how it should be organized, staffed, and operated.[18] He would recast the traditional courses into phases that reflect the student's ability at a given moment, as well as the intensity needed in order to learn particular materials. When readiness for the next phase is shown by the student's willingness to advance, he is encouraged to move to the next phase. Dr. Brown's ungraded program at Melbourne High School has five phases in four basic intellectual disciplines: English, history, mathematics, and science. Phase one is remedial for those who need intense help. Phase two is for those who need work that emphasizes the skills of the basic subject area. Phase three is for those who indicate a readiness to deal with the material of the subject involved. Phase four is for those who can go into the subject matter in depth. Phase five is one of independent work, and is reserved for the learner who can, with the supervision of a teacher, assume responsibility for pursuing his own work. All the courses of the curriculum have been adapted to fit these phase levels. Freed from the structures of the traditional curriculum, with a library as "large as a gymnasium," and a new intellectual atmosphere, the students at Melbourne High School work in the "flexibility of the nongraded structure," which in turn "gives a new image to both the learning process and the educational establishment." Chapter Four of Dr. Brown's book goes into the nongraded program at the secondary level in detail. Case studies of secondary schools are included in Chapter Three.

Nongrading at the high school level is on the increase in the United States. In addition to the cycle plan, we have what we call a linear plan of nongrading in the high school. A typical plan of this sort is found in Middletown, R.I., and in an altered form in Ridgewood High School, Norridge, Ill. It is becoming increasingly clear that differential opportunities and differential intensities of learning may be needed more at the high school level than was hitherto thought to be the case. If nongraded education is a success at the elementary school level it is because of the extended readiness necessary to underpin future learning without failure. If it is to be successful at the secondary school level it will be because the added time needed to achieve success in learning will not be prejudicial to the youngster who attacks his educational program at a slower rate. For this reason, modification of curriculum and temporization of input in subject matter areas are necessary if the high school is to reflect the true needs of our adolescent society.

A Summary and Some Conclusions

It is not within the purview of this chapter to support the nongraded school movement by adducing what now seems to be unequivocal evidence in its favor. Both descriptive and empirical research indicate very strongly that youngsters in nongraded programs perform significantly better in all measures of school achievement than do their

counterparts in randomly assigned or paired regular graded classrooms. A study that I conducted revealed that certain gains were made
in attitudes and social and mental adjustments as a result of nongrading.
A by-product of that study was a common agreement among teachers on
a long list of benefits that accrued to them and to the school administration because of nongrading. The literature of education, with its discussions about the organization for instruction, has turned the nongraded
school movement into a ubiquitous one. This type of change in educational organization cannot be sustained by mere enthusiasm, however.
By necessity it must rest on the evidence that clearly indicates it to be a
better way of doing things.

In the last ten years there has been an acceleration in the accumulation of research concerning the nongraded school, continuous progress
education, collaboration in teaching, and the allied areas of innovative
continuous progress education. We now have a growing body of evidence of better academic performance and sounder mental health as a
result of nongraded programming. In all of the research published in the
last several years, not one article of a substantive nature has indicated
that youngsters in a well-conceived nongraded program are anything
but better off or significantly more able than their graded counterparts.

There are many bibliographies to help the reader make up his mind
about the evidence. The three given here may be useful in developing
background on the nongraded school:

> Maurie Hillson. *Continuous Progress Education.* Distributed
> through EDICT, Fresno County (Cal.) Regional Planning and
> Evaluation Center (11 pages). A selected bibliography on the
> nongraded school and other reorganizational plans.
> William P. McLoughlin. *The Nongraded School.* The University of
> the State of New York, State Education Department, Office of
> Research and Evaluation, Albany New York, 12224. (32 pages).
> An annotated bibliography.
> Robert H. Anderson. *A Bibliography on Organizational Trends in
> Schools.* Center for the Study of Instruction (CSI), National Educa-
> tion Association (33 pages).

In summing up the impact, direction, and intensity of this bold new
venture of nongraded schools, one must understand that the graded
school is a static organization imposed on a dynamic evolving process.
School organization must emanate from and, in turn, serve the needs
that are shown experimentally to be worthy and germane to the vast

educational endeavor. To accept the graded-school organization as the environment for this endeavor is like accepting the idea that the roads and highways of 1910 are sufficient to carry the vehicles, traffic, and aspirations of the American people today. The nongraded schools fit our space-age needs more realistically. At this moment in history, they represent a better organizational design for carrying forward the intellectual traffic that must travel through our schools.

Notes

1. Alexander Frazier, "Needed: A New Vocabulary for Individual Differences," *Elementary School Journal,* 61 (Feb. 1961), 263.

2. Robert H. Anderson, *Teaching in a World of Change* (New York: Harcourt, Brace and World, Inc., 1966), p. 51.

3. William H. Burton, "Basic Principles in a Good Teaching-Learning Situation," *Phi Delta Kappan,* 39 (March 1958), 242–48.

4. Edgar A. Doll, "The Four I.Q.'s," *Exceptional Children,* 24 (Oct. 1957), 56–58.

5. John I. Goodlad and Robert H. Anderson, *The Nongraded Elementary School* (New York: Harcourt, Brace and World, 1959), p. 20.

6. Lee J. Cronbach, *Educational Psychology* (New York: Harcourt, Brace and World, 1963), p. 263.

7. Jerome S. Bruner, *The Process of Education* (Cambridge: Harvard University Press, 1962), p. 33.

8. Luella Cole, *Psychology of Elementary School Subjects* (New York: Farrar and Rinehart, 1934), pp. 6, 7.

9. William S. Gray, "The Teaching of Reading," in *Encyclopedia of Educational Research,* 3rd ed. (New York: Macmillan, 1960), p. 1118.

10. Cronbach, p. 262.

11. Goodlad and Anderson, p. 226.

12. Fred J. Weaver, "A Non-Grade-Level Sequence in Elementary Mathematics," *Arithmetic Teacher,* 7 (Dec. 1960), 431.

13. Maurie Hillson, et al., "A Controlled Experiment Evaluating the Effects of a Nongraded Organization on Pupil Achievement," *Journal of Educational Research,* 57 (July-Aug. 1964), 550.

14. These six objectives and several others concerning the development of expanded nongraded programs are fully developed, along with examples, in Maurie Hillson and Joseph Bongo, *Continuous Progress Education: A Practical Approach* (Palo Alto, Cal.: Science Research Associates, 1971). Additional critical insights on various elements of nongrading are offered in Maurie Hillson and Ronald T. Hyman, *Change and Innovation in Elementary and Secondary School Organization,* 2nd ed. (New York: Holt, Rinehart and Winston, 1971), pp. 33-106.

15. Van Dyke, Mich., Public Schools, "Bulletin to Parents," mimeographed (n.d.).

16. Kimball Wiles and Franklin Patterson, *The High School We Need* (Washington, D.C.: Association for Supervision and Curriculum Development, National Education Association, 1959).

17. Jean D. Grambs, Clarence G. Noyce, Franklin Patterson, and John C. Robertson, *The Junior High School We Need* (Washington, D.C.: Association or Supervision and Curriculum Development, National Education Association, 1961).

18. B. Frank Brown, *The Nongraded High School* (Englewood Cliffs, N.J.: Prentice-Hall, 1963).

CHAPTER 3

Establishing Nongraded Reading Programs
by

CARL BERNARD SMITH

Dr. Smith is a professor of education and Director of the Measurement and Evaluation Center in Reading Education at Indiana University. He has taught in junior and senior high schools and has served as a public school reading consultant and as a textbook editor. Among his recent publications are Treating Reading Disabilities: The Specialist's Role *and* Correcting Reading Problems in the Classroom. *He has contributed articles to* The Reading Teacher, Instructor, *and publications of the University of Dayton, and has written magazine stories for children.*

IT HAS BEEN a good many years since educators began talking about continuous progress education. Recently the organizational concept of the nongraded school seems to have captured the imagination of enough educators to make this type of teaching a closer reality. All across the country, school systems are experimenting with nongraded plans, especially in reading.

If you walked into some of the Portsmouth, Va., schools, for example, you might find children working on a variety of tasks, though the classrooms themselves look like any other classroom in the country. Portsmouth has adopted nongraded classes in reading and language arts for the bottom half of its students, from first grade through the secondary school. Nongraded classes generally are not developed for slower students to the exclusion of better students; the Portsmouth schools concentrated on slower students because they had special funds for that group.

The age divisions used by Portsmouth are primary, intermediate, junior high, and senior high. On the basis of their scores on standardized reading tests and the recommendation of classroom teachers, those children who have not kept pace with the mean of the graded classes are placed in nongraded groups. Three different basal readers are used in the elementary grades to carry students through the various levels. Which basal reader series the teacher decides to use depends on the student's previous achievement and the speed with which he is able to make progress. The three reading series are categorized by the Portsmouth supervisors as difficult, medium, and slow. The size of the vocabulary used in the series and the frequency of repetition of words and concepts are the main criteria for judging how difficult the series are.

Portsmouth teachers supplement the basal texts with exercises that they devise themselves. In hopes that the teachers will analyze the specific needs of the children, Portsmouth authorities do not purchase additional workbooks. Rather they train their teachers to construct practice exercises and tests and expect them to produce items that will benefit individual children. It is evident, of course, that the success of that approach depends largely on the training of the teachers, the amount of time set aside for lesson development, and the supply of clerical assistants to type and run off practice exercises each day.

As the children in the Portsmouth program get older, they may remain in the nongraded classes if they are still not able to read well enough to keep up with the graded classes. In other words, there is a corrective flavor to the nongraded program in Portsmouth. A child can move from the nongraded class at any time that the teacher determines from standardized tests and other inventories that he can perform at a level and at a speed adequate for the graded class. Portsmouth views this aspect of the program as a kind of competition that encourages children in the nongraded classes to work diligently. If a student does not catch up to "grade level," he is regrouped when he moves from primary to intermediate, or from intermediate to junior high. In order that nongraded students are not ostracized or stigmatized, they participate with the other students in physical education, social studies, art, and music.

Before examining other approaches to nongraded teaching of reading, it would be wise to look at what constitutes a nongraded reading program and what considerations one makes in setting up such a program. Reading is used often in nongraded pilot programs because it can be arranged easily in a neat sequence of skills with a scope that most people can understand. Another reason for using reading is that the public is so concerned about reading instruction that any attempt to provide more individual attention is greeted with much favor.

Anyone concerned with effective teaching of youngsters should have an interest in the nongraded concept. Even if supervisors and administrators do not foresee an immediate switch to a nongraded organizational plan for children, it is certainly desirable to "ungrade the teacher." To get a teacher in the frame of mind in which he sees reading as a continuous development over a number of levels rather than a book to finish during the course of a year would be a major advance toward differentiated instruction. In order to accomplish the "ungrading of the teacher" or the nongrading of a school several things have to be worked out: (1) In-service education is needed to inculcate the principles and the attitudes of teaching specifically described reading behaviors. (2) A curriculum committee must describe the reading behaviors to be accomplished over several levels. (3) Materials have to be identified and purchased in order that teachers may differentiate instruction for the children in their classrooms. (4) Organizational problems, such as keeping records and reporting, must be worked out in detail before a nongraded plan can be put into operation.

In-service Training

In-service education for nongraded teaching must treat practical concerns as well as principles and attitudes. Teachers must know, of course, that basically nongraded instruction includes (1) continuous progress along a sequence of steps toward reading competency, (2) pacing of instruction to the style and drive of the individual learner, and (3) maintenance of reasonably comparable age groups. But in addition to those general concerns, the teacher must know how to survive in the day-to-day world of the nongraded classroom. There are inevitable questions, such as: How do I know where to place a student? Do I have to arrange a separate plan for each student? How can each one work at his own pace without having thirty-one different activities go-

ing on at the same time? When will the students have time and opportunity to share their joys and insights if each is working on his own?
Won't I need a full-time secretary to keep records with such a variety
of activity? Since comparative grades are almost impossible in a nongraded situation, how will I report to the parents and to the school
about the kind of work the child is doing? What am I going to do with
the child who goes through all the reading levels before his time in the
primary group is completed? These questions are not only practical
worries of the teacher but are important considerations in the operation
of any nongraded reading program. The answers can be found in the
discussion that follows.

Ways of Establishing Nongraded Reading Programs

Success in nongraded reading programs depends heavily on having
clearly defined steps or levels that the students accomplish in their
march toward reading competency. New York City published a booklet
entitled, "Sequential Levels of Reading Skills, Prekindergarten—Grade
12," which identifies levels of performance ranging from prereading
skills to critical reading and the mastery of work-study skills for secondary school students.[1] Prereading skills are described under the headings
of (1) developing word power, (2) getting and interpreting meaning,
and (3) developing work-study skills. Each heading contains a series
of performance objectives. One objective under Getting and Interpreting Meaning is "Develops the ability to identify the main thought in
material presented orally and through pictures." Specific stories and
pictures are then recommended.[2]

Having described the initial levels, the bulletin presents a matrix or
chart to show how the same basic reading skill could be developed at
different levels. For example, under the heading "Acquiring a Sight
Vocabulary," the guide gives a single description of what this skill
means at levels ranging from the beginning (typically first grade) to
more advanced (see Figure One). This matrix approach to setting up
the scope and sequence of skills at various levels shows the teachers
where the student is heading and what the limits of a given level seem
to be.

Evaluation of progress is then based on the student's ability to demonstrate that he can do what the instructional objective describes for

ACQUIRING SIGHT VOCABULARY—VERTICAL PROGRESSION

Level	Objective
I	Uses shape of words, position of words in familiar context, and pictures to recognize words on sight.
II	Uses all reading experiences to recognize words on sight.
III	Recognizes the Dolch list.
IV	Distinguishes words that are very similar in appearance, such as *then–them.*
V	Recognizes more frequently used technical terms from other curriculum areas.
VI	Continues to add to sight words through a variety of reading experiences.

FIGURE ONE

that given level. Tests made up by the teacher are the most likely instrument for determining success. In many cases no formal test need be administered. An observation that the child can perform the task is sufficient. A simple checkmark in the child's folder will indicate that he has accomplished a given item and can concentrate on other facets of that level.

In designing a curriculum guide for nongraded reading more is involved than simply listing skills showing a gradual increase in the level of difficulty. At each level of progress, word skills, comprehension skills, and related attitudes, interests, and life-long reading habits should be included. A complete curriculum guide (or at least a complete view of reading development) should include a strand showing the development of reading skills, another strand that calls for systematic review and practice of what has been learned, and a strand that identifies evaluation milestones at each level (see Figure Two).

STRANDS FOR DEVELOPING A CURRICULUM GUIDE IN READING

Level	Sequence of Reading Skills	Review Skills	Tests and Evaluation
I	Readiness	Systematic	Tests,
II		practice should	inventories
III	Word recognition	be built into	and criteria
IV		curriculum guide.	should be
V	Literal comprehension		recommended
VI			at each level.
VII	Critical reading		

FIGURE TWO

Using the Basal Reader

Two basic techniques are used for establishing levels of performance in a nongraded reading program. One method is to divide the sequence of material in a basal reading series into a number of logical parts for the primary unit and an additional number of parts for other age groups. The other way is to define levels on the basis of a definition of the reading process and on the needs of a specific population. Some schools, such as the Immaculate Conception School in Dayton, Ohio, use each book in a basal series as one level. Thus the primary program may have eight or ten levels, depending on the number of books in the basal series that serves as the source of materials (see Figure Three). The

USING A BASAL READER TO ESTABLISH ACHIEVEMENT LEVELS

	readiness	*pre-primer*	*primer*	*first reader*	*second reader*		*third reader*	
l					1	2	1	2
e v e l s	I	II	III	IV	V	VI	VII	VIII

FIGURE THREE

scope and sequence chart produced by the publisher then identifies the skills and competencies to be achieved at each level. The Dayton schools place a systematic word attack program into each level (basal book) in order to provide rather clear performance objectives to accompany the broader objectives stated in each book of the basal readers. Some publishers are now producing books that are organized in "levels" instead of grades. One book can then be assigned to each level in the nongraded program.

Richmond, Cal. (near San Francisco), involved many of its teachers and administrators in building a reading and language arts curriculum. They started with the needs of the student population in Richmond to make sure that language factors and background concepts were built into the guide. For each of the specific objectives that they established, the curriculum writers developed recommendations for teaching and practice sheets to assist in accomplishing the objectives. The advantage of setting up a nongraded curriculum in this way is that every teacher thinks about what constitutes competent reading performance and the means for carrying out the objectives. The curriculum writers in Richmond are committed as a group to building their own exercises for specific objectives when they are unable to locate suitable exercises in commercial materials. The obvious disadvantage of this approach is that it requires considerable time and money to complete the task. Expert guidance is also necessary to insure meeting the needs of the school population.

Whether a school decides to use basal reader texts as the means for physically dividing levels or whether it first defines levels and then builds materials around each level, it is important that those levels be clearly defined in performance and behavioral terms. What is the child expected to be able to do when that level has been achieved? A curriculum committee wrestles with the heart of many related operations when it sets up the performance objectives for each level, for without those specific objectives, the teacher cannot determine whether a child should proceed to the next level. Without those clear behaviors, an accurate evaluation report cannot be given to the school or to the parents. Perhaps the most crucial factor is that without those objectives the teacher does not know precisely how to direct the student and therefore the student may fumble and falter instead of stepping surely to achievement and success.

Those who wish help in writing behavioral objectives for reading can find assistance at the Center for the Evaluation of Instruction at U.C.L.A., where a large number of behaviorally stated objectives are stored. The Evaluation Center in Reading Education at Indiana University publishes a *Taxonomy of Evaluation Techniques* (1970) for reading programs, which includes a section on behavioral objectives for student performance in reading. An article in the April 1969 issue of *Elementary English*, "Selected Objectives in the English Language Arts (Pre-K through 12)," by Enders, Lamb, and Lazarus, leans heavily on reading skills. The catalog of reading skills given below indicates some of the elements that go into a reading skills program. The list should not be misconstrued as a complete K through 12 sequence of reading skills, nor should it be thought of as the entire reading program. As mentioned above, attitudes and interests are included in the content of a good reading program.

CATALOG OF GENERAL READING SKILLS

Perceptual Skills

AUDITORY SKILLS

Matching rhyming words
Identifying consonant sounds
Identifying vowel sounds
Hearing word variants
Recognizing syllable length
Listening for accent

VISUAL SKILLS

Noticing similarities and differences
Noticing differences in upper and lower case
and between letters
Developing spatial discrimination

MOTOR SKILLS

Developing left-right eye movement
Developing hand-eye coordination
Developing motor awareness and coordination

Word Identification Skills

SIGHT VOCABULARY

Recognizing 220 common words
Recognizing words appropriate for level of development

PHONIC ANALYSIS SKILLS

Recognizing consonant sounds
Recognizing consonant blends
Recognizing consonant digraphs
Recognizing vowel sounds
Recognizing vowel diphthongs
Recognizing vowel digraphs

STRUCTURAL ANALYSIS SKILLS

Recognizing affixes
Recognizing compound words
Recognizing roots
Recognizing contractions

CONTEXT CLUE SKILLS

Using definition clues
Using experience clues
Using comparison clues
Using synonym clues
Using familiar expression clues
Using summary clues
Using mood clues

SYLLABICATION SKILLS
  Recognizing syllables
  Using syllabication generalizations
COMPREHENSION SKILLS
  Matching words and pictures
  Recognizing meaningful phonograms
  Matching definitions and word symbols
  Recognizing antonyms, synonyms, and homonyms
  Following directions
  Using context clues
  Recognizing sequence
  Recognizing main idea and supporting detail
  Recognizing meaning in larger units—sentence, passage, chapter
  Making generalizations and conclusions
  Analyzing and categorizing while reading
  Making evaluations on the basis of expressed criteria
COMPREHENSION RATE
  Using correct left-right eye movement
  Rapid recognition of sight vocabulary
  Using little or no regression
  Using little or no vocalizing or subvocalizing
  Using correct phrasing to read
  Adjusting rate to purpose
ORAL READING SKILLS
  Adjusting rate to purpose
  Using natural phrasing
  Using sufficient eye-voice span to read
  Using pleasing pitch and volume
  Enunciating clearly
  Pronouncing correctly
  Using punctuation cues
  Being a relaxed reader
Study Skills
ORGANIZATIONAL SKILLS
  Arranging in alphabetical order
  Interpreting diacritical marks, symbols, and abbreviations
  Using the Table of Contents
  Using the Index
  Taking good notes
  Developing a sense of sequence
  Using summarizing and outlining
  Synthesizing materials from several sources
LIBRARY SKILLS
  Knowing the arrangement of the library
  Using the card catalogue
  Using the vertical files

Using the dictionary and glossary
Using the encyclopedia
Using the atlas
Using the *Reader's Guide*
INTERPRETATION SKILLS
Using pictures for information
Interpreting graphs
Interpreting diagrams
Using time lines
Interpreting maps
INTERPRETATION AND APPRECIATION SKILLS
Inferring and concluding
Recognizing the author's purpose
Recognizing the difference between fact and opinion
Seeing cause and effect relationships
Recognizing the mood of the story
Using figurative language to visualize
Identifying literary styles
CONTENT AREA READING SKILLS
Knowing the specialized, technical vocabulary of the area
Knowing symbols and abbreviations in the area
Knowing the organization of the content area
Interpreting maps, charts, graphs, and tables in that area
Adjusting rate according to purpose and difficulty
Using research skills for study in that content area

Materials for Nongraded Reading

It has been a maxim in education for some time that every classroom should have a wide range of materials to meet the needs of all the children in the class. That maxim applies more stringently to a nongraded reading program than to a graded class. Levels here imply the ability to perform within a certain vocabulary and using certain concepts. But in addition to the fact that there would be several levels of activity in every nongraded classroom, there would likewise be a wide variety of interest at each level. So the skill program would have to have a set of materials and be matched with books that appeal to a variety of individual interests within that level. In the modern classroom tapes, records, and filmstrips become part of the materials for the operation of a nongraded reading program.

Some administrators might think that the expense of materials makes the nongraded program prohibitive. For some school systems the cost may be too great under current funding, but there are ways of reducing the cost of materials. Many nongraded schools, such as the middle school in Orange, Va., operate around a learning center. A combination of library and materials center, the learning center acts as a source of material and a place for a variety of individual learning activities. After the child has received direction from his teacher in the classroom, he can go to the learning center to select a book, worksheet exercise, tape recording, filmstrip, newspaper, or other material to assist him in accomplishing the reading skill for the day.

There is no way of setting a price tag on the materials needed to conduct a nongraded reading program. Some schools have spent as much as $2,000 per classroom for books, workbooks, tape recorders, projectors, and study carrels. Other schools have added practically nothing, relying on the individual teacher to find ways of supplying children with an adequate supply of books and materials for efficient learning in a nongraded structure. Though $2,000 is probably extravagant for most school systems, the other extreme of adding nothing to the materials budget and expecting the classroom teacher to find materials is unrealistic.

The Teacher's Role

The teacher's role is to assess the child's continuous performance, diagnose problems, organize interest group projects and discussions, and map an instructional plan that will lead the child across the various reading levels. Some teachers make "contracts" with the students to give them personal goals and to have checkpoints at which teacher and child can assess progress. The contracts vary from achieving a certain number of skills, as evidenced by a successful achievement of 20 or 30 pages in a book, to reading and reviewing a story or series of selections, thus revealing competence in such comprehension skills as interpretation, analysis, and evaluation.

An adequate evaluation of a student's progress will necessitate the use of some kind of checklist of the various subskills and objectives within a level. As the teacher is able to identify the child's performance of these skills, he can check them off in the child's folder. Interest inventories and attitude inventories should be part of the teacher's standard equipment (see Figures Four and Five).

INTEREST INVENTORY

Name_____ Address_____

Grade_____ Age_____ Date_____

1. Check the four items you like to do most in school:
   - a. Act in plays
   - b. Build things
   - c. Draw and paint
   - d. Go to assemblies
   - e. Study arithmetic
   - f. Write lessons
   - g. Listen to music
   - h. Talk about things

2. Check four things you like to do on Saturdays:
   - a. Play outdoors
   - b. Watch television
   - c. Work on a stamp album
   - d. Read a book
   - e. Help mother
   - f. Help father
   - g. Go to dancing lessons
   - h. _____

3. Check the game you like most:
   - a. Marbles
   - b. Cops and robbers
   - c. Space men
   - d. Dolls
   - e. Puzzles
   - f. _____

4. Show your preference (1, 2, 3, and 4) for what you want to be when you grow up:
   - a. Doctor
   - b. Teacher
   - c. Nurse
   - d. Policeman
   - e. Rancher
   - f. Scientist
   - g. Space traveler
   - h. _____

5. Check the country you would like to see:
   - a. England
   - b. Mexico
   - c. Switzerland
   - d. Canada
   - e. France
   - f. Japan
   - g. _____

6. Check the one you would like to collect:
   - a. Foreign money
   - b. Stamps
   - c. Rocks
   - d. Butterflies
   - e. Dolls
   - f. _____

7. Check four foods you like very much:
   - a. Vegetables
   - b. Candy
   - c. Fruit
   - d. Cake
   - e. Ice Cream
   - f. Puddings
   - g. Pie
   - h. _____

8. Check the ones you like to read about:
   - a. Adventure
   - b. Science
   - c. Fairy tales
   - d. Travel
   - e. Sports
   - f. Animals
   - g. People
   - h. _____

FIGURE FOUR

CHECKLIST OF APPRECIATION

	Jim	Jan	Jerry
1. Visualizes enriching imagery			
2. Recognizes the author's intent, purpose, and mood			
3. Appreciates literary style			
4. Appreciates figures of speech			
5. Understands semantics			
6. Understands approaches to poetry			
7. Understands approaches to drama			
8. Understands approaches to the novel			
9. Understands approaches to the essay			

FIGURE FIVE

One instructional strategy for nongraded reading is *teach, test, teach, test, teach.* After the student completes the first instructional task, the teacher checks to see whether he has learned the generalization or the skill. If he does not show sufficient competency, the teacher presents some new insight and practice based on his observation of what seemed to cause the difficulty in the more general task. If at Level 3 the child fails to perform well in identifying the sound of the vowels in the consonant-vowel-consonant (*c-v-c*, cat) spelling pattern, a new instructional task might include making rhyming sounds with a variety of words in the *c-v-c* pattern, *bat, bet, bit.* The purpose of such an exercise would be to provide the sound discrimination base on which the *c-v-c* generalization can build. If the child fails to achieve rhyming discrimination satisfactorily, the teacher may want to teach him the short sounds of the vowels in isolation and make sure that he realizes that the alphabetic symbols represent sounds (phonemes). In other words, the teacher keeps taking the student back to skills that underlie the one he cannot perform.

The task analysis described above gives an example of the kind of diagnostic teaching the nongraded organization encourages. This is not to say that the same kind of teaching cannot be done in other settings. But the nongraded arrangement makes teachers and students focus on the accomplishment of a series of behaviorally defined tasks, the performance of which are recorded in the students' record folders.

Evaluation

Evaluation forms a crucial part of the operation of any nongraded reading program. Evaluation must be a continuous process, and the only way it can be accomplished with objectivity is for the teacher to have a file on each child and to use a series of checklists and inventories in addition to the usual kinds of achievement tests that the teacher constructs or buys from a publisher. In addition to the daily observation, certain milestones should be established so that the teacher and the student can set their sights for a more formal kind of evaluation. Certainly the final activity for each level should be such a milestone. For most children, however, the major subgoals of each level should likewise have milestone evaluations. Each level should contain subgoals relating to word recognition, comprehension, and attitude factors.

In any evaluation of the child's performance in reading, his capacity for achievement guides the teacher's expectancy. Academic capacity is often measured through I. Q. tests or previous performance in school subjects. Thus the teacher should not create a negative impact by informing a child with a fairly low expectancy that his reading is not on a par with the other children. He must always be evaluated in comparison with himself. The primary question is: Is he responding at a speed and at a level that coincides with his own native capacity and the background that he brought to the learning task?

The fact that the child is being rated according to what he can achieve indicates that the child himself should be personally involved in evaluating his achievement. The performance contract is one way. Self-evaluation ratings, such as the one in Figure Six can help the student gather evidence on himself. In a personal conference the child should be asked about his own opinion of his performance. Did he do what he set out to do? Is his work representative of what he can do? Is there some way that he can improve or stimulate better responses? In group work, the child's classmates will offer an evaluation if given an opportunity, but the teacher must provide the group with some criteria on which to judge the performance of the members. "Did he read clearly enough for everyone to understand him?" "Did he have a natural inflection in his

SELF-EVALUATION

PRIMARY READING CHECKLIST

Circle the answer that best describes what you do when you read.

A S N   1. Do I read silently without moving my lips?

A S N   2. Do I read groups of words rather than one word at a time?

A S N   3. Do I usually read forward from left to right and down the page without looking back to words I have already read?

A S N   4. Do I fit my speed of reading to my reading purpose and to the type of material I am reading?

A S N   5. Do I read easy material rapidly but with understanding?

A = Always

S = Sometimes

N = Never

FIGURE SIX

voice?" "Was the reading smooth enough to show that he had practiced?" These and similar criteria can be supplied to allow the class to assist in peer evaluation.

It follows naturally that the child should learn quickly about the evaluation placed on his performance. The more immediate the reinforcement the more likely it is to influence the behavior of the child. When possible the child should see or hear about the judgments the teacher has made. If they are made soon after the performance of the task, no matter if they are positive or negative, the child has a sense of immediacy that enables change, but if he has to wait for a quarterly grading period, the evaluation seems so general that it does not tell him anything about a specific task performance.

Reports to the parents and to the school are likewise a necessary part of evaluation. They should indicate the achievement the child has made along the sequence of objectives, as well as qualitative remarks about the child's work. If the parent and the school knows what tasks the child has performed, then they can provide continuing direction and assistance without boring the child with unnecessary repetition or without skipping important steps. The home report may even contain suggestions about books that may help the child or about his interests and ways of relating those interests to his reading. Checklists similar to those used in the classroom could form part of the home report. They could indicate what learning is taking place: skills, joy of reading, sense of inquiry through reading, industry in reading tasks, and similar concerns. Figure Seven shows a sample of the kind of evaluation form that not only helps the teacher plan instruction but also can be used as a school record and a home report.

RATING SHEET
WORD ATTACK SKILLS

Student's name_____

Date_____ Teacher_____

		Ratings					
	1	2	3	4	5	6	7
1. Hears all blends or digraphs (bl, pr, ch, ph,) and identifies the printed letters that represent the sounds.							
2. Selects the appropriate printed letter of a vowel sound contained in a word he has heard.							
3. Selects the appropriate printed letter of a consonant sound contained in a word he has heard.							
4. Discriminates words that contain the same vowel sounds from those that have different vowel sounds.							
5. Sounds out whole words by blending identified vowel and consonant sounds.							
6. Uses pronunciation key to determine the pronunciation of unknown words.							
7. Employs the common rules of syllabication to divide words into syllables.							
8. Identifies prefixes, roots, and suffixes.							

Ratings
1. No grasp and/or rarely uses the skill
2. Some mastery and/or rarely uses the skill
3. Below expected mastery level and/or has some difficulty
4. At expected mastery level and/or uses the skill with moderate success
5. Good mastery and/or has difficulty with some aspects
6. Skill almost perfected and/or rarely has difficulty
7. Complete mastery and/or uses skill successfully when necessary

FIGURE SEVEN

Organizational Problems

The teacher in a nongraded program must work out certain organizational and instructional concerns very carefully. In fact some of these organizational considerations may occupy most of the teacher's and the administrator's attention during the early stages of the program's operation. Seating plans, instructional plans for each child, keeping records, and the child who moves extremely fast or quite slow are practical matters that need to be settled.

SEATING PATTERNS

Seating arrangements should have flexibility. Even though nongraded instruction implies much individual work, opportunities for project work in groups, interest reading groups, and skill practice groups should be foreseen. With these in mind, the teacher can arrange the room so that areas are defined for different activities. A conference corner for private discussions with the teacher is a necessity in a system in which there is continuous individual evaluation. Some teachers may be fortunate enough to have a small office as part of the classroom. An area for group instruction or group meetings as well as a rather permanent area for personal work should be set aside. An area for informal study, for reading practice games, for free reading, or for expression through art or chalk board activity provides a needed outlet for children to stretch their bodies and their imaginations—what better place than a library and games corner? A listening post or an audio-visual center in the classroom makes a lot of sense in these days of multi-media learning of language and reading concepts. Figure Eight depicts an arrangement that served one group.

INSTRUCTIONAL PLANS

Individual instructional plans for each child should be constructed on the basis of test data and an informal reading inventory. The teacher's observations through an informal reading inventory can give him a better indication of the needs and present performance of the child than most standardized tests. This analysis should enable the teacher to place the child in an appropriate level and to begin with a task that the

FIGURE EIGHT

CLASSROOM GROUPING

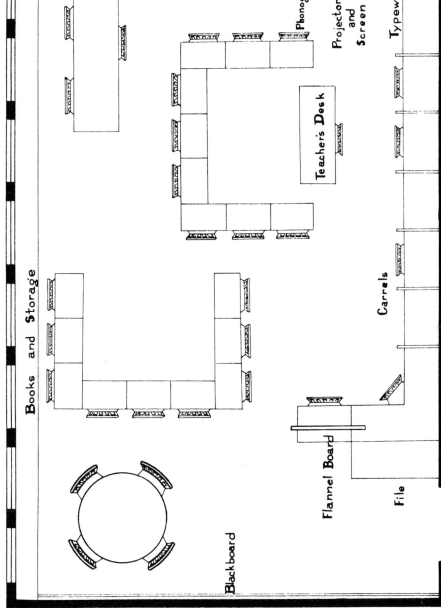

child can perform. The teacher may find several children who need instruction in the same skill at the same level. They can work together until their individual pacing or interest separates them. Wherever the student is placed, the child's individual instructional plan should include word recognition and comprehension directions associated with his level of achievement, as well as directions on how to capitalize on his interests and his motivational makeup for maximum productivity. In other words, some individual goals have to be set for each child.

KEEPING RECORDS

Keeping records will bother teachers forever because they must record a great many behaviors for many children. There is no easy solution to keeping records, but there are ways of making it systematic and of reducing the time and strain it takes to maintain good records. Having a duplicated set of forms, checklists, and inventories makes notations a fairly simple matter. These instruments enable the teacher to make checkmarks next to appropriate categories instead of writing out every observation. They also force the teacher to define the behaviors he is looking for as a measure of progress in reading. Some sample checklists about oral reading, interests for book selection, word analysis competencies, and silent reading behaviors have been included in this chapter to guide the teacher in preparing checklists for his pupils.

THE EXCEPTIONAL CHILD

There will always be those children for whom checklists seem hardly necessary. They finish their task quickly and accurately and easily complete all the levels normally associated with their age group. For these children the teacher must find projects and books that expand the knowledge, interests, and tastes that they bring with them. This kind of child can benefit from a personal enrichment program, but the teacher should be careful not to burden him or bore him with tasks that simply repeat what he already knows. The teacher should use the child's interests and send him searching for new ideas through reading—ideas that he can share with other members of the class.

The teacher will also find children who cannot seem to make any headway on the tasks as defined in the nongraded program. It may be necessary to refer non-learning students to the remedial reading teacher for a more specific diagnosis of their reading problems. If a child is not successful with the task-oriented objectives of the nongraded sequence, the chances are that he has difficulties that require the attention of the reading specialist. The specialist may visit the child in his home class-room to encourage transfer of learning to the subjects all the students deal with. Flexible classroom arrangements, such as the one shown in Figure Eight, make special learning activities convenient and unobtru-sive. It seems especially important that nongraded classrooms have a conference area where private meetings are always possible.

Conclusion

Even though research and evaluation have not demonstrated that a nongraded organization solves all reading problems, the principles of a nongraded program certainly seem conducive to better instruction in reading when self-pacing and daily diagnosis are prime concerns. Thus pilot studies in nongraded reading seem appropriate if American schools are going to accomplish successful learning for all children. Almost every major city in the United States has one or two pilot classes that are experimenting with the nongraded structure. The few examples de-scribed in this chapter were chosen to show the variety of approaches that can operate under a nongraded organization. They are not pre-sented as blueprints for everyone to follow.

Each school (system) will want to plan its own nongraded reading program on the basis of the needs of the children and the resources available. Administrators, teachers, and parents should be involved in the development of the nongraded curriculum. Reading teachers and reading specialists have the particular obligation of setting the specific objectives for each level in a continuous progress toward reading com-petency. In order to do that they must work with a list or catalog of reading skills, but they must also remember that those skills are de-veloped for use in books and magazines. Skills are not ends in them-selves. Part of the goal, therefore, is to create interest, develop tastes, and show children the treasure house reading unlocks for them. In de-veloping a curriculum outline, a curriculum committee might use a worksheet similar to Figure Nine. It shows the various kinds of objec-tives to be established for each level, and gives a sample of desirable goals at several levels. Naturally, a full set of goals would require much more detail, as in the catalog of reading skills listed earlier in this chapter.

Planning Sheet for Nongraded Reading

Sample Levels	Word Skills	Comprehension Skills	Attitudes
I Readiness	Build auditory and visual discrimination skills. Develop perception of self and immediate world around him.	Learn to identify a story line through pictures and stories read to child.	Words and books are fascinating things to work with.
II Initial Reading	Build a basic sight vocabulary and apply letter-sound patterns.	Learn to identify main idea and follow directions through chart stories and very short stories.	Reading is fun.
III Basic Meaning	Structural and linguistic analysis of words, e.g., roots, prefixes, suffixes.	Grasp literal comprehension of larger units, such as a story or chapter.	Books and reading can be used in a variety of ways.
IV Higher Competencies	Expand vocabulary from variety of general and technical sources	Use analysis and criteria to evaluate and use reading selections.	Reading enables one to tap all knowledge and human emotion.

FIGURE NINE

The effectiveness of nongraded reading programs will gradually improve as we determine which children function best under which instructional conditions. That, after all, represents the goal of all instructional plans—to find the circumstances that best suit an individual to learn most efficiently.

Notes

1. Curriculum Bulletin, 1967–68 Series, Number 4 (New York: Bureau of Curriculum Development, Board of Education of the City of New York).
2. Ibid., p. 6.

Bibliography

McLoughlin, William. *Nongraded Schools—Where to Find Them, A Directory of Nongraded Schools in the United States.* Bloomington, Indiana: Phi Delta Kappa, 1968.

Smith, Carl B.; Carter, Barbara; and Dapper, Gloria. *Reading Problems and the Environment: The Principal's Role.* Newark, Delaware: International Reading Association, 1969.

New York City Curriculum Bulletin, 1967–68 Series, no. 4. "Sequential Levels of Reading Skills, Prekindergarten-Grade 12." Bureau of Curriculum Development, Board of Education of the City of New York.

Measurement and Evaluation Center in Reading Education. *Taxonomy of Evaluation Techniques for Reading Programs.* Bloomington, Indiana: Reading Program, Indiana University, 1970.

Enders, Mary; Lamb, Pose; and Lazarus, Arnold. "Selected Objectives in the English Language Arts (Pre-K through 12)." *Elementary English,* vol. XLVI (April 1969), pp. 418-25.

CHAPTER 4

Science: Focus on Process

by

ROGER CUNNINGHAM

Dr. Cunningham is presently on the faculty of Early and Middle Childhood Education at The Ohio State University. He has also been a member of the faculty of Indiana University. In the capacities of elementary school classroom teacher, junior high school science teacher, science consultant, and curriculum director, as well as university methods instructor, Dr. Cunningham has been actively involved in elementary school science education for 13 years. He has served as science consultant for the State of Illinois and several local school districts in Illinois, Indiana, and Ohio. When the program described in this chapter was developed he was science consultant for the Fairview Schools, Skokie, Illinois.

Why Not Science?

IN THE LITERATURE of nongraded programs one would be hard pressed to find descriptions of nongraded organizations for science in the elementary school curriculum. It is apparent that attempts to design and implement this type of organization for science have been avoided. There may be many reasons for this, but three are most obvious.

First, instruction in science has placed more emphasis on content. It is very difficult to identify levels of progress with content, for there is no common agreement as to which content belongs at a particular level. Research studies have shown that it cannot be assumed that one area is intrinsically more difficult than another. When content is viewed as factual knowledge rather than conceptual schemes, there is no sound basis on which to describe a sequence for progress based on the content alone. Consequently, when content is the basic emphasis for science instruction in the elementary school, a longitudinal sequence is difficult to describe.

A second reason that there have been few attempts at nongraded science has been the assumption that certain advantages derive from having children of diverse abilities studying the same topic at different conceptual levels, and that the resulting interaction leads to a more complete understanding of that topic. The assumption is that the less capable learn from the more capable. The whole class can more easily study the same topic, at the same time, than they can in one of the "skill areas."

Closer examination of this line of reasoning, however, reveals that the argument is more of an excuse for avoiding a nongraded design than a sound basis for instruction in science. The reason for dealing with science in this manner may be based more on convenience and tradition than need. This reasoning also ignores contemporary trends. Present-day developments in the elementary school science curriculum emphasize individualizing instruction and developing skills in the processes of science. Science has not been recognized as one of the skill areas of the curriculum. To consider it as a non-skill area is not in keeping with current developments, in which skills closely connected with the processes of science and cognitive abilities of children are stressed as instructional goals.

A third reason for avoiding a nongraded scheme for science is the view that it is more difficult to put into operation. Obviously, to provide some sort of levels program in science creates additional problems for the teacher. By tradition, elementary teachers have feared and avoided teaching science because of a lack of content knowledge, poor preparation, shortage of time required to gather and organize materials for instruction, and the lack of acceptance of science as a major part of the curriculum. A levels program, with children at several different stages, and with a variety of topics, concepts, and activities, would merely compound an already difficult area of teaching. Consequently, it is easier to stay with the "whole-class hang-up" characteristic of the graded structure.

A Need for a New Focus

As we assess and reassess what we do in education today, it becomes increasingly apparent that we cannot do enough to develop the potential of each and every child. We have continued to be concerned with the individual—the way he learns, what strategies he employs in his learning, what we can do to enhance individual qualities and develop identifiable potentials. The problem is at least twofold: We do not know enough about how the child as an individual learns, and we do not know how to identify and describe with accuracy the strategies he employs in his learning processes.

We do know, of course, that the child's learning involves interaction with his environment. The mental processes he engages in as he reacts and interacts are remarkably similar to those that a scientist uses when he is involved in the investigation of phenomena. Thus science activities are quite natural to the child's everyday activity. One fallacy of our educational system is that we have tried our best to direct him to do otherwise.

What Is Science?

Science is not easily defined, but the greatest injustice is to think of it only as an organized body of knowledge. It is more than the facts that are its product. It is both product and process. The essence of science is its methods. It is an intellectually active process that involves the search for new information. Science is a way of dealing with and solving problems. It is a way of gaining knowledge and utilizing this knowledge. It is the processes that constitute the search that are important for the teaching and learning of science. It is the mental activities related to observing, describing, inferring, measuring, classifying, generalizing, and experimenting that constitute its true nature. Viewed as an intellectual activity, science provides a major contribution to education.

To present science to children in an intellectually honest manner, it must be presented in its true form. To present it as factual information misrepresents it. The facts of science are constantly and rapidly changing, but its processes are stable. Understanding the nature of science develops from firsthand experience with scientific problems and leads to the discovery of the processes employed by scientists. To learn how scientists learn is to learn what science is. To fulfill the contribution that science can make to education, the teacher must bring about an understanding of its structure, values, and processes. To understand the meaning of science is to experience the questioning, doubts, frustrations, successes, failures, and joys of discovering new ideas and information for oneself. As a dynamic process of inquiry, the ultimate outcome of science experiences is the fostering of a questioning attitude and an inquiring mind.[1]

Science and Children

Science in the elementary school is nothing new, but it is only in recent years that we have come to recognize the significance of the child's experiences with the phenomena of science. Only in the last decade has it become an established part of the elementary school experience. In the past, we have failed to realize the contribution science makes to stimulating the child's intellectual growth. We have recognized the product of science—an accumulation of factual knowledge—but have failed to recognize and utilize its most important element—its processes.

Traditionally, elementary school science has been fact-oriented, resulting in a dropping-off of interest as the children progress through school. Children come to school scientifically oriented. They are very interested in science and science-related questions, and many of the questions they raise originate from observations of their environment. Their many "why" questions are indicative of their curiosity about their world. The satisfaction of answering these questions through experience is highly motivating. However, expository teaching, stress on minutiae, and textbook-centered science have done much to destroy the children's initial interests. Science teaching that is limited to vicarious learning, sometimes accompanied by verification demonstrations, is meaningless, and is an illusory kind of science.[2] The "read and talk about" science is contrary to the way children learn. Children are "doers." For the most part, their thinking and learning are highly active experiences.

In fact, psychologists have suggested that thought is a direct function of activity, of doing, of handling, of seeing, and of experiencing.

Science is fun until teachers force children into the deadly, stereotyped rigor of the traditional approach. The convenient simplicity of this approach is a threat to children's natural tendencies to use their senses, minds, and skills for meaningful learning.[3] Teachers must provide continual and sequential experiences to enhance these traits.

The concrete-investigative experiences of testing, touching, smelling, lifting, twisting, and seeing are necessary prerequisites to the abstract thinking children do later in their learning.[4] Surprise, doubt, wonderment, and bafflement are challenging and stimulative to children's natural desire to investigate. Most children possess an urge to experiment, build, change, and discover for themselves. Psychologists claim that a child's intellectual growth is hastened by his experiences in investigating his own environment.

How Children Learn Science

Knowledge of children's modes of learning is limited, but today we have more to base curriculum decisions on than we have had in the past. The findings of developmental psychologists like Jean Piaget have shed new light on the way children learn. Piaget's theory describes a sequence of stages of intellectual development that all children go through. At each of these stages, observable behaviors representative of cognitive patterns can be described. It is apparent from Piaget's research that where variations do occur it is more a result of experience, or lack of it, than other factors.

Contemporary Piagetian research highlights some important considerations. First, we cannot force development on children through instruction, whatever the focus. Secondly, for young children, learning is based on perceptions of their environment, and as long as learning experiences remain at this level, they are fruitful. It is when we attempt to push them into logical reasoning that instruction proves inappropriate. Cognitive change on the part of the child is dependent on extensive interaction with objects of his environment. This learning is one of the actions, manipulating things without having specific knowledge about the things being acted upon.[5] The cumulative effect of his actions take on significance as his apparently meaningless and repetitious actions in one setting are combined with actions in others, and lead to a more generalized system of functional operations.[6] As the child's experiences are broadened his cognitive activity takes on a more formal nature. This takes time, and as Piaget proposes and research substantiates, no amount of instruction will speed up the process.

The significance of the Piagetian theory lies in the fact that most of the child's learning is one of activity—exploring and manipulating his object world. He is not a passive receiver of external stimuli.[7] Cognitive change is influenced by social as well as physical experiences. Therefore situations in which children interact with one another as they learn are important. Activities become cognitively useful when they provide for maximum involvement of the child with materials of his world. Understanding is a result of an invention of principles of the object world on the part of the child. The real gain is in the derivation of the methods by the child and not in his mastery of a concept or fact.

Knowledge of the Piagetian levels of development helps us prescribe appropriate science activities for children of different ages, purposeful instructional goals, and a suitable sequence for learning. A hierarchy of skills can be outlined so that in following the sequence of learning tasks the child could gradually incorporate new information into the cognitive structure he already possesses. To make this learning sequence more purposeful basic content ideas (concepts) and cognitive processes must be developed simultaneously.

The approximate age considerations in the Piagetian stage of development are not commensurate with the typical school age and grade considerations. Piaget's stages are important only for the way they describe the child's cognitive growth and not as a basis for categorizing children.[8] It is additionally significant that Piaget's notion of operations matches the idea of process skills. In view of his theory there is an obvious demand for firsthand experiences during most of the child's elementary school experience.

To ignore the intrinsic value of firsthand experience in motivating children to investigate is almost criminal. Children want to explore, to construct, to mess with, to move about, and to take chances. These activities form the crux of contemporary science curriculum developments. What children perceive and how they perceive it grows out of direct experience. No curriculum area can offer as many varied opportunities for their direct experiences as science.

Firsthand experiences provide the raw data for investigation. It is true that children form misconceptions and display gaps in their thinking, but direct experience does much to dispel them. A prime example is the misconception that heavier objects fall faster. Both adults and children are convinced that this statement is true, but a few experiences with objects, testing this theory, does much to eliminate this false idea. The child does not learn everything from observation or direct involvement but the importance of reality cannot be denied.

Learning Science Concepts

Science education based on reality is important in grasping of science concepts. Concepts become the organizers of the child's knowledge. He uses them to interpret new observations and experiences. They are the constructs he uses to relate new information to his previous experiences. The child's knowledge of the content, as represented by his understanding of the concept, will enable him to see more relationships, to make his observations more relevant, and to apply this concept to new experiences. Therefore, understanding the concept permits him to transfer his knowledge more readily.

Concepts are not facts and cannot be taught as facts. It requires time and a wide range of experiences for concepts to be formed, become thoroughly entrenched in the child's cognitive style, and be workable for him. There is much evidence to support simultaneous development of concepts and processes of science through direct experience. As a result of the many activities that utilize and develop the process skill of classifying, children understand how objects of their environment can be organized into related groups. Conceptual development emerges from a wealth of concrete experiences. The child must have contact with the concept in several different contexts. Reading about a concept and verbalizing about it does not indicate understanding. The quality of a child's learning can be judged by the extent to which he uses conceptual patterns and their related process skills in new contexts. Planning for a child's learning requires knowing the gaps in his conceptual understandings and guiding him through a curriculum sequence according to *his* needs. In any case, the link between process skills and conceptual patterns is significant for meaningful learning.

Learning and the Processes of Science

The child learns science by doing science. He becomes skillful in its processes only as a result of using them. The inquiry processes that characterize science are the cognitive operations the child uses to gain scientific knowledge. When he classifies, predicts, infers, or hypothesizes the child is using mental operations that can be identified with observable behaviors and can be developed logically throughout a sequence of related experiences. These processes are the tools of his thinking.

Initially, a child goes through a data-gathering process. His observations on objects and events are the initial phase of his concept formation. His first observations arise out of sensory experiences, but as he is able to interpret these observations, relate them to one another, and employ some of the other process skills, his observations become more sophisticated and discriminatory. When he is able to distinguish between the properties of objects, noting similarities and differences, he begins to develop a coding system. Children develop the rudiments of classification very early in their development, even before they come to school. Categorizing objects or events stimulates new observations. As the child makes discriminations, he begins to quantify his observations. When he thinks of objects in a numerical sense and comes to understand concepts of weight, space, and time, he is developing skill in the process of measuring.

As the child becomes more discriminatory in his observations, he begins to distinguish between direct observations and inferred observations. To make inferences or predictions he has to relate and use observations he has previously made. When these predictions are tested by investigation, the results may produce a whole new set of observations that may cause the child to modify his thinking. In the first place, of course, to construct a prediction he had to interpret and clarify the meaning of his previous observations. As the child begins to distinguish spatial and time relationships, using the skill of measuring, his observations become more definitive and improve the quality of his predictions. When the child tests his predictions, he may identify variables that influence the outcome. When he is able to isolate these variables and test them one at a time, he is developing the skill of constructing an experiment. Drawing from his previous observations, he may be able to generalize and predict the expected outcome when each variable is investigated. When he does so, he is hypothesizing. A hypothesis is a high-level inference since it remains to be verified by observation.

Throughout the development of this hierarchy of process skills the skill of communication is interwoven. The intellectual gain made through communicating cannot be denied. It is one thing for a young child to see and feel an object, but it is quite another for him to describe it. Representing his observations verbally and symbolically adds much to the organization of the knowledge he is gaining. It takes on more meaning by helping him to visualize relationships. Research further substantiates the intellectual gain made by having children testing their thinking through verbalization of *their* ideas.

To assume that these process skills can be taught directly would be foolish. It would be equally foolish to consider them as separate entities and to assume that they can be developed when they are divorced from meaningful science content. Children do not come upon these skills intuitively, nor do they develop them from brief experiences. They must be developed over an extended period of time with repeated use. Science has the distinct advantage of permitting each of these skills to be tested in a variety of ways. In social studies one can infer, predict, and hypothesize, but these processes usually cannot be subjected to a test or direct observation. If the processes of inquiry are not major concerns of our teaching and learning, then we are cheating the child of his right to strive for the prime goal of education—developing the ability to think. Emphasizing a body of content in teaching and learning science in the elementary school can only result in ignoring the intellectual skills. To be effective, an elementary school science curriculum must provide activities and events that develop these intellectual skills logically throughout the child's elementary school experience. Because higher-level skills depend on lower-level skills their development cannot be left to chance.[9]

Science and the Graded School: The Mismatch

The graded, self-contained classroom is notorious for its contribution to a fact-oriented curriculum, which has become a series of timed, predetermined packages that lack sequence as well as purpose beyond learning facts. A certain amount of work is to be completed in a year.

This in turn is divided into smaller, usually totally unrelated, self-contained packages called units of study. In addition, during each day the classroom learning and teaching are designed around a fairly rigid timetable. When teachers in self-contained classrooms tend to dwell more on factual information, teaching and learning are reduced to a "timed race over facts." Of course, it falls to this level because of the concern for coverage, the inadequate preparation of teachers to do otherwise, and dependence on the textbook. Teaching factual information is of course much easier with the aid of a textbook. Progress in the graded school is judged in terms of coverage, and fear of failure motivates both children and teachers. When stress is placed on factual knowledge, thinking does not rise above recall, rote memory, or convergent thinking. The emphasis is on getting the right answers rather than on deriving ideas and developing the processes of thinking from direct experience. The nature of science as a dynamic, open-ended process of investigation is overlooked.

The fallacy of this approach lies in the fact that not everyone can keep the same pace. Children do not develop conceptual patterns and process skills at the same rate or in a specified period of time. To develop relationships and integrate ideas requires time and meaningful experiences. The segmented organization characteristic of the curriculum in a graded scheme is not suited to the logical development of these concepts or processes. There is little hope for real progress as long as it remains that way. The gaps between units of study and between the levels of instruction are alien to the developmental aspect of science. Science has evolved by building gradually on what has already been found, and children's learning of science should evolve in the same way.[10]

The most delimiting factor of effective learning is reliance on textbooks. The teaching and learning of science in the self-contained classroom is bound up in the security of the authority represented by the book. One only needs to look at a number of textbooks written for a given grade and note the variety of content and approach to realize the senselessness of this dependency. Science lessons are often no more than lessons in reading, phonetics, or spelling; and demonstrations, when conducted, are used to verify textbook ideas. The same facts could be derived by the children, utilizing the methods of the practicing scientist. The significance of searching, hypothesizing, questioning, and experiencing is lost, and thinking is ignored. The textbook, by its very presence, tends to negate a functional understanding of the processes of science.[11] It very seldom suggests situations that lead to using the processes of inquiry, nor does it provide for different ways of finding answers, communicating these answers, different points of view, and sharing findings. Children in elementary school should be involved in learning how to think and for this very reason science should be approached as a mode of inquiry.

Elementary School Science and the Nongraded Philosophy

The modern view of elementary school science has much in common with the philosophy of the nongraded scheme and its demand for radical change in elementary school education. This match is no surprise since they are both deeply rooted in the contemporary view of child development, which is concerned with constructing a learning atmosphere more conducive to individual progress and providing for the wide range of intellectual abilities demonstrated by young children.

The nongraded view of the curriculum, organized longitudinally, with common organizing elements running vertically through the curriculum, is compatible with present proposals for a K–12 science sequence. Science educators see the curriculum based on sequential development of the conceptual schemes and the processes of science. Their proposals stem from the learners' behavior and the structure of the discipline: learning by inquiry is sequential; building complex skills depends on the development of certain prerequisite skills, continuity and sequence are important. Using their senses, minds, and emerging skills, children build on initial observation experiences to develop higher-level process skills. The investigative process characteristic of inquiry gives meaning and power to the child's emerging conceptual understandings. These conceptual structures emerge only through use in a variety of contexts and concrete experience. A curriculum based on conceptual levels, arranged in a graduated order, affords greater utility of conceptual structures and permits "multiple tracking" where children in the same class progress at different rates.[12]

The materials and approaches used in the "newer" programs in science are designed so that each child can explore at his own pace. The pacing of learning processes is more important than grade placement of specific learning tasks. The press for individualizing instruction and learning in science is highly compatible with the true nature of science—

the way scientists work—as well as the nongraded philosophy and its commitment to enhancing individuality.

One of the major goals of science education is to encourage children to be independent inquirers, a goal that requires teaching and learning the inquiry processes. The nongraded school stresses learning heuristic skills, by which it is believed, the child gains knowledge that is meaningful and long-lasting. Autonomy in learning is a major objective. The success derived from discovery of the autonomous reward on the part of the child stimulates faith in his ability to think, bolsters independence, and reduces inner conflicts because he is no longer passive in his learning.[13]

The child's investigations are designed to lead him to specified goals and the resource materials provide new questions or contexts for investigation. The child's own observations, discriminations, inferences, classifications, and measurements become the basis for further learning. These processes are valuable because they are transferable not only within the area of science but also across all areas of the curriculum. A broad range of resource materials is made available to provide information related to the investigation and to satisfy differences in interest. In the philosophies of both modern science education and the nongraded school the textbook is seen as only one of several resources.

Evaluation of progress is a continuous process and focuses on the progress of the individual, not as he compares with others, but in comparison with his own previously developed skills and concepts. The child's demonstrated achievement is not based on learning specific content. Evaluation is part of the learning experiences. It involves periodic check points to inform the learner of his progress toward the desired goals. Significant gains are made when the child can help assess his own progress, for self-assessment contributes to autonomy in learning. These ideas are consonant with both the nongraded philosophy and contemporary elementary school science education.

Developing a Nongraded Science Program

In the fall of 1963, the Fairview School District #72, Skokie, Illinois, set up a modification of Dr. George Stoddard's Dual Progress Plan,[14] a plan that offers a semi-departmentalized organization for the elementary school years. The Dual Progress Plan utilizes the favorable aspects of both the graded and nongraded schemes. The social concomitants and other elements of the graded organization usually cited as advantages are retained in what Stoddard identified as the "cultural imperatives." Each child spends half the day in a core that focuses on language arts and social studies. Children are grouped to advance on a graded basis, resulting in fairly heterogeneous groups.

The other half of the day is spent in a nongraded segment studying what Stoddard called the "cultural electives." Science and mathematics are the basic content areas of this block, where the advantages of nongraded advancement are served. The nongraded phase is designed to group students separately for each of the subject areas, resulting in fairly homogeneous groups and curricular sequences that extend above and below the usual grade offerings.* The sequence is based on the idea that all students, despite their learning ability, would follow the same sequence but with different rates of progress. Consequently, students of different ages and grade levels are found in the same group. The teachers in both the graded and nongraded phases of the program are specialists in their areas of the curriculum. Teachers in the nongraded segment provide subgrouping and individual work in lieu of whole-class teaching. The curricular sequence offers horizontal and vertical enrichment for the more able student, and frees the less capable student from the prospect of failure by permitting him to learn at a pace commensurate with his ability.

At Fairview, the decision to place science in the nongraded segment was a clear one. This was not only as Stoddard had intended but it was also homologous with contemporary philosophies for elementary school science education. Because of a commitment to individualizing instruction through a process-oriented curriculum, the self-contained classroom clearly did not provide a setting conducive to the modern view of teaching and learning science.

To provide a scheme for nongraded advancement, traditional grade-level demands and limitations had to be removed. This called for a series of levels that would allow a logical unfolding of the child's education and clearly defined goals for each level. In the early stages in the development of the Dual Progress Plan, Dr. Glen Heathers, director of the program at New York University,[15] proposed that advancement in science be based on progress along a sequence of stages based on the

---

* See above, p. 38, footnote.

scientific processes of inquiry. Taking a lead from "Science: A Process Approach,"[16] an elementary school science curriculum development project developed by the American Association for the Advancement of Science, we selected nine basic process skills to be the organizing threads for the curriculum. These skills, defined in specific behavioral terms, became the goals for each level of progress, along with correlating conceptual schemes. They were defined in order of increasing sophistication. Unlike the A.A.A.S. program, however, each process skill was defined within the context of a selected content to bring about logical mastery of the conceptual structures also. The content areas selected for study required scrutiny. Some content areas offer a greater potential for variety in laboratory activities and, in view of the general stages of child development, allow a more suitable context for developing a working knowledge of the conceptual schemes. The real key to the Fairview program, however, were the laboratory activities. They were the vehicle for developing the process skills, the means by which the child could demonstrate his mastery of these skills, and the mode for building on the conceptual structures.

The nine processes are: observing, classifying, measuring, communicating, inferring, predicting, hypothesizing, making space-time relationships, and constructing an experiment. A few of these skills are defined here in a general way.

> *Observing*: The child should be able to make distinctions between objects, citing similarities and differences in their physical properties by using all his senses. The child shall be able to make distinctions related to properties of color, shape, size, temperature, and hardness. The child shall be able to identify the stages of a given event.
> *Classifying*: The child shall be able to use his observations of physical properties to categorize objects or order them on the basis of the differences or similarities in their properties. The child should be able to categorize events on the basis of direct or inferred observations. He should perceive the arbitrary nature of a classification system and be able to construct such systems.
> *Measuring*: The child should be able to make comparative and descriptive measurements using both his own system of measuring and standard units of measure. The child should be able to distinguish between objects on the basis of measurable properties and relate two to more measures.
> *Communicating*: The child shall be able to communicate descriptions of objects and events using language that is his own as well as

scientifically correct. The child shall be able to demonstrate this skill by a variety of means—verbally, in writing, pictorially, by demonstrating, or by graphing. Descriptions should be accurate and complete and include quantifying dimensions.[17]

The descriptions of the processes are not intended to be specific or to be all-encompassing, but only give an idea what they might include.

Organizing for Instruction

The five-year block of time ordinarily described as grades four through eight was divided into three mastery levels. Mastery Level I, which was divided into three subdivisions, constituted what had ordinarily been described as grades four through six; and Mastery Levels II and III corresponded in a very loose way to grades seven and eight. So far the arrangement was not very different from a graded organization. Next we defined five levels for each of the five main divisions, or a total sequence or levels program of 25 sequential steps. The real difference between this arrangement and a graded program lay in the process goals established for each of the 25 levels. Because the number of process skills varied, the levels were not necessarily equal in duration or scope.

The basic scheme (shown in Figure One) served only as a frame of reference to facilitate design of the levels program. There is nothing fixed about these levels or the amount of time a child spends at any level. They are designed to be flexible and describe general expectations. In actual operation, children in the same classroom may be working at two or three different levels. Instead of the lock-step design of a graded scheme, progress is continuous, without restraints imposed by time considerations.

The first fifteen levels of the sequence were set up because it was expected that the less capable children (intellectually) would not progress beyond Mastery Level I in the five years. They should not have to plod through a program at a snail's pace, however. The Mastery Levels provided convenient check points to define and assess a program that would give these children an adequate and wholesome science experience before entering high school. In time, it was found that these expectations held true for many, but certainly not for all. For this sequence to be meaningful, purposeful, and challenging for the less

BASIC ORGANIZATION FOR NONGRADED SCHEME

Level of Advancement	Curricular Sequence	Rapid Learner	Average Learner	Slow Learner
Mastery Level I Stage A Levels (1–5)	General	(Year) 1	1	1 / 2
Stage B Levels (6–10)	Science	2	2 / 3	3 / 4
Stage C Levels (11–15)		3	4	5
Mastery Level II Levels (16–20)	Life Science	4	5	
Mastery Level III Levels (21–25)	Earth Science	5		

FIGURE ONE

capable learner, the goals set for each of the first fifteen levels required more time and the use of several different but concrete experiences with the process skills. In this way the less capable child would not spend a long time struggling with a single problem, but would tackle related ideas in smaller doses with the aid of many short, pointed investigations.

The complete sequence of levels was designed with the more capable learner in mind. It was expected that many of these children would progress as far as the twenty-fifth level before entering high school, and that some might go beyond it. No attempt was made to make any learner achieve a certain stage in a specified period of time.

Nongraded Advancement

The twenty-five levels constitute a sequence, since the nine basic process skills recurred and were defined with increasing sophistication, as were the conceptual schemes, with the child building on previous experiences and understandings. Even the less capable child had numerous experiences with each of the processes and the opportunity to develop these skills to a level commensurate with his ability. All the children went through the same sequence, striving for the same goals, but in different ways and at varying rates. Figure Two illustrates the levels scheme used to permit nongraded advancement.

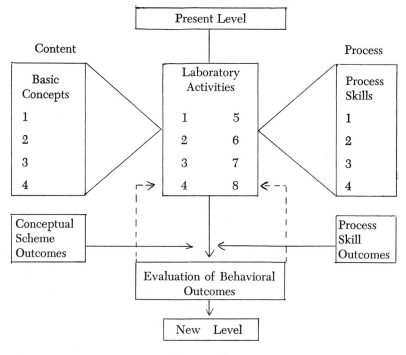

FIGURE TWO

The laboratory activities were the vehicle for nongraded advancement. The content, as represented by the basic concepts, and the process skills, defined for a given level in the sequence, provided the basis for selecting the investigations to be conducted. The time spent on these activities, the number conducted, and the type of activities carried out also depended on the child's ability. Since not all children would need the same kinds or same number of experiences to accomplish the objectives prescribed for a level, they would do different kinds of investigations. This arrangement permits both horizontal enrichment as well as longitudinal growth. The value of the laboratory activities lies in that they provide the concrete perceptual base for relating the conceptual structures and the processes of science. In this way, the basic content understandings and the process skills can be developed simultaneously.

The variability of the design increases the potential for individualizing learning. The goals for this sequence were always defined behaviorally and communicated to the child, so that he had a clear picture of what he was striving for. To illustrate these ideas and expand on the design shown in Figure Two, the organization for one level in the nongraded sequence is outlined below:

ORGANIZATION FOR ONE LEVEL OF PROGRESS

Mastery Level I
  Stage C
    Level II
      A. Content context: animals, animal behavior and environments
      B. Process skills: (1) observing, (2) making space-time relations, (3) classifying, (4) predicting, (5) measuring, (6) constructing an experiment (using variables).
      C. Concepts: (1) Animals can be classified according to common physical characteristics. (2) Animals adapt to their environment. (3) Animals and their environments are in constant change. (4) Animals respond to stimuli from their environment and changes in the environment. (5) Animals reproduce themselves and develop by responding to their environment. (6) Animals interact with other living things and their environment.
      D. Laboratory activities:
        (1) Structure-observing: activities with bones, describing physical features of many animals in room, microscope study
        (2) Organization-classifying: make an insect collection, aquarium study
        (3) Behavior-observing and experimenting: population study—snails, earthworm behavior, mealworm, housefly investigation, crayfish study
        (4) Environments-observing, making space-time relationships surveys of school yard, pond, marsh, lakeshore and woodland, constructing microcosm
        (5) Responses to environment-measuring, predicting and experimenting: experiments with brine shrimp, daphnia, planaria, earthworms, slugs
      E. Conceptual outcomes
        Application of conceptual schemes is demonstrated through performance on process measure. Illustrative schemes shown:
        (1) Living things are in constant change. (2) A living thing is a product of its heredity and environment. (3) Living things are interdependent with one another and their environment.[18]
      F. Process outcomes
        An example of a behavioral objective for a process skill: Given an animal and the necessary materials, the child will be able to

identify at least three variables and test these variables in experiments with the animal.

G. Evaluation

Evaluation devices consist of situations oriented to laboratory-type activities that cause the child to apply both the conceptual schemes and the processes.

H. Provisions for variability in children's abilities

The basic difference lies in the number and type of activities that are conducted. Obviously, many will be the same. However, the less capable child may do several that are limited to one basic concern.

Level II was one of the more involved levels. Although all its aspects are not given here, this outline does illustrate the nature of the sequence. The activities described are representative of the many possibilities.

If a child was unsuccessful in demonstrating his skill with the goals for which he was striving, he was not directed to repeat the activities he had done before. He was given a new set of laboratory experiences in the hope that they would bring success. Most children did not see this as failure but were often challenged by the new activities. This also accounts for differences in rate of advancement. The result of this feedback procedure was that in any given learning center (science laboratory classroom) children were not only working at different laboratory activities but also at different stages of development, despite homogeneous grouping to narrow the range of differences.

Because most laboratory activities were highly success-oriented, motivation to continue was high. In time, children who had been conditioned to the competitive aspect of learning in previous school experiences began to see that it was neither important nor necessary. The focus of their competition changed, for they began to see it more as a competition with themselves to improve their ability to progress longitudinally in the curriculum sequence. They could see that the new experiences gave them breadth in their understanding of the concepts and skill with the processes.

Grouping Children for Instruction

To make such a program possible it is necessary, at least initially, to group the children. Using measures of mental ability, tests of special abilities, and teachers' judgments of ability, the children were grouped according to their anticipated ability to advance further in the science sequence. Within these groups, they were regrouped on the basis of how far they had progressed along the sequence. To a large extent this grouping depended on teachers' judgments. As would be expected, children of different ages were found in the same learning center working together on the same stage in the sequence.[19]

Problems to Consider

The emphasis on individuality sometimes presented difficulties. Group activity was difficult to arrange since children were often pursuing quite different problems. Fortunately they could occasionally share their findings and improve their skills by working with others. This communicating period also raised new questions that often led to other investigations. Since not everyone views a problem in the same way, much was gained from this interaction.

There is a danger in overemphasizing laboratory activities. They can become as uninteresting or overtaxed as the "read and talk about" approach of textbook teaching. Care must be taken to prevent the experiences from degenerating into an "activity for the sake of activity" program. Small-group discussion often served as well as individual investigation. Scheduling problems limited the movement of the children between groups, but in many cases, a child's program was changed or he was moved from one group to another as he progressed to a new level in the sequence. Children did not move as a group from one teacher to another or from one stage to another at the end of a year. Some children whose progress was not rapid met with a particular teacher for as long as three years.

The Role of the Teacher

Children at all levels of ability and achievement spent a minimum of 200 minutes a week with a teaching specialist, a person who knew the area well, was well-versed in how children learn, and was able to construct meaningful learning experiences in science. For the low-ability child to learn the same skills and concepts as the more capable pupils takes more teacher preparation, more time, many more illustrations, concrete experiences, and pupil-centered activities. For more capable learners the teacher must provide opportunities for horizontal enrichment as well as vertical development. For all children enrichment experiences are necessary, but for the more capable child they need to be more challenging and broader in scope, and must stimulate curiosity and critical thinking.

The success of a curriculum of this type depends greatly on the teacher's ability to teach according to the nongraded pattern, his flexibility, and his ability to adjust to an entirely new classroom procedure. Whole-class teaching is out of the question, and so is taking a group of children a fixed distance along a given sequence. The teacher must overcome the tendency to expect certain end-points to be completed at specified times. He must also understand that the major goals are learning how to learn and developing the ability to think, rather than mastering a given body of content.

The teachers were responsible for defining the sequence and behavioral goals that were the basis for the sequence, constructing inquiry activities, guiding the students through the activities toward the desired goals, and assessing the achievement of these goals. The success depended on their ability to motivate children in a variety of ways, to prescribe activities that would meet individual needs, to judge individual progress correctly, to provide new activities if progress was not adequate, and to be flexible in dealing with the wide range of working levels that would exist in any given learning center.

To meet the needs of the slower learner or less capable child and to place his learning on a more individual basis, he was placed in a learning center with a small group of 10 to 18 children. A team of two teaching specialists, instead of one teacher, was assigned to each of these groups to lighten the teaching load. Because all instruction in the Dual Progress Plan is conducted by specialists, generalists did not exist.

Evaluation of Progress

Evaluation is an extremely important responsibility of the teacher. It must be done by comparing the individual with himself, and must be based on clearly defined behaviors. The teacher must be skillful at observing, questioning, and discussing with the children on an individual basis. He must be specific in his assessment of individual needs, progress, and abilities. He must see evaluation as a continuous process, and be able to encourage self-evaluation by the child. In every sense of the word, the teacher's inquiries into individual differences and needs are comparable to the inquiries the children make in their everyday learning.

To assess the child's mastery of the process skills, mastery tests or competency measures were designed and used by the teachers. They were rarely paper-and-pencil tests, but were purposely designed to match the activities the child investigated as he worked toward the desired goal. It would be extremely difficult for him to demonstrate a process skill by means of a paper-and-pencil test. Because the goals were stated in behavioral terms, these measures usually required some manipulation of materials. The teacher determined the child's success in a particular skill from his performance on this measure. Evaluative check points were an integral part of the child's progress and occurred almost daily.

Progress was not reported by using grades, but consisted of an indication of the level the child had achieved and a description of the degree to which he had accomplished the prescribed goals. Since children were progressing to different levels at different times, reports of progress were not made at specified times. Teachers were not averaging and tabulating grades every six or nine weeks, but were reporting progress to parents as the child progressed through the program. A portion of a progress report is shown in Figure Three.

PROGRESS REPORT	Excellent	Satisfactory	Inconsistent	Unsatisfactory	No Basis for Evaluation
Observation:					
a. Utilizes all possible senses for making pertinent observations					
b. Immediately and accurately records all observations made during an activity					
Measurements:					
a. Effectively uses measuring devices					
b. Describes objects and events in terms of standard units of measurement					
c. Understands and utilizes the Metric System					
d. Makes comparative measurements					
e. Describes a change with two related measurements					

FIGURE THREE

Science in the Primary Grades

Although the purpose of this chapter is to describe an innovative science curriculum for children 9–14 years old, it is necessary to describe what preceded it. A viable science program was very much part of the K–3 curriculum at Fairview. It would be philosophically and psychologically inappropriate to thrust all nine-year-olds into the nongraded sequence, with its process skill and conceptual expectations, without developing the prerequisites represented by motor activity, mental images, and language. The organizational break between the third and fourth grades presented an unnatural division, which placed limitations on effective initiation of the child into the nongraded sequence. Many of the children in the age range of seven to nine years were undergoing significant cognitive changes. It would have been more appropriate to start them in the sequence at different stages.

Most of the children in the early primary grades (K–2) are in what Piaget calls the pre-operational stage. In this stage the child is primarily concerned with ". . . establishing relationships between experience and action; his concern is manipulating the world through action."[20] These basic considerations provided the rationale for science in the K–2 curriculum at Fairview. For children in this school system it meant numerous multisensory experiences involving the processes of observing, classifying, and communicating. No attempt was made to sequence learning or set specific goals. The emphasis was on doing science with little regard for content or conceptual considerations. Capitalizing on children's interests, questions, and natural curiosity to develop a positive attitude about science and learning, the program consisted of a great variety of activities with rocks, animals, plants, liquids, shells, ice cubes, buttons, and many other objects of the child's environment. Opportunities for children to verbalize about their experiences was considered valuable. The child builds on his observations, tests his thinking, learns the meaning of words, and identifies relationships through oral communication. The child becomes more definitive in his observing by describing objects in detail. As a result, he begins to quantify his observations and builds on his basic ability to classify the things of his environment.

The program for third grade children emerged from summer experiences involving 40 children entering this grade and those entering the nongraded sequence. They and their teachers engaged in an activity-oriented program that built on their earlier experiences. In terms of Piaget's developmental stages, these children could be considered to be in a transitional period in their cognitive growth. Sensory experiences were still valuable, but these basic experiences could be broadened to build other process skills. The children collected data and conducted simple experiments designed with some attention to conceptual structures. Basic experiences with measuring and predicting proved fruitful. Two summers of this special program resulted in a few units for broader application during the academic year. However, the program continued to be an emerging one, changing as children and teachers explored these units.

Conclusion

In this program both conceptual structures and methods of science are important. Content takes on more meaning when one can experience it through his own investigations. When children can construct their own investigations, much in the way that a scientist would, they are truly experiencing the essence of science. Greater breadth of understanding of content is achieved when one has the opportunity to view it from several vantage points and at a pace that is commensurate with one's thinking ability and learning style. Children do not have automatic learning devices to grasp the concepts or processes in specified periods of time. Individuals vary greatly in the way they think and in the progress they make toward developing the processes of thinking. No two children are equal in their ability to solve problems, to plan strategies for solving problems, to complete a series of investigations, or even to respond to their teacher's encouragement. By ignoring these differences and failing to stipulate a variety of learning experiences to enhance them, we are reducing science learning to mediocrity.[21]

If the schools are ever to meet the needs of children, the curriculum must be geared to the diverse range of abilities that exist. In a sound curriculum sequence, all children should have the opportunity to investigate subjects and the processes of learning in a way that brings success. The *entire* curriculum should not be within the range of all the children, but *some part* of the curriculum should be obtainable for every individual. Today's demands require radical changes in the curriculum.

The world of the future will be a world beset with problems, and even more scientifically oriented than today. If today's children are to be prepared to live in tomorrow's world, we must give them something of lasting value. For the science curriculum, this means skill with the processes, the intellectual abilities that will enable them to deal with their world, and the conceptual structures that add productivity to their knowledge. Science must be taught and learned as a process of inquiry and a way of thinking.

Notes

1. Louis Kuslan and Harris Stone, *Teaching Children Science: An Inquiry Approach* (Belmont, Cal.: Wadsworth Publishing Co., 1968), p. 5.

2. Ibid., p. 242.

3. Ibid., p. 163.

4. Ibid., p. 74.

5. Edward Chittenden, "Piaget and Elementary Science," *Science and Children*, vol. 8, no. 4 (Dec. 1970), p. 14.

6. Ibid., p. 15.

7. Ibid., p. 15.

8. Ibid., p. 15.

9. Paul de Hart Hurd and James Gallagher, *New Directions in Elementary Science Teaching* (Belmont, Cal.: Wadsworth Publishing Co., 1968), pp. 13–14.

10. Robert Karplus and Herbert Their, *A New Look at Elementary School Science* (Chicago: Rand McNally, 1967), p. 20.

11. Kuslan and Stone, p. 128.

12. Paul Brandwein et al., *Concepts in Science* (New York: Harcourt Brace and World, 1966), pp. 1–13.

Theory Into Action . . . in Science Curriculum Development (Washington, D.C.: National Science Teachers Association, 1964), 48 pp. This publication describes the major processes and Conceptual Schemes of Science and sets a rationale for a K-12 science curriculum based on these two components.

Conceptually Oriented Program in Elementary Science (COPES) is a curriculum development project designed to test the feasibility of a K–6 science program based on the conceptual scheme.

School curricula based on the conceptual schemes are in operation in St. Mary's County, Md., and in the Nova Schools, Fort Lauderdale, Fla.

13. Kuslan and Stone, p. 97.

14. The plan was conceived by George D. Stoddard, Chancellor, New York University, and was directed by Glen Heathers, former Coordinator, Dual Progress Plan, School of Education, New York University. It is de-

scribed in George Stoddard, *The Dual Progress Plan* (New York: Harper and Row, 1961), 225 pp.

15. Glen Heathers, "A Process Centered Elementary Sequence," *Science Education*, vol. 45 (April 1961), p. 204.

16. This plan was developed by the Commission on Education, American Association for the Advancement of Science, Washington, D.C., in 1962 as a result of a Feasibility Study in 1961.

17. Adapted from *The Psychological Bases of Science: A Process Approach* (Washington, D.C.: American Association for the Advancement of Science, 1965), pp. 13–21.

18. Brandwein, pp. 14–15.

19. Joseph Zafforoni, *New Developments in Elementary School Science* (Washington, D.C.: National Science Teachers Association, 1963), pp. 13–15.

20. Jerome S. Bruner, *The Process of Education* (Cambridge: Harvard University Press, 1962), p. 34.

21. Kuslan and Stone, p. 41.

CHAPTER 5

Social Studies: Dynamics of Change

by

DOROTHY J. SKEEL

Dr. Skeel has taught at the elementary, high school, and college levels. She is presently an associate professor at Indiana University responsible for the development and coordination of an Early Experience Program with Triple T and an Intern Program for doctoral students in teaching methods of elementary social studies. Dr. Skeel is the author of The Challenge of Teaching Social Studies in the Elementary School, Children of the Street: Teaching in the Inner-City, *and* The Process of Curriculum Change *(with Hagen).*

CURRENT PROBLEMS of society that create turmoil in our neighborhoods, cities, college campuses, and international relations force us to ask the questions "Why? What has caused this situation? What can educators do? What is the role of the school?"

As educators, we frequently ask ourselves, "Do schools reflect the changes in society or do the schools effect changes in society?" Actually the answers to both these questions might well be in the affirmative. The curriculum area that can most readily fit into both categories is that of social studies.

Social studies are intended to aid the child in understanding man as he relates to himself (psychology), to truth (philosophy), to his spatial environment (geography), to groups or institutions (sociology), to his heritage (history), to governing himself (political science), to cultural expressions (anthropology), and to the resolution between his wants and needs (economics). Social studies help the child to a better understanding of himself, his actions toward others, and the effect on him of his social, political, physical, and cultural environment. This understanding is necessary if the child is to become a useful member of society and develop his individual potential. Like any other facet of the curriculum, social studies add to the child's body of knowledge, increase his understanding, affect his attitudes and values, and develop his creative and intellectual skills and abilities.

If these are the major goals of social studies, then the content of the area is unique, since it describes human actions in the translation of the social science disciplines, in a manner that is understandable to the elementary school child. The techniques of teaching, or the process, include posing problems for the child to solve, involving him in the inquiry process, presenting situations in which he can make decisions and value judgments, and involving him in activities in which he expresses his creativeness, learns what builds effective human relationships, and acquires a body of knowledge that will further his understanding of human actions.

In viewing social studies in this way, we can see the possibilities for a careful analysis of society as it exists at any particular time. Thus societal changes can be recognized as they occur, and facets within our society that should be changed can be identified. The analysis may be approached as problems to be solved, decisions or value judgments to be made, or knowledge to be acquired about previous societal conditions that will affect understanding of the changes.

Social studies in the graded or nongraded school have frequently been relegated to a backseat. The emphasis on group activities and the lack of identification of convenient steps or levels of achievement in the social studies curriculum have created this situation. From the previous discussion it is obvious that considerable use of group activities is necessary if the child is to learn about and participate in effective human relationships. It would be difficult for him to observe human reactions and actions if he participates in individual activities only.

The most frequently used plan for social studies in a nongraded, and often in a graded, school is the topical approach (also known as expanding horizons theme). Teachers who work with primary children might teach The Family, Home, and School the first year; The Community and Holidays the next; and Cities, States, and Nations the following year; and then go back to the beginning of the cycle. Intermediate programs generally focus on the study of different cultures with the same type of cyclical pattern. However, this scheme fails to meet the nongraded philosophy in that the children do not proceed at their own rates of progress, capitalizing on their strengths and improving on their weaknesses. More often the whole group proceeds through the units together; the only individualization takes the form of tasks, such as art projects, written reports, or committee membership, which are assigned according to ability. Other alternatives must be pursued; one might be the development of behavioral objectives based on the major goals of social studies.

A behavioral objective includes (1) the expected behavior of the child, (2) how he will achieve it, and (3) the accepted level of achievement. One of the major goals of social studies is for the child to understand himself. An example of a behavioral objective based on this goal at the beginning level is:

> Through observation the child will discriminate between man and other animals by describing two characteristics that differentiate him from animals.

For each sequential level these objectives would include cognitive and affective domains as well as skills. The example given specifies the development of the skill of observation and the acquisition of specific knowledge. Another will specify an affective or attitudinal development.

> The child will demonstrate his acceptance of different ethnic and racial groups by his positive statements describing their contributions to our society.

The specific objectives for any nongraded school social studies program would be determined by the overall major goals established for that school.

Since the content of social studies results from the actions of man, its study relies extensively on the experiential background of the children and their level of understanding. Therefore the age and experiential level of the children will affect the type of program established. I will first pursue alternatives for programs at the primary and intermediate levels and then discuss special considerations for children from experientially deprived backgrounds.

Primary Programs

Children at the primary level have a limited understanding of people's motivation and their actions. They may have viewed war scenes, racial disturbances, and the ravages of poverty and malnutrition on television, but they have difficulty understanding the situations and motivations of the people who caused them. The appearance of people with different customs and actions, whether in their neighborhood or on television, confuses children, particularly when they observe adult reaction to them. They ask, "Why do people dress and act differently than I do?" Another problem for the primary level child is that many of the resource materials explaining human actions are written in a form that is much too difficult for him. How then can a teacher approach social studies in a primary nongraded unit?

One alternative is the program planned by the California Statewide Social Sciences Study Committee.[1] The entire program covers kindergarten through senior high school. It encompasses three modes of inquiry: analytic, integrative, and policy, with specific skills included under each mode. The analytic mode involves broadly applicable generalizations that require the skills of observing, classifying, contrastive analysis, communicating, generalizing, and defining. Each process is developed gradually. The integrative mode involves generalizations that are not as broadly applicable, but are refined to fit specific situations by using the processes of comparing, integrating, and generalizing. The policy mode in the primary grades is limited to valuing.

In each inquiry mode the teacher should define the specific behavioral objectives based on the content and process. The following are examples of some that might be outlined for each topic:

Behavioral Objective	Process	Content
The child will contrast the clothing worn by the early Indians of the area and the members of his class, giving two reasons why they are different.	Analytic Contrastive analysis	Early Indians
The child will describe the several customs of the Japanese tea ceremony after seeing a film about it.	Analytic Communicating	People of Japan
The child will define several similarities between his life and that of the children of Mexico.	Integrative Generalizing	Children of Mexico

At the first level, regardless of age, the teacher will find a range of abilities in the skill processes. As he would in any other area, the teacher works with small groups of children to determine their proficiency in the first skill of observing. Under the first topic suggested by the California Committee, "What is a man?", the teacher would begin with a series of pictures of animals and men: birds, reptiles, mammals, fish, members of the class, people in the community. Both animals and people should be shown with their young. The teacher might ask such questions as "What do you see in the picture?", "What are some features of each?", "What is the animal or person doing?"

The next skill, classification, is introduced by asking the child to establish groups in which each animal could be placed. What criteria should he use to separate the groups? As the teacher works with small groups of children, he notes which children have no difficulty in observation and are able to move along quickly to classification. Those who have difficulty are presented with a fresh set of pictures, and continue working on the skill of observation.

The children who have made progress with classification move to the integrative mode of inquiry and begin to compare the animals in the pictures with those in their own experiences. When they have no difficulty distinguishing animals and have grasped the concept of man as opposed to animal, they move on to observing and classifying groups of men—those in their own community, those from a totally different culture—and comparing their characteristics.

Once the teacher has established certain procedures of observing, classifying, and comparing, the child can continue these activities on his own. The teacher can return to check on his progress after he has spent some time with the materials. A variety of activities can be used—viewing filmstrips of people and animals, reading stories, drawing pictures, and small-group discussions. Frequent small-group discussions are important because they provide an opportunity for the child to perceive how others react to the differences between man and animals, and between different cultures of men. Individual children who express a special interest in one or another of the animals or cultures should be encouraged to pursue them in more detail.

Topic two as suggested by the California Committee is, "How are man and animals affected by the land they live on?" It uses the skills of observing, classifying, comparing, and the additional one of communicating (which is the ability to use appropriate language labels and translate from one language to another, i.e., picture or graph to verbal). In this topic the children observe local phenomena, landforms and water, photographs, or models.

The subsequent topics, "Why do things have names?", "Why are there rules for everyone?", "How are people alike and how are they different?", use the various skills in a variety of settings. This inquiry approach requires many visual and concrete materials as well as written materials at different reading levels. The child uses the analytic mode of inquiry to acquire a broad perspective about a topic and then uses the integrative mode to focus on specifics.

At the next level, the policy-making mode is used for valuing, that is, choosing between alternatives on the basis of values to be realized. The child learns to recognize the alternatives based on different sets of values and the consequences of selecting each alternative. The decision-maker should recognize what he values and the priority these values have over others. He then makes a rational choice. In their daily lives children make value decisions constantly—about friendships, or use of time, as well as about weightier issues like honesty, prejudice, and democratic procedures. As the child uses the process of the policy-making mode of inquiry, this process should transfer to the decisions he makes in his daily life.

The advantages of this approach over the purely topical one are that the child can proceed at his own rate from one skill to another within the topic, and the teacher can begin a skill with one child or a group of children at any time. It also helps children understand themselves and others. This inquiry approach can be continued throughout the elementary years, and includes all the social sciences. However, alternative approaches will be discussed for the intermediate programs.

Intermediate Programs

By the time children enter the intermediate program, they have acquired research skills, and with adequate guidance they are capable of working through a problem approach to social studies. For the process to be significant and relevant to the child, he should identify the problem to which he will seek a solution. To begin the process, the teacher may guide small groups of children toward the identification of problems centered around one topic, such as "Community." It is also possible that the pupils will initiate their own problem search. Racial unrest, unfair employment practices, poor housing, and insufficient recreation areas are examples of problems that are of interest to children and can be investigated. The research may require reading local newspapers, interviewing public officials, using public and school libraries, and consulting local budgets and company reports. Many educators question the validity of having children seek solutions to problems such as these when the actions they can take are limited by their age and experience. However, any reasonable solutions can be conveyed to public officials by letter, which action is probably the best one open to children. The important lesson to be learned is the effect that the children's actions have in a realistic setting. Of course, the teacher will need to follow up the experience with activities appropriate to the ensuing consequences.

As the small group pursues its particular problem, the teacher can note strengths, weaknesses, and interests on which future attention can be focused. As a child searches for solutions he may come upon other problems, and he may need guidance toward resources to answer these new problems. If the children do not uncover new problems, the teacher may again initiate activities to produce problem situations in another topic area. It is conceivable that every child in the classroom could be pursuing a different problem. The teacher should direct their activities so as to include many kinds of social studies materials: maps, charts, graphs, primary sources, diaries, logs, simulation games, and numerous books. Problems requiring information from different social sciences should be included. The objectives defined by the teacher for each individual problem will include the knowledge to be acquired, the skills to be achieved, the attitudes to be developed, and the value decisions to be made.

Different individuals pursuing the solution to the same problem might have different objectives, based on their particular needs. For example, in studying the reasons that new businesses fail to locate in the community, the behavioral objective for Student A might be: "The child will exhibit skill in critical reading by his ability to distinguish between facts and generalities when given several sources of information." The objectives for Student B, who is pursuing the same problem, might be: "The child will demonstrate his ability to hypothesize by suggesting several possible solutions to the problem."

When utilizing the problems approach, the teacher should define specific objectives for each child according to his strengths and weaknesses.

The objectives should be prepared in the form of a list to be checked off as each one is achieved. It is impossible to suggest a series of sequential abstract objectives to be achieved at each intermediate level, since the objectives are developed according to specific needs and problem content.

The results of the search for problem solutions should be shared with at least a small group of children, if not with the entire class. A sample presentation might be:

> Problem: Why does our town have such high unemployment?
> The child discusses the hypotheses he tested: (1) lack of new industry moving into town after the mines closed, (2) not enough money in the community to build new industries. He then discusses the methods he used to check his hypotheses—interviewing local public officials (such as the secretary to the mayor or town manager), reading local newspapers, interviewing a number of townspeople, and talking to local businessmen. His findings indicate that the town does not have the resources for new industry and that the townspeople will have to show outside industries that their town is a good place to start a business. The other members of the group may want to ask him questions or supply additional information. It is possible that they may disagree with his findings and decide to investigate the problem themselves.

There should be opportunities for children to work on their individual problems, but they should also be encouraged to investigate other problems with small groups. Nongrading social studies does not preclude the possibility of the entire group working on a problem together, at times.

Another approach at the intermediate level is the development of a data retrieval bank. It requires organizing an extensive amount of information on one topic. The information may be in the form of slides, films, filmstrips, and tapes, as well as in written form. It must be catalogued carefully and should be simple enough for intermediate children to use.

For example, to illustrate a topic such as Mexico, the teacher will need the assistance of an audio-visual center to establish the bank of data. Slides showing various aspects of the culture—cities, small towns, people, topography, Indian ruins, products, artifacts, clothing, schools, and manufacturing—must be labeled and filed. They should be informative and should provoke questions. Important information about the country should be typed and photographed on slides. Information in the form of primary sources and differing viewpoints about problems should be reproduced. The written information should also be taped for those children who have difficulty with reading. After the children have acquired sufficient skill in the use of the catalog system and the slide projector, they can investigate questions about Mexico on their own at their own rate. Initially, the teacher may have to stimulate questions for the children's research.

The purpose of such a data retrieval bank is to permit children to work individually to improve their research skills—critical reading and thinking; generalizing; reading maps, graphs, and charts; solving problems; developing attitudes; and making value judgments. Children soon learn independent work skills, show more interest in research of their own choosing, and move along at their own rate of progress. The data bank provides easy access to information, makes individualization possible, and permits the teacher to observe the difficulties encountered by individual children as well as the strategies they use.

Behavioral objectives for the specific goals for individual children should be developed. An example of a cognitive objective might be: "The child will investigate a question on Mexico independently, utilizing a data retrieval bank, and will demonstrate the independent work skills of moving ahead on his own, locating information easily, and displaying confidence in his ability to seek answers." In the affective domain the objective might be: "The child will acquire appreciation for the Mexican culture and exhibit it by his positive statements about the people of that country."

Even though much of this activity will be accomplished in individual activities, a discussion of the information acquired should be planned. It will provide the opportunity to draw conclusions, generalize to new situations, and argue points of differences. It can be accomplished in small groups, or with the entire group after the research has been completed.

Storage of materials may be a difficulty in setting up a data retrieval bank. A learning resources laboratory would alleviate this problem. If the learning center acquires a number of banks of data on varying topics and sufficient equipment for several children to use the bank at the same time, it may be helpful to use individual study carrels with record players and slide machines. As computers become more a part of the educational scene, the data can be stored in them and the children can be taught to operate the computer terminals.

Regardless of the approach, children at the intermediate level begin to search in depth for answers to some of the problems of our own and other societies. They need to use the skills and information from all the social sciences to help them understand the intricacies of human relationships.

Special Considerations for Children
from Experientially Deprived Backgrounds

Disadvantaged children need special consideration in their social studies program. A disadvantaged child is described as one who through no fault of his own arrives in school with insufficient language skills, a paucity of enriching experiences, a poor self-concept, and a lack of accepted skills. These disadvantages create problems for him in the average school situation. Too often he encounters teachers who do not understand him or his learning problems, and expect to make him over immediately into an individual who accepts the school's middle-class values.

The typical social studies program requires sophisticated skills and background experiences that are not part of the disadvantaged child's repertoire. To alleviate this situation special considerations are suggested. Language skills are a prerequisite for success, and major emphasis should be placed on them in the primary programs. Disadvantaged children do not have much difficulty expressing themselves about experiences and activities that are within their realm. Therefore topics discussed at the beginning should be very relevant to their lives. For example, when studying the family, the typical family should not be portrayed as having a mother who stays home to care for the children and a father who goes out to earn a living. Often these children have working mothers, no father, or an extended family of aunts, uncles, and grandparents. All homes should not be exemplified as neat suburban ones with lovely lawns and trees.

An opportunity to talk about their own experiences within the family and discuss the reasons that families are different will improve language skills as well as help them understand their own circumstances. Discussions of feelings of hate, love, and prejudice, and the importance of the individual improves the self-concept.

Small-group experiences to improve social skills should take the place of individual activities at first—learning to take one's turn to speak, really listening to others, and being listened to are important social skills to acquire. The opportunity to complete a task with the assistance of a classmate, learning to share materials, and the pleasure of having one's own special place may be quite new experiences for many of the disadvantaged.

Enriching and concrete experiences are vitally needed by these children. Even though they may live within a teeming metropolis, the child's world is often limited to the ghetto environment. Meaningful trips to parks, museums, theatres, and the close rural environs are important. How can a child conceptualize the meaning of a city if he has no experience with which to contrast it? Research indicates that the learning style of the disadvantaged responds to physical contact with materials and thus requires many concrete experiences to maximize immediate reinforcement. Textbooks often present experiences that are unrealistic for the disadvantaged. Materials for their early experiences should be selected with care to insure that they are relevant and understandable.

Nongrading, with continuous progress, presents many advantages for these children. The feeling of failure has been eliminated, there is concern for their individual problems and needs, close personal contact with adult models are provided; and they may progress at their own rate.

Summary

The goals for social studies as outlined at the beginning of the chapter focus on the humanistic aspects of learning. The processes and content presented to achieve these goals in a nongraded program, whether primary, intermediate, or for the disadvantaged, emphasize these humanistic aspects. However, cognitive development and skill building have not been ignored, but are related to the major focus. Through this humanistic approach social studies can become the dynamics of change in our society.

Notes

1. Statewide Social Science Study Committee, *Progress Report* (Sacramento, Cal.: State Department of Education, March 1968), pp. 23–30.

CHAPTER 6

Nongrading the Middle Years
by

ANN GROOMS

Dr. Grooms is known nationally and internationally for her work in assisting school systems to customize their educational programs. She has worked with some 600 school systems in the United States, Latin America, Europe, and Asia. A former teacher, administrator, university professor, and writer, Dr. Grooms is now president of Educational Services Institute, Inc., and has received much acclaim for the "most praiseworthy" school programs that the Institute has helped to develop. Perspectives on the Middle School *is perhaps her best-known work.*

Introduction

A COMPENDIUM concerning the middle school can serve a useful purpose. While the thrust of this writer's thinking is directed specifically at the problem of improving educational programs for ten- to fourteen-year-old students, the ideas expressed here have implications for American education from nursery school through adult programs. The dominant message of this compendium is learning support. All the sub-systems of an educational program—facilities, personnel, procedures, techniques, and materials—must be tailored to accomplish the support end. It is felt that proper mixture of the sub-systems will result in a system of education that enhances rather than circumscribes the learning capabilities of students. It is to the enhancement of learning capabilities that the middle school program is dedicated.

Until now the American public has placed much confidence in the premise of school achievement level. One question that is of paramount importance to all Americans is: Can the type of education afforded students significantly affect their learning achievement levels? Recently, several documents, including the Coleman Report,[1] purport to present findings indicating that present school program characteristics have little effect on student learning. Their findings are based on data that refute existing educational practices.

Ample evidence exists to suggest that American education has been in a long slumber, but it appears to be awakening; theoretical and technical bases for a new education are emerging. The new education promises to realign student/institutional relationships: Educational institutions will exist to facilitate student learning, not to impart knowledge in a predigested form. In the twentieth-century world, learning has become a life-long process rather than an activity that is terminated by a certificate award.

The millennium for public education is not yet at hand, for there must be improved changes in facilities, materials, procedures, techniques, and personnel. These changes must be supported willingly by the populace, and although the change process is beginning to be understood through behavioral science studies, the time frame for implementing change is becoming critical.

The educational segment that is changing most rapidly is the middle school program, which was developed during the last decade and is designed for 10-to-14-year-old students. While some middle schools are just slightly altered upper elementary and junior high schools, a unique program is described in the book *Perspectives on the Middle School*.[2]

Middle School Organization

Since the ten- to fourteen-year-old student differs from his counterpart of a generation ago, what type of grade organization would serve him best—5–8, 6–8, 7–8, or 7–9? Within the last fifty years we have seen a proliferation of grade arrangements all based on the premise that educational experiences can be neatly packaged into single-year programs, and that the single-year programs can somehow be integrated into a total package without an integrator being involved. Hence, it really has not made too much difference how the present organization was structured. The advocates of a given grade arrangement are often hard-pressed to identify the differences between elementary, intermediate, middle, and junior high school programs.

None of the arrangements listed are adequate for the education of the 10–14-year-old. A different approach is needed. For want of a better description, this approach will be called middle school, but the middle school discussed here will differ significantly from the institution presently identified as "middle school."

In recent years authorities have written voluminously about the inability of the junior high school to satisfy the educational requirements of preadolescent and older children. Among the more vocal has been the eminent American anthropologist, Margaret Mead, whose writings project an image of dull, uninteresting, and unchallenging programs for all students regardless of ability. Her readers are led to conclude that students are under-achievers, that they have more esteem for the social rather than the intellectual facets of school programs, and that their spirit of inquiry and experimentation are adversely influenced. For 10–14-year-olds the school years are something to be endured and passed through as rapidly as possible.

The middle school, then, must provide a solution to the dull, uninteresting, and unchallenging program problem. The task is complicated by the constraint that the middle school program must afford equal opportunity for all students. The dedication of the Fox Lane Middle School, Mount Kisco, N. Y., eloquently expresses a fundamental tenet of middle school education: "This school is dedicated to each pupil who enters—that each may discover his own talents for learning, for growth, and for service."

Knowing the Middle School Student

Middle schools provide a system of education that supports the learning activities of 10–14-year-old students, and they have distinctive programs that differentiate them from other educational institutions. Adherents of the middle school believe that the student must be responsible for his learning and share in the selection of learning activities. What is likely to result in the way of attitudes toward self and love of learning from student participation in middle school programs as contrasted with conventional upper elementary and junior high schools where the curriculum is fixed (established) for the student?

SELF-INITIATED LEARNERS

In this chapter the term "middle school" is limited to those institutions that recognize that the development of self-initiated learners is their contribution to the school's patrons. This middle school, by definition, accepts older children who have given achievement levels in basic skills, guides and supports them through the most rapidly changing periods of their lives, and sends them out as self-initiated learners. Since the middle school recognizes the worth of each student and adheres to the virtues of equal education opportunities, it is challenged to establish and maintain excellence throughout the school to assure that all students emerge with a capability for independent study and confidence in their ability to achieve realistic learning goals.

It is axiomatic that the middle school exists to serve its patrons—parents, community, state, nation, and world. This idea might startle readers who are familiar with the idea of students as consumers of education, that is, that the process of education consists of passing information on to students. School patrons see educational institutions as devouring ever-increasing amounts of available tax resources. They see some of the resources wasted in the form of school dropouts, who are unable to contribute effectively in a complex scientific/industrial society. They are alarmed by findings such as those of the Coleman Report concerning the correlation between socio-economic factors and school success. They are disparaging in their attitudes when they are informed that if the products of education can no longer serve its patrons, alternatives to public education will be proposed.

The middle school serves its patrons through the development of self-initiated learners. Self-initiated learners do not happen by chance. Students must discover not only that they have a capacity for learning but also that they need to learn how to succeed in a given discipline in a satisfying manner. This suggests that the structure of whatever is to be learned as well as the particular student's learning style must be identified. The middle school may never be able to make learning easy for all students, but it can strive to make independent learning possible.

Since the organization must focus on the individual student (in this instance a student who is moving from learning dependence toward a state of learning independence during the most changing years of his life), the implications for organizational structure are clear: (1) the structure must accommodate students spanning the dependence-independence spectrum from total dependence on the professional for learning support and guidance to specific independence, (2) the educational program must be centered around learning to learn rather than on the mastery of discipline facts, (3) communication within the school and between the school and its patrons must be free and open, (4) provisions must be made for controlling change, and (5) decision-making opportunities must be accorded to patrons and school personnel.

MAJOR PREMISES

The middle school is concerned with looking at its students in terms of what they are, how they are functioning, and what they are feeling and thinking, as well as with their endogenic behaviors and activities. The emphasis is on the current, the inherent, and the intrinsic, with a focus on the satisfactions and joys of being a youngster, as well as on their problems, their difficulties, and their conflicts.

The following paragraphs offer a few major premises in looking at youngsters in general. Included in these premises are some other types of general and specific concerns dealing with human development.

1. The human brain is not a mirror of the curriculum or of the occupational structure. The human brain or the human organism is not initially endowed with parts or functions that are the direct counterpart of different parts of the curriculum. The human brain or human organism must be pulled and pushed and stretched in order to conform eventually with the artificial way we have established of functioning either at school or at work. The hierarchy of important aspects of the curriculum, the priorities assigned, are not the counterparts of the priority hierarchy that the organism assigns. Yet it is precisely during the middle school years that the priority conflict is most critical. This conflict has the potential for inducing permanent disfiguring of natural and spontaneous bents. However, there is a second potential. It is evident that in order to develop an *individual's* hierarchy potential the curriculum must be sharply revised to provide a curriculum for students with similar hierarchies and priorities.

2. Development is not the same as growth. Development refers to the emergence of new, *different* characteristics rather than *more* of the old ones. The emergence of new characteristics—the transformation of people—is a far cry from the processing of individuals in order to produce more of a certain kind of entity or dimension.

3. Development is not steady, continuous, or linear. During the years 10–14 internal development is of utmost importance because of the student's fantastic developmental discontinuity, as evidenced by unsteadiness, instability, and unpredictability—unpredictable except to the extent that educators make it predictable, by channeling it away from discontinuity into an artificial continuity.

4. Whatever has been thought about human potential is now a thing of the past. We are on the threshold of a new understanding of the vast potential of all people. The IQ and the normal curve should be abandoned because they tell us very little about the real potential of men. The intelligence quotient and the normal distribution curve are frequently detrimental to the understanding of man's nature because they describe very limited functions and very limited groups of people exposed to rather limited and segmented experiences.

Children's Rights

It is because of the new visions that arise about human potential in general that a significant corollary should be made here with regard to children: the development of the children's rights movement—something which is very new in the thinking of humanity. Children, as Golding pointed out, have typically been objects of exploitation—exploitation of various needs. The fantastic success of the novel *Lord of the Flies*[3] is significant. Along with many other works of fiction or drama it calls attention to the fact that children are growing in their sense of importance, significance, autonomy, and ability to function. Any discussion of curriculum change that does not recognize that the general social movement towards human rights has, as an inevitable counterpart, the movement of children's rights is missing an important understanding of how much children are capable of doing. The significance of the Red Guard Movement in China is that Red Chinese culture obviously thinks of its children as being significant participants in the overall social movement. Several other countries have assigned the same importance to involvement.

CHILD DEVELOPMENT

Let us consider some themes, concepts, ideas, and paradoxes about child development and the way the individual emerges. The first is the notion of variability with the focus on intraindividual variability, that is, the tremendous pattern of differences within a person. The important considerations are not individual differences from person to person or from group to group, but the intraindividual differences in rates of metabolism and percentiles of audio acuity, visual acuity, color sense, and binocular vision. Roger Williams, a biochemist, has charted at least two hundred significant types of scores that truly describe the intraindividual patterns that account for the different kinds of tempo and pace of learning, the motivation and the ability to sustain effort, and the ability to move up and down.[4] When we understand that the human being cannot be reduced to five, ten, or even fifteen scores, and that he functions as a person in more than two hundred different ways, we begin to comprehend the fact that we are probably not only overlooking the whole idea of variability but are also blatantly violating it by constructing curricula whose objectives are to turn out the "well-rounded" person.

In any significant school experience there must be an opportunity for the individual's variability to be utilized. Test scores presumably describe how the tested individual is functioning at the time of the test. People not only develop their individual patterns of functions differently but they also develop at different rates. One day, even that fifth percentile in numerical ability may be changed.

The second theme is the problem of continuity and discontinuity. No one in our complex society needs protection and understanding in the light of this general principle of the development of human beings as much as the middle school student and the adolescent. In our society the typical six-year-old functions at a much more complex level than the full-grown adult in primitive society. He moves rapidly through a series of experiences that catapult him into becoming a highly differentiated, fragmented individual. He is moving helter-skelter by the time he reaches the older childhood and preadolescent years. He is moving into a highly fragmented educational experience at a time when he has certain understandings of his own abilities that are not recognized by the adult world. The individual is not likely to understand the qualities of changes affecting him. He does not understand why he moves so quickly from one area to the next and nobody makes connections for him. He does not understand the meaning of the math for which he has marginal ability and indifferent interest or why he should even learn it. Frequently, he is told that the reason he should study math is that he needs it, the reason he needs it is that it is good for him, and the reason it is good for him is that he has to have it.

Spontaneity does not come when one piles fragmentation on the learner and justifies the action by platitudes. Instead of searching and probing for the reason for studying certain content that the student does not feel he wants to learn, be honest and tell the individual that perhaps the only reason he needs to learn it is that it is in the curriculum. Also, when the curriculum becomes fragmented, nothing is done to protect the individual's fantastic curiosity and exploratory drive by helping him understand the relationship between the various subjects and the different aspects of the curriculum.

It is my belief that what happens to the student in college is a result of his never having had a chance as a middle student to think about the connection between the individual fragmentations of the curriculum— what they add up to, what they mean, or how they can motivate him to learn. When the day comes that he must be a self-starter, he is incapable of it. If he goes through a series of such discontinuous experiences from day to day, year to year, from one school to the next, from one style of teaching to another, and no one talks to him about it, then even the finest curriculum, individually put together, with the best faculty, the most flexible scheduling, and the best facilities cannot educate him. Although it is not always necessary to break the discontinuity, there is definitely a need to talk explicitly with youngsters about continuity, to engage them in a dialogue about it constantly so that they have a chance to understand the quality and meaning of what is happening in their current life.

A third important theme in the development of young people's lives is the one of differentiation and integration. This theme is an obvious concern in all developmental psychology. During the ages 10 to 14 significant differences are emerging between male and female students. There is a serious question as to whether educators should begin earlier than they ever have to provide somewhat different experiences for boys and girls, both to help them develop a clear sense of identity and to take into account the fact that the whole culture is at work telling boys and girls simultaneously (1) that they are different and (2) that they must learn exactly the same things. This does not mean a dual system of education, or completely segregated schooling, such as Margaret Mead recommended.[5] What is meant here is that it is a well-known fact that until the fifth and sixth grades, girls' mathematics and arithmetic scores are either slightly better or the same as boys. Beginning around the sixth or seventh grade, girls decline significantly in math scores. The decline in mathematical ability does not result from any serious brain damage that is sex-linked, but is the result of a continuing cultural reinforcement that girls are supposed to develop a math block. If a math block is being developed on the one hand and the same curriculum is being imposed on the other, the school is not being successful in reversing what the rest of the culture is doing. There is no easy answer for alleviating this situation; however, it is important to examine the possibilities of accommodating some differentiation in curriculum to allow for sex differences.

At any point in the child's development there is an increasing differentiation and a breakdown of ability to finer and finer degrees. It is possible not only to talk about general math ability but also to talk about five or six different types of numerical or mathematical ability, each of which have a different pattern. One no longer talks about verbal ability; nevertheless, as differentiation proceeds some children find dealing with vocabulary easy while others find handling paragraphs very simple. Paragraph- and word-meaning scores begin to split far apart: Poetry, fiction, drama, expository writing, spelling, and other skills increasingly branch off into individual patterns. Who is to say that some could be writing ungrammatical poetry?

With the amount and rate of differentiation increasing, what can be done to effect integration? Integration must come from the concern for the theme of independence. The ability and capacity for 10–14-year-old students to function on their own, to be independent learners, to take hold of their own tasks and schedules is currently being eroded. It is important to know that as development occurs from the 10 to 14 age interval to ages 15 and 16, a point is reached where realism about different aspects of our society is increasing. Almost any 10-year-old in our society knows more about the principle of the jet engine and the way space vehicles work than practically any upper elementary or junior high school teacher, with the exception of professionals in the math and science disciplines.

The capacity for understanding reality, for knowing the real world, must be perceived as a function of the fact that a 12- or 13-year-old has lived approximately a sixth or seventh of his life span. It is important to realize how much experience the student has had (rather than how much he has not had), how much he knows, how much he can master, and how much he can control. The repertoire of skills and functioning capacity of a 10- or 11-year-old in our society is so great that further perception results in declining confidence in his ability to manage himself, until the day arrives when he is permitted to see that he is ready to function in the adult world. Despite the occurrence of earlier sexual maturity (approximately a year to a year and a half earlier than fifty years ago), despite superior physical, cognitive, and other functions, children are placed in limbo around the age of 11 or 12, from which they have a hard time emerging until the day comes when they begin to get the signals and are ready to emerge.

This particular flexibility is applicable to all areas of learning and functioning, even to such things as discussing intelligently the meaning of curriculum. One startling example is afforded from my experiences in the Soviet Union. Beginning in the first and second grades, children are members of youth organizations, which play a major role in the conduct, behavior, and learning of children. These young Octoberists in the primary years (at the age of eleven, during our middle school years) later become the young pioneers, and the young pioneers have an across-the-board membership in just about every classroom in the Soviet Union. They take the responsibility for discipline and learning problems: for instance, if a youngster is not doing well in math, the other children decide who is good in that subject and then it is up to that child to tutor the poorer student. If someone misbehaves the other children talk to him about his behavior. An English observer, Nigil Grant, in his book on Soviet education,[6] has pointed out that it is the easiest job in the world to be a teacher in the Soviet Union because discipline and learning problems are typically handled by the children. There is very little need for guidance counselors, school psychologists, therapists, or even for remedial work simply because all these functions are performed by the children. It is very cheap labor and very effective in terms of education. In the midst of a totalitarian and authoritarian regime a participating democracy operates at the grass-roots level, where it counts. There is very little question about the capacity of young people to learn and to initiate behavior side by side with a strategic, unimaginative curriculum.

One cannot spend any time in the Soviet Union without being impressed with the fact that the students learn and read. And do they read! One-fourth of all books published in the world are published in the Soviet Union. The tremendous drive for publishing comes from a trust and a faith in the capacity of children to learn and to teach each other. Children do not instinctively learn to use the criteria for full success. In his books on the adolescent society and the adolescent in school, James Coleman shows that among such criteria as being popular, well liked, attractive, or athletic, learning and the drive for learning come last in both American society and the American high school.[7] Learning and the drive for learning are extremely high and fully accepted by the preadolescent and the adolescent in the Soviet society. Children are not just athletic, they do not just have fun, or look for popularity only. Children are just as much driven to learn.

Consider now a fourth theme—the theme of competence rather than that of achievement. They are not synonymous. It is not always possible to judge how effective an individual will be in controlling and dealing with his environment from his achievement test scores. A youngster's drive is to be competent, to master his environment, and to function effectively. The problem is how to keep this drive for competence in his mind during the discontinuity of growing up. Limited, segmented, and fragmented experiences do not always move the individual to try to become competent in the things he feels he can do and would like to do. A child should be given a chance to master those things that he feels he can do before he takes on the challenge of those he cannot do as well.

Records of later school years often reveal any one of a number of blocks or disabilities. The history goes something like this: At some strategic point in the student's learning (frequently in the years 10–14) a teacher told him that he had to drop everything else and learn some specific materials, even if it meant sheer drill. The fear of not being able to accomplish this unnecessary, traumatic experience was cumulative, and it usually deterred the student from that particular subject area. Disabilities or blocks happen, in part, because there is a misdiagnosis as to the ways in which people achieve competence. People achieve competence because they want to master something, and once they have mastered it by self-direction it frequently releases them to master other things. For this reason we should listen to our students when they try to tell us what they would like to do.

Managing the Middle School

The middle school must accommodate students who span a wide range of dependent-independent learning capabilities. Since studies of individual differences show that these capabilities do not correlate positively with age and that both younger and older students benefit from student tutorial assistance, an ungraded structure is required. Because it is mandatory that close student-professional relationships be established, developed, and maintained, maximum student team size of 125 should be established. The minimum team size will depend on the competence of the professional staff, student capabilities, and the availability of material and facility resources.

The composition of the learning team affects the success of the middle school operation. Procedures must be determined and implemented to optimize peer influences. It is necessary to know not only the student's present academic achievement but also his learning models—his aptitude for benefiting from particular instructional approaches, his desire to achieve, and his special strengths that can be related to the structure of a certain discipline. Establishing optimum teams is a management challenge. Plans should be made to establish student teams that will maintain continuity throughout the middle school years. New students enter the team at the lower end of the dependent-independent learning spectrum every year while others depart from the upper end, but for the students involved in team activities, the learning process flows on, the characteristic esprit de corps of the team remains.

PROFESSIONAL STAFF

The principal thrust of the middle school's educational program must be toward learning to learn rather than on the mastery of subject matter facts. A few years ago Emmett Williams[8] described the curriculum of the middle school as the staff of beautiful people, and he may have posited a truism. Learning to learn implies a professional staff thoroughly competent in particular disciplines—generalists, rather than specialists, who are thoroughly skilled and knowledgeable in instructional theory.

The professional staff, operating in the disciplines, is organized into teams to guide and support the learning endeavors of individual students. A professional team consists of a professional from each of the disciplines (mathematics, science, social studies, and communication skills) and a team coordinator. The team should have the services of a guidance counselor, specialists from the learning and language laboratories, professionals from the unified arts areas, and paraprofessionals. The professional team members are responsible both individually for supporting learning in their given disciplines and collectively for producing self-initiated learners capable of self-development in the academic disciplines.

Having generated student teams and professional teams, the school must then see that they spawn learning teams. Middle school management must integrate student teams and professional teams into a cohesive unit in which self-initiated learners are developed. The preferred manner of forming student teams has already been indicated. Developing professional teams involves professional training, internships, personnel selection, and staff induction and development activities. The members of a professional team must not only be academic generalists and instructional theory application experts *but* they must also be personally compatible with the other members of the professional team. Middle school management must integrate the learning team(s) and supply the required resource support.

COMMUNICATION

Communication channels within the school and between the school and its patrons must be open and kept free from harmful interference. The middle school depends on achieving effectiveness through school communication; therefore, its organizational structure is flat rather than pyramidal in form. Information flows down from the top (the manager or principal) directly to the team coordinators and staff, and is a two-step process at the most. There is no intervening staff to filter and/or impede information flow. Information moving up from the learning teams flows directly to the principal. Information freely passes laterally between the learning teams and the other professionals in the school.

The internal communications network makes all the personnel resources of the school available to work out problems.

Middle school patrons are described as being parents, community members, the state, the nation, and the world. The extent of the patronage points up the need for managing patron communications. The scope of possible problems is of sufficient magnitude that a school-and-community-relations expert is needed. The school must interact with its patrons; it must have individual and collective patron support. Communications and a communication management program are stressed, in part, because of the ways schools are likely to be financed in the future. They will depend on donations from individuals, foundations, industry, and grants from the national government, as well as local and state taxes.

CHANGING INSTITUTION

The middle school is a changing institution. The school either must manage the change process or it will be in the unfortunate position of trying to react to it. The compensatory programs of the 1960's furnish excellent examples of the failure of schools to respond to changes and then belatedly responding with educational approaches that proved unsuccessful in the regular school programs.

One member of the middle school staff, the change catalyst, is responsible for stimulating change and evaluating its effect on the school program. He is a knowledgeable change-process technician, who assists the school's professional staff, its manager, and its patrons in bringing about changes that will accomplish the school's objectives more effectively.

In the 1960's the inadequacy of centralized decision-making in American public education became apparent. Traditionally, decision-making has been centralized; the central office, far removed from the individual school's patrons, students, and professionals passed down programs to be administered. The schools were only partly managed by their administrators, who monitored programs and performed supervisory functions. The planning and organizing aspects of management were retained by the central office.

Centralized management is antithetical to middle school philosophy. If middle schools are to be productive, management must be decentralized. The middle school must be free to develop its own educational program. The responsibility for its success must rest in its local management and professional personnel. When the school system's central office delegates responsibility to middle school management and establishes policies that are compatible with middle school philosophy, a middle school can become operational. With decentralization, the principal can call on his school patrons to help develop school policy peculiar to that middle school, and his staff and students can make decisions as the need arises.

A typical middle school structure is shown in Figure One. The orga-

MIDDLE SCHOOL ORGANIZATIONAL CHART

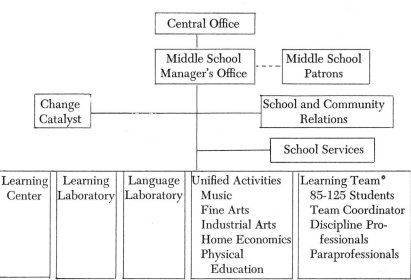

* School population and size of learning teams will determine number required.

FIGURE ONE

nization reflects the requirement that the middle school be a separate management entity, and the close relationships of all the people involved.

IMPLEMENTATION

After a management plan for the middle school has been determined, the feasibility of implementation must be considered. Will the current state of the education art support a middle school program? Are materials sufficiently developed to support many different levels of achievement and learning rates? Bruner[9] suggests that a student can be taught anything at any time in an intellectually honest way. Do we have sufficient knowledge about the structure of disciplines to support Bruner's claim? If teachers have been trained in conventional institutions and are experienced in conventional pedagogy, can they be developed into the type of professional staff members required by middle schools? Will present research in educational psychology support the varied learning styles of 85–125 students, when each style is unique? Learning styles will influence the extent to which a student becomes a self-initiated learner in particular disciplines. What about learning continuity? Since the middle school assumes a four-year period of continuous progress in learning how to learn, what happens when students change schools, as frequently as they do in central city schools? These problems are typical of those facing the middle school manager.

Many systems have foundered on the shoals of inadequate scientific and technical support. It can be stated, for the benefit of middle school innovators, that middle schools need not be among the defunct. The reason is that the middle school does not have to become fully operational all at once. Middle school managers must be realists. They must realize that the success or failure of a middle school depends greatly on school patrons and staff. Therefore, a school system planning to implement a middle school should bring together its tentative middle school manager, school-and-community-relations expert, and change catalyst long before the contemplated opening of the school. The school patrons, staff, and students should be brought into the planning activities as early as possible. Experts in structuring disciplines, child and early adolescent psychology authorities, and developers of individualized materials should be included in the planning sessions. The location for the middle school must be chosen carefully. Since many withdrawals from central city school result from arbitrarily drawn school district boundaries, the new middle school must be located so as to minimize student withdrawals because of family relocation within the geographic area served by the school system.

It is apparent that the management of the middle school does not start with the initiation of the operational phase, but rather with the conceptional phase. The middle school manager must be a creator as well as an operator. Middle school management is not for the unimaginative and not for those who lack the fortitude to face challenges. It is for those professionally prepared managers who realize that a new system of education for 10–14-year-olds is mandatory, and who are willing to accept the risks inherent in undertaking any innovative enterprise for which the scientific research and technology to support it are still evolving.

The Middle School Curriculum

In the beginning stages of developing the curriculum for the middle school, certain guidelines need to be established.

The first essential for a successful program is a staff of adults with uncommon talents and abilities. The teachers should be creative, imaginative, inspired, and inspiring. They should be knowledgeable in academic fields and gifted in understanding older children, preadolescents, and younger adolescents. A program of selection, recruitment, and special training is necessary to develop a staff with these special qualifications, but the school should settle for nothing less.

The curriculum of the middle school must honor the preciousness of every child. If the new middle school organization is to be worthy of all the talent and energy that will be required to effect a true reorganization, on the order of the movement that produced the junior high school, serious emphasis must be placed on the worth and dignity of every individual. Every curriculum offering, every technique and procedure, and every school policy must be planned to enhance the development of a positive self-concept. The fully functioning adult is a person who sees himself as able to cope with problems and challenges and as an important and contributing member of groups. Experiences that foster these attitudes belong in the curriculum; experiences that seem to destroy or negate these attitudes do not belong.

The design of the middle school must emphasize discovery. Opportunities must be planned for the pupil to discover himself—his potentials and limits, his interests and aversions. They should include opportunities for him to discover other people, his own world, his heritage, and his future. Discovery should be a dominant motif running through the curriculum.

The middle school curriculum must foster self-direction. This guideline is accepted as a desirable goal of education, but self-direction is one of those goals toward which *everyone* is supposed to be working, and as a result almost no one regards it as urgent. Those planning the curriculum of a middle school must believe in the importance of self-direction and provide opportunities for the pupils to practice it.

The middle school curriculum must emphasize continued learning. This emphasis has at least two dimensions: a *zest for learning*, which comes from the mood, environment, and philosophical and psychological orientation of a school, and the *skills* of continued learning, which include instruction in the use of various modes of inquiry and the discovery method.

The middle school program gives high priority to the intellectual components of the curriculum. There is a planned sequence of concepts and skills for the general education areas of the curriculum. This plan does not imply an emphasis on mastering content in a narrow range of academic disciplines, but rather on creating a climate in which learning is exciting and rewarding. The personal and humanistic values of learning are as important as the academic, practical, and vocational. Intellectual integrity does not require identical minimum standards for all. What is required is that every learner be challenged to perform well at whatever level he is capable of. All children are capable of intellectual growth, regardless of differences in ultimate intellectual development. In such an environment, intellectual pursuits are as respected as the social and athletic components of the school program. Habits of scholarship are formed and children are helped to see that learning can be its own reward, uncluttered by any extrinsic system of grades. A series of planned opportunities for developing both creative and disciplined thinking is scheduled for every student.

Human values underlie all aspects of the middle school program. The real aim of the middle school program is to develop people who love beauty in all its forms—the beauty of a plant in a small garden space, a cell under a microscope, a well-written paper, a project made with one's own hands, a friendship discovered or deepened. The middle school years are a uniquely advantageous time for helping children to formulate personal values and standards, and to analyze and question social attitudes and group behavior. Children in the 10–14 age interval are undergoing physical and psychological changes that they are striving to understand. They are increasingly aware of discrepancies between stated ideals and observed actions. Intellectually honest and emotionally calm exploration of these value areas must be provided for in the middle school curriculum.

The design of the curriculum may take many forms, and the content will certainly vary, as curriculum workers plan and implement middle school programs, keeping these guidelines in mind.

MAJOR CURRICULUM COMPONENTS

A curriculum might have three major components or areas: General Studies, Learning Skills, and Personal Development. Of course, there will not be classes bearing these names. In fact, the whole concept of classes and classwork in the usual sense might be done away with in the middle school. In operation, these components are often integrated as an individual pupil draws on content, skill processes, and data from several academic disciplines and sources to solve a problem, write a theme, or build a project. It is necessary to identify and assign tentative priorities and some sequence to those essential curriculum elements to assure a balance in the total curriculum offered.

General Studies. This area includes learning experiences that give the student a heightened awareness of his *cultural heritage* and *other common learnings* essential to civic and economic literacy. The content and methodology of the General Studies Area would be drawn, for the most part, from the large-scale, national curriculum projects. In mathematics, any of the modern approaches, with their teaching aids and student materials, for which teachers have been or may be trained, might serve as a base for learning and understanding the quantitative aspects of the world. In the sciences, programs like Paul Brandwein's[10] could be followed. They include concepts from earth and space sciences—physics, biology, and chemistry—and have the pupils working as scientists to discover inductivity using methods of inquiry appropriate to the particular science. In social studies, several concepts would be identified and developed, particularly those dealing with self-understanding, living in a family and a community, and the interdependence of mankind. Language arts would have three components—an inductive approach to language study following the newer linguistic developments, a program focusing primarily but not exclusively on a close reading of literature appropriate for 10–14-year-olds, and a well-defined composition program.

How does this area of the curriculum differ from any standard curriculum of mathematics, science, social studies, and English? It differs in this important way: There are no quantitative requirements and no mythical, minimum group standards. There are no courses and no classes. There is no delusion about jurisdiction, no frustrations, and few hypocrisies of competitive grading. There is just a curriculum plan—

freed of trivia and focused on key concepts and underlying relationships —that allows skillful professionals to choose from a vast reservoir of possibilities those learning experiences most appropriate to a given individual at a given moment.

It was stated that there would be no classes. A school without classes? Have you ever been to a good, happy summer camp? Have you been to a camp with a minimum of required activities but a great many exciting and challenging opportunities for individual and group participation, where the camp staff are healthy, happy, intelligent, older youths and adults with whom the children want to identify and whose counsel they value and follow? This is the atmosphere that is desired for the middle school.

How can the middle school be sure that pupils will receive a balanced program of general studies by following the highly voluntary approach proposed? First, every pupil should have a teacher-counselor who knows him well and who loves and respects him. Second, at frequent combined meetings, all the teacher-counselors and other staff members should examine and evaluate the progress of individual pupils and plan opportunities and activities accordingly. Third, the middle school should provide a wide range of possible ways of achieving the goals of general studies with a rich store of materials and resources for individual and group use. Fourth, it should abandon the myth that requiring a student to study a subject means that he learns. A balanced curriculum is achieved by providing opportunities, environment, resources, motivation, and skilled guidance, and not by requiring coverage of any particular selection of courses.

Learning Skills. Learning skills are being developed as boys and girls read, write, solve problems, study, and work in and out of school. A certain level of development is presupposed for all academic work beyond readiness-program stages. Some of the pupils will not have reached that presupposed level. The middle school curriculum must provide diagnostic testing to discover specific deficiencies and remedial programs to overcome them. These measures call for highly trained specialists and well-equipped laboratory centers. For example, educators are just beginning to discover the relationship between certain neurological functions and specific language difficulties. This area of the curriculum is individually prescribed, just as a physician prescribes medication for a patient based on his diagnosis.

Personal Development. This area of the curriculum includes those experiences that fulfill personal and remedial needs, permit exploration of personal interests, and promote physical and social growth: health and physical education; individually planned experiences in foreign languages, typing, technical training, music, art, dramatics, and journalism; student-managed enterprises; community work projects; and advanced work in science, mathematics, and other fields of individual special competence. Special interest centers, competently supervised and operated on a flexible time basis, will allow students to pursue hobbies, work on projects connected with their studies, or an outside interest. Scout merit work and other youth programs may be incorporated into the school program.

Summary

The middle school is designed to serve the needs of older children, preadolescent, and early adolescents. Pupils are accepted in the middle school around the age of ten and progress to the upper or senior level of high school around the age of thirteen. Children in this age bracket need freedom of movement, opportunities for independence, a voice in the running of their own affairs, and the intellectual stimulation of working with different groups and with different professionals. They are eager and ready for experiences quite different from those of elementary school. A congenial school environment for preadolescents is free of the departmental rigidity, the pressures of interschool competitions, and the tensions of older adolescent social functions, which loom so large in the typical junior high school. The organizational arrangements of the middle school foster growth from childhood dependence toward a high degree of self-sufficiency. During this stage of their growth, children have to adjust to dramatically changing roles and they need a school climate that is tolerant to trial and error and that permits children to make mistakes and profit by them without fear of embarrassment.

Notes

1. James Coleman, *Quality of Education* (Washington, D.C.: Office of Education, 1966).

2. Ann Grooms, *Perspectives on the Middle School* (Columbus, Ohio: Charles E. Merrill Books, Inc., 1967).

3. William Golding, *Lord of the Flies* (New York: Coward, 1965).

4. Roger Williams, *Biochemical Individuality* (New York: John Wiley and Sons, 1956).

5. Margaret Mead, "Early Adolescence in the United States," *The Bulletin of the National Association of Secondary School Principals,* April 1965, pp. 5–10.

6. Nigil Grant, *Soviet Education* (Baltimore: Penguin Books, 1964).

7. James Coleman, *The Adolescent Society* (New York: Crowell-Collier Publishing Company, 1961).

8. Emmett Williams, *The Emergent Middle School* (New York: Harper Row & Winston, 1968).

9. Jerome S. Bruner, "Liberal Education for All Youth," *Education Digest* 31 (Feb. 1966), p. 5.

10. Paul Brandwein, *The Gifted Student as Future Scientist: The High School Student and His Commitment to Science* (New York: Harcourt, Brace and World, 1955).

CHAPTER 7

The Nongraded High School
by
JOHN M. JENKINS

Dr. John Jenkins has been actively associated with the non-graded movement since 1963, when he was an NASSP intern at Melbourne High School, Melbourne, Florida. He served for five years as principal of the nongraded Miami Springs High School, leaving that position to become an associate professor of education at the University of Miami, Coral Gables. At present, Dr. Jenkins is principal of the highly innovative Wilde Lake High School in the new city of Columbia, Maryland.

INDIVIDUAL DIFFERENCES are something that all educators talk about but very few ever really attempt to translate into action-oriented programs. Despite considerable research indicating that students differ both within and among themselves, programs that attempt to take these findings seriously are relatively scarce. Those that do exist are at best educational halfway houses where students are grouped into Procrustean molds on the basis of a variety of quantitative and qualitative criteria. These criteria, when analyzed, "spell" such futuristic notions as ability and/or potential.

The nongraded high school is a serious effort to deal with the present behavior of young people. Its form is a tacit recognition that if individual differences are indeed real, then they can only be reckoned with intelligently if one considers what the students know at their initial entrance into a school.

The popular belief that the nongraded school is merely an organizational shift in which students are placed into different administrative groupings is incorrect, and any facsimile of this fallacious model should be exposed for the imposter it is. The nongraded high school is something more than administrative manipulation. It is a blending of "proper" pupil placement with appropriate curriculum and instruction. Changing the organization only results in students going to different places in the school. It is more important to change what happens to them when they get there.

The ultimate goal of all education is to help students function more independently. In this context, the nongraded high school can be viewed for what it genuinely is, a way for students to become increasingly less dependent on outside stimulation for action. Any approach designed to free the student from outside dependence would therefore be construed as a type of nongraded education. Two theoretical models appear most frequently. In actual practice, most schools pioneering in this field utilize aspects of both models.

The first model is probably the easier of the two to establish, and provides a framework from which a truly individualized curriculum can be spun. It establishes a loose type of grouping properly called *phasing,* which permits a student to move from one group to another at any time it will benefit him. The use of the label, phase, is deliberate. It implies a temporary stage of development, a plateau, or point of departure, not a self-fulfilling prophecy. The phase becomes another name for a course of study, or better, an environment into which students are placed on criteria other than chronological age. Phases are sequentially numbered and are built on the notion that students need to develop competencies in the basics of a discipline before they are ready to ask more sophisticated questions. It is an inquiry model that recognizes the importance of students gaining more and more control of their academic destinies as well as their learning heuristics. Each phase of instruction in a subject area bases its *modus operandi* on what students are able to do. A subject required of all students for graduation may be offered at as many as five different phases, each phase being a separate course with separate assumptions about incoming student behavior and separate expectations of exiting behavior. Figure One summarizes the idea of phasing in relation to a school's program of studies.

The first model leads naturally into the next—a process that is properly called continuous progress education. In this model, which is a good deal more difficult to establish initially, students work through any

DESCRIPTION OF PHASING IN A NONGRADED
HIGH SCHOOL

Phase One	Courses at this level are designed to help students who are quite deficient in basic skills. Classes are small so that individual assistance can be given.
Phase Two	Courses at this level are designed to help students who are somewhat deficient in basic skills and who will profit from additional help with these skills.
Phase Three	Courses at this level are designed for students who are achieving in an average way.
Phase Four	Courses at this level are designed for students who desire to study a subject in depth.
Phase Five	Courses at this level are designed to give a student the opportunity to take a college-level course while still in high school.

FIGURE ONE

program as rapidly as they are able, without regard to length of residence. Time is considered a variable, not a constant. As students complete the requirements of one program they move on to the next. The curriculum permits a student to begin the study of a subject at the point of *his* entering behavior and allows him to go as deeply as his time, talent, and motivation permit. Failure is virtually eliminated for all practical purposes since the students are not attempting to complete the requirements of a course within a specified time. All that is required of each student is that he meet any local and state requirements for high school graduation.

In some schools the continuous progress units are referred to as Learning Activity Packages or LAPS. These packages are systematically developed by teachers who must consider the variables of pace, background, depth, and learning styles of the target population. LAPS deal with major ideas and, in combination, form what traditionally can be labeled a course of study. Major ideas are supported by any number of secondary ideas. The number of secondary ideas per major idea depends on the teacher, the group of students, and/or the idea itself. Primary ideas and their appropriate secondary ideas constitute the Learning Activity Package.

LAPS begin with the objectives for the major idea and include subobjectives for each of the secondary ideas. Following the objectives are lists of various activities designed to help the students achieve the specified ends. They work through these packages naturally, selecting those learning activities that fit their own idiosyncracies. Some students learn best by viewing, others by listening, and still others by reading. The key is the blending of the accomplishment with the process, not one against the other.

In continuous progress programs advancement to more challenging environments is based on demonstrated achievement. Students can enter or exit from programs at any time during the "normal" school year. Traditional marking procedures are usually replaced by some type of system whereby students and parents are kept informed of a student's mastery of the ideas included in the program.

An example of a course taught using the continuous progress approach is outlined in Figure Two.

Both phasing and continuous progress education are an outgrowth of the idea that learning environments should accommodate the

Continuous Progress Learning Model

Course: A Way or a Path to Achieve Given Ends
    I.   Rationale
   II. Objectives (stated behaviorally)
  III. Activities: Units of learning activity packages selected to achieve course objectives
       A.   Learning Activity Package "A"
          1. Rationale
          2. Objectives (stated behaviorally)
          3. Activities: secondary ideas selected in terms of LAP objectives
             a. Rationale
             b. Objectives (stated behaviorally)
             c. Activities
                (1) Differentiate for individual backgrounds
                (2) Differentiate for individual learning styles
             d. Evaluation: in terms of objectives* for secondary ideas
       B.   Learning Activity Package "B"**
  IV. Evaluation—in terms of course objectives

   * Students attempt the evaluations or tests when *they* are ready for them, and not at some specified time.
   ** Learning Activity Packages represent primary ideas. There will be as many learning activity packages for a course of study as there are ideas to support the objectives of the program.

Figure Two

learners. Most nongraded secondary schools utilize a combination of both models. Of the two, phasing is more easily established because it requires a change in the conventional grouping practices with an accompanying change in the curriculum. Once the faculty, student body, and community understand and accept phasing, steps can be taken to develop some continuous progress education. In contemplating the latter, it is wise to begin with those aspects of the subject matter disciplines that are skills-oriented.

A Plea for Relevance

If the curriculum is inextricably related to the school organization, it is only natural that consideration of courses or content follow the adoption of the philosophy of nongraded education and its objectives. Who determines what should ultimately comprise the school curriculum and the content of the courses? Educators would like to think that they have some control over the learning experiences designed for youth, and indeed they do. However, curriculum alternatives are subject to certain restrictions. Graduation requirements are prescribed by the states; parents want students to perform well on certain standardized tests; college entrance requirements generally present a standard menu; state legislatures often prescribe specific course offerings;[1] and even the students, at least at the high school level, come with built-in expectations. In spite of these obvious limitations, all is not lost. Some effective action can be taken at the building level to adapt the curriculum to the interests and needs of each student.

For example, schools can take the rubrics of graduation requirements and refine them. While it is perhaps true that all students must receive a Carnegie unit in English, what constitutes the course in English is not prescribed. It is my experience that a wide latitude is possible if school officials would only attempt to test the limits.

In the nongraded program, process becomes more important than product. Therefore, curricular packaging is given much thought and emphasis. The quest to adapt curricula to the student, and not vice versa, requires that one take a hard look at the insistence of equal educational requirements for all. Such a position fails to consider the differences within and among students and the reasons for which a student wishes to study a particular subject. The nongraded program understands these differences, and within state and local requirements, attempts to tailor educational experiences to fit individual students.

Despite the admission that the nongraded school takes a different view of the "process of education," it is still necessary to examine the relevance of curricular content. Much of what is now considered essential for all students could be dropped from the curriculum without impairing a student's chances for a successful life. Mastery of the skills of communication are primary, and probably some mathematics is needed to function effectively, but one would be hard-pressed to establish the universality of other content areas. Yet, the schools give students very little voice in the direction their education takes.

Students need to see the relationship between what is happening inside the school and what is happening outside the school. Too frequently the correlation between the two is zero or even negative. The curriculum in the nongraded school gives more than lip service to what is important to the student. Student values are not subservient to those of the teacher. Textbooks are usually replaced by a myriad of interesting materials; an abundance of elective areas exist; and the students are given a great deal of latitude in determining how they will spend their time. The thrust is toward relevance, for unless a student is motivated to learn, no curriculum, regardless of the level of sophistication, will make a difference.

Accent on Individuality

It is essential that learning activities are designed to assist students toward the internalization of desirable ends. This is accomplished best when the students are considered as individuals and when learning environments are developed that are appropriate to each student's *present* level of operation. A student's readiness for confronting knowledge at a variety of depth levels needs to be based on *his* background— on what he knows about a given subject or area. Caution must be exercised, however, to prevent the interpretation of a student's present level of knowledge as an end unto itself—a trap from which he cannot escape.

Currently a student's background is diagnosed by utilizing some combination of standardized achievement tests, pre-tests constructed by the teacher, and the student's previous success or lack of it in a similar area of study, as determined by school records. The notion of testing a student to determine his breadth of knowledge in a specific academic area needs to be broadened to include devices other than paper-and-pencil tests. After all, a test is a demonstration of one's understanding (read internalization) of learning *vis-à-vis* the cognitive, affective, and psychomotor domains. While paper-and-pencil tests can probably be devised to assess students in these areas of knowledge, they are not used extensively today.

Truly individualized or nongraded programs should extend beyond these criteria, and include data gathered from personal involvement with students. Ways can be devised to enable teachers to get to know students better—if this end is important. For example, the use of flexible scheduling, not necessarily modular, can facilitate a variety of student-teacher groupings. Different types of teacher aides can free teachers from non-professional duties and provide them with more time to get to know students better. This responsibility presupposes that teachers are sensitive beings, capable of making valid observations about individual students. Such an assumption might be judged presumptuous. Nevertheless, the administrator and the faculty can work together on realistic ways to become better acquainted with students. It is necessary for the success of the nongraded program that it be done.

In this setting, the role of the teacher shifts from a didactic model and a source of all wisdom to one of a teacher-advisor. As such, he becomes a guide in a journey, an analyzer of student performance, a prescriber of activities to fill in learning gaps, an alter ego, a confidant.

In extending the teacher's role to include some of the responsibilities hitherto associated with the guidance counselor, we are acknowledging that no guidance counselor, under the usual counselor-student ratio, can get to know all his counselees well enough to assist them effectively in decision-making activities. Teachers must be enlisted to assist with these functions if the charge of individual differences is to be met. Moreover, if the decision is related to a specified academic area, the teacher is in a better position to assess the student's knowledge in that area than the guidance counselor is. Decisions involving a student's movement from one learning environment to another are highly personal. They require an individual who understands the nature of the new learning activity and the nature of the client who will confront it. As builders and/or adapters of curricular programs, teachers are in a better position to offer constructive assistance to the student.

While the teacher may be the best individual to assess the background of the student and prescribe appropriate learning environments, it is the student himself who must ultimately do the learning. He needs to develop certain competencies in order to make sense out of the "blooming, buzzing, confusion" called twentieth-century society. The school can assist in this formidable task by building into its programs activities that involve the student in inquiry, discovery, and the heuristics of the disciplines.

The nongraded secondary school accentuates those aspects of learning in which the student realizes that he must discover for himself—that he must uncover, rather than cover, the contents of a course. He learns how to inquire into the structure of the disciplines, utilizing methods and techniques germane to the respective areas. The way of the mathematician differs from the way of the social scientist, and the way of the linguist differs from the way of the natural scientist. The student needs to learn how to recognize these differences, and how, when, and where to employ them for maximum effectiveness.

The Coleman Report, as reviewed by Dr. Edmund Gordon, indicates the importance of a student's gaining control over his own destiny and the relationship of this success to his achievement in school and society.[2] In the nongraded school, learning is perceived as a matter of helping students learn how to deal with new environments. This developmental process pervades the school program. New environments are created out of familiar events and materials so that students can gradually develop less trepidation about venturing into the unknown. As students gain more competency, they become more successful, and as they become more successful, they develop more positive attitudes toward themselves, their school, and their community. Like the poker player with a sizable quantity of chips at his disposal, the successful student can afford to take more chances. In today's complex, changing world the "spoils of victory" belong to those individuals who can face uncertainty with confidence. The strategy of the nongraded program is fashioned to produce these characteristics in *all* the students.

The Affective Is Effective

The atmosphere in the school is as important to the success of the nongraded program as the curriculum. Inquiry-centered learning requires a special type of environment in which to flourish and grow. Students who are frightened rarely venture far from home base, and a school that changes the externals and ignores the atmosphere within only tends to reinforce what the students already suspect: "They don't trust us."

Any serious attempt to invoke a new curriculum, based on a student's background and readiness for learning, must, by necessity, begin by considering the psychological well-being of the student. Subject matter (externals), no matter how sophisticated, can never be taught in a vacuum. Its validity is always in terms of a given population of students. How a learner is functioning at a given moment and in a given place affects the shape, form, and meaning of any external stimulus. This is why it is so crucial for the nongraded secondary program to consider the learner as important to the success of the program as the teacher or the content. Each impinges upon the other.

A repressive, threatening school environment tends to constrict the perception of the students, and forces them to place external stimuli into preconceived patterns. Furthermore, teachers who fail to "see" the importance of individual students to the success of their program doom the school program to a mild form of mediocrity at best.

Extrinsic learnings are more effective when they follow an attempt by students to come to grips with who and what they are. When students know what they want and where they are going, they tend to develop an altogether different attitude toward learning. The nongraded school endeavors to develop an appreciation for learning within all its students, but such a realization takes time. If the primary characteristic of the nongraded school is the acceptance of the student on his own terms, then it must acknowledge personal differences as requisite to cognitive undertakings.

Inquiry-centered learning, particularly, demands that students be free to expose areas of weakness, and with adolescents this is asking a great deal. As a general rule, the adolescent is not likely to share himself personally with anyone, let alone "someone over thirty." Thus, a special type of student-teacher involvement is implied. The beginning of inquiry is the realization that the right answer is not yet recorded, at least not by the inquirer. A non-defensive, non-judgmental atmosphere permits more students to drop their guard and open up. At this point the truly sensitive teacher is able to discover the personal differences between students.

A visitor to a nongraded secondary school would be immediately impressed by the relaxed atmosphere and the sense of purpose apparent in the student body. It is a personification of disciplined spontaneity:

students moving in a variety of directions simultaneously, their purposes clear, their eye on a resource. Students could be seen just passing time, waiting for a moment of insight to move them further along in their inquiry. The nongraded school is an intelligent environment, and above all a state of mind that focuses on experimentation and innovation. The school is viewed as a spacious learning laboratory in which students are free to "hammer," "paint," "tear down," "build up," and use the building as a means to many ends. Out of this potpourri of activity comes an identification with the school and a school spirit that transcends the traditional athletic variety.

Staffing the Nongraded High School

THE PRINCIPAL

Much has been written recently about the changing role of the secondary school principal. The gist of it is that he must indeed become the instructional leader of his school. Inasmuch as all the ramifications of the tradition underlying his position support what he does, his actions matter. What he *does* determines the élan of the school. If he busies himself with bus schedules, budgets, and the athletic program, he cannot expect to become a mover of teachers, an instigator of change. The nongraded high school demands a new breed of administrator, an *agent provocateur* who poses significant questions to teachers about teaching and learning, and helps them think more clearly about (1) what they want to do, (2) why they want to do it, and (3) how to bring it about.

Informal communications between the teachers and the principal are best. The principal in the nongraded high school gets out of his office and reaches the teachers and students on "the streets where they live." No principal ever improved instruction by greeting salesmen at the front door or peering into classroom windows. The fear so prominent in conventional high schools is replaced by a new spirit of cooperation. A teacher-administrator relationship based on mutual respect is paramount if the school is to take a serious step toward establishing an environment that encourages individualized instruction. The principal *is* the principal-teacher. He should practice the art of good teaching in his dealings with the staff.

What the principal does with the staff seems crucial. How does he get them to gain visceral acceptance of all the implications of nongraded education? Charisma? Eugenics? In-service education? The answer to this knotty problem probably lies in a fortuitous combination of all three. The probability of charisma residing in many principals is rather slim, and the adage that teachers are born, not made, appears too deterministic and leaves much to chance. A more realistic approach, and one within the control of all administrators, is an in-service education program aimed at re-educating teachers about the nature of young people and how they learn. The faculty meeting is one form, which has traditionally served only to prove that the principal does not understand what learning is all about. Instead of being dominated by the principal and dealing with items that are just as readily communicated in written bulletins, faculty meetings ought to provide the teachers with examples of superior large-group instruction. Their purpose should be the re-education and continued development of a staff of professional workers. Films, student presentations, resource speakers, and teaching demonstrations, selected as illustrations of good practices of individualized instruction, should be used. They should be succeeded by charges to teachers to try to implement an idea to improve their own instruction. The principal should follow up these "assignments," and when teachers are successful, broadcast the results for all to hear. Encouraging teachers to write about what they do is equally effective. Frequently these reports are duplicated and disseminated to the entire faculty, or are published. Teachers, like youngsters, want recognition and for many the mark of success is the principal's perception of their professional behavior. In the nongraded school, the principal uses the weight of his office to give dignity to teacher behavior that best exemplifies individualized instruction.

One large-group session per month is enough. It should be supplemented by small-group discussions and informal meetings between teachers and administrator. The small group can serve many purposes, but seems most effective when it is used to bring teachers face to face with themselves and their colleagues. It is amazing how poor communication can be in schools, especially large ones. Techniques for helping teachers to know each other are most important. Analysis groups focused on instructional problems and tasks are often very effective in opening channels of communication previously blocked.

Administration is a service-oriented function. The wise administrator comprehends that he can only be as effective in improving instruction as he is able to relate effectively to his teachers. His words or actions mean very little if they do not fall on a receptive audience, many of whom have adopted a "show me" attitude. Part of his good teaching practice is to show the necessity for establishing a proper relationship with the person being taught. Above all, the administrator in the nongraded high school should be ever mindful of the administrator's prayer, *Ne Sim Obex*,* as professed by John Culkin, Director, Center for Understanding Media, Fordham University.

THE TEACHING FACULTY

Probably the most critical aspect of developing a nongraded school is the selection of teachers. It should not be done in haste. The nongraded school entails a new look at teacher selection and deployment. In selecting staff the prime considerations are the teacher's preparation in his subject and his ability to work closely with young people. Since the main thrust of the nongraded school is experimentation and innovation, teachers with a proclivity to seek newer ways are highly prized. However, there are few clues to assist the administrator in locating such people. Some research, mostly in fields other than education, has uncovered characteristics that differentiate the innovative from the non-innovative person, but these characteristics are often poorly approximated when used for purposes of selection.

A Chinese proverb reminds us that "when two thieves pass on the street, they immediately know each other." Perhaps the innovative administrator can judge intuitively the likelihood of a teacher fitting into and contributing to the creative environment of the nongraded school. Even though there is a paucity of specific cues to aid with this process, the task is not hopeless. One recommended practice calls for involving more than one person in the selection. Assistant principals, department chairmen, other teachers, and even students can all provide the administrator with valuable data for making this important decision.

The emphasis in teacher deployment is on placing teachers where they can facilitate learning, not impede it. This is team teaching in its true sense. The entire staff is considered a team of teachers to be deployed throughout the school. Every effort is made to match the teacher with the specific task to be undertaken. Some teachers work

---

* May I not be an obstacle.

better with reluctant learners, while others have a talent for challenging the gifted. No teacher is expected to be good for all students. Of all the assignments, working with slower learners seems the most difficult, and should be rewarded by being considered the most important status position in the school. It has been said that if a school had one good teacher, he should work with the students who need him most, namely those students with learning difficulties. This philosophy is appropriate for the nongraded high school. The commitment is to the total student body, but in varying degrees, according to the students' needs. Unfortunately, educational practice often works against the implementation of this rule. Historically, administrators have assigned the "poorest" students to the most inexperienced teachers, saving the instructional "plums" for the teachers with longest service, a practice analogous to that of the university, where the best professors rarely see an undergraduate.

Although teachers must be involved in the process of teacher assignment, it is the administrator, by virtue of his elevation, who can see the total configuration. He "plays" on the faculty as a musician plays an instrument or an artist strokes a canvas. In this sense, administration is an art, not a science of manipulating dials and mechanisms according to some preconceived formulae.

Fixing Responsibility

Legal responsibility for the success or lack of success of any school activity resides in the principal's office. However, if professional responsibility also resides there complications can arise. Ideas for improving the school should flow in many directions, up as well as down. Moreover, teachers must feel free to try out their ideas in their own classrooms without first getting clearance from the office, or fearing reprisal if the results are not successful.

How can possibilities for decision-making among the staff be broadened? There is no substitute for communication, but proper communication requires time, and unfortunately time is a precious commodity in a school. Time must be found, however, for teachers to face each other regularly—and on company time. At least one school, Meadowbrook Junior High School, whose profile appears in the last section of this volume, has been able to do so. Others are just going to have to do better. If meeting on school time is not feasible then some form of flexible schedule must be devised to allow teachers to work together. Common planning zones also help.

The nongraded school considers curriculum and instruction the administrator's primary function. If the principal is to be the instructional leader, then he must be willing to delegate responsibility to other members of his administrative staff. Possibly a reorganization of the entire administrative order would be most desirable. Building maintenance, discipline, attendance, public relations, parental complaints, and other daily demands of the principal's job should be the major responsibility of other members of the staff. Other positions may need to be created to make this possible. Such job titles as Director of Community Relations, Director of Dissemination, Director of Pupil-Personnel Services, and Administrative Assistant for Building and Grounds frequently appear on the organizational chart of a nongraded high school. The principal has a line relationship with the teachers. Devoting a minimum of seventy-five percent of his time to activities that will improve instruction is an imperative the principal cannot overlook.

Space Designed for Learning

Flexibility is the *sine qua non* of the nongraded school. It is equally important in the building and furnishings. Students are expected to be active. They will move to appropriate learning activities and appropriate areas as the needs arise. Ideally the learning zones will be as flexible as the programs they facilitate. However, the desirability of maximum flexibility in the building should not deter the administrator and staff who are housed in more conventional quarters.

If a new building is to be constructed one might consider the MODU—BUILDING, a new concept in building design and function, which allows teachers, administrators, and students to modify the building practically on demand. The MODU—BUILDING contains demountable walls to allow for large groups, small groups, and quiet areas for private study. It provides for maximum interaction between the many learning networks in the school. In an already existing building certain modifications can be requested, but they should reflect the *raison d'etre* of the school.

When they are described in these terms, money for improvements and modifications is often easier to obtain.

Students are disposed at individual learning stations for much of the school day. Furniture, such as wet and dry carrels, trapezoidal and rectangular tables, and comfortable chairs, is designed to fit the respective learning activities. Many of the programs are situated in learning laboratories in which students are surrounded by materials to aid them in their individual quests.

The most important center in the nongraded high school is the library or media center. It is furnished with individual student carrels, some equipped with electronic devices that enable students to use non-printed data. The study carrel provides the student with a quiet, private station in which to learn on his own. In addition to the study areas, the library provides space for student groups and offers a lounging area for perusing magazines and newspapers. The library is the most active space in the school. It is busy from morning until night, and is even available for student use in the evenings and on weekends. A new staff member, the Independent Study or Quest Director, assists those students who have decided to study a subject entirely on their own. He schedules periodic seminars to help them develop research skills, and works with individual students in solving their research problems.

Evaluation—Some Considerations

Evaluation and feedback have become important notions in education, at least they are important to those individuals who are reluctant to accept the new and the different without challenge. Does the nongraded school improve learning opportunities for more students? Is it better than its conventional counterpart? Questions such as these often plague the proponent of the nongraded approach. While he has a responsibility to evaluate and disseminate the results of his findings, it is interesting that those individuals who demand immediate evaluation of the non-graded high school have been so tardy in requiring it of conventional programs. In education, by and large, there is a dearth of research to buttress even traditional practices. Nevertheless, educators continue to employ them, and what is worse, defend their decisions with fervor. No research data supports the 900-square-foot classroom, or the teacher-dominated program, or a student-teacher ratio of thirty to one.

As a relatively new development in educational circles, the nongraded high school can offer little conclusive evidence that its practices significantly improve education. What evidence does exist is of the home-grown variety, and often simply reports the reactions of students, teachers, parents, and visitors. These reports are considerable, however, and definitely establish an aura of concern for determining the future direction of the nongraded movement. The nongraded practitioners give more than lip service to the need for constant appraisal of innovative programs. There is a problem of implementation of this appraisal, which requires but a shift in strategy. Teachers engage in action research as they look for evidence to strengthen or modify entire instructional programs or for new methodologies. Students participate in educational diagnostic groups that feed back to teachers the results of their teaching. An air of openness pervades. At one nongraded school a random selection of students meets with the principal each week to analyze what is happening to them and to offer suggestions for improving the school.

The pure researcher may ask for more valid and reliable evidence than presently exists, but the plain fact is that it is difficult to define the nongraded variable with sufficient clarity. It is much too global an entity to serve as a powerful independent variable, and in those instances where it was used to compare graduates from a nongraded high school with those from a conventional program, little light was shed on the issue. A better approach might be to break down the nongraded variable into its component parts in order to make a series of independent investigations of its various dimensions. This tactic would at least allow for some generalization of the results to environments outside of a particular school.

While the more formal types of evaluation are being planned and conducted, teachers must still go on planning for individual students, and educators must still make decisions that will have a resounding effect on a vast number of young people. It becomes a matter of waiting until all the data is in or going forward with programs based on existing evidence of how youngsters learn. Until more formal evaluations are available, teachers can build action-oriented evaluations into their instructional strategies, and they can assess the effectiveness of the environment of a specific group of students; school-wide assessment can be predicted on follow-up studies of graduates' academic and attitudinal objectives; and teachers and administrators can continue to ask the students how they feel about the school that places intelligent student response above all other behavioral outcomes.

Notes

1. In 1961 the Florida State Legislature passed a bill requiring all high school students to complete a unit in Americanism versus Communism.

2. *IACD Bulletin,* III, no. 5 (Nov. 1967), Ferkauf Graduate School, Yeshiva University.

CHAPTER 8

The Curriculum in the Nongraded High School: Restoration of Curiosity

by

JOHN M. JENKINS

> *A curriculum should involve the mastery of skills that in turn lead to the mastery of still more powerful ones, the establishment of self-reward sequences.*
>
> —Jerome Bruner

B Y NOW the knowledge explosion and its exponential implications are no secret to the professional educator. Schools that stress only the accumulation of knowledge at the expense of the process of accumulation are committing the students to an early obsolescence. Possibilities for the future literally stagger the imagination, and while the future cannot be predicted, students can be prepared to deal with whatever uncertainties they might meet. This end is best accomplished when students are assisted to live more richly in the present.

The purpose of nongraded education, and properly of all education, is to develop within each student a confidence in his capacity to act appropriately no matter what the circumstances. Such an end product implies a student who can trust himself to act intelligently, that is, to adapt, to understand, and to cope with rapid changes in his environment. This process is somewhat akin to the physiological principle of homeostasis, whereby certain bodily functions are committed to automatic functioning, enabling conscious attention to be directed to more creative matters. As the student gains additional power over the skills of a given discipline, he can delve more deeply into the rigors of the discipline. It is a practice that acknowledges that intuitive thinking is the highest form of thought.

The nongraded high school makes a commitment to educate all the children of all the people. It starts from the basic assumption that every youngster has a right to the best mankind can offer. Dropouts are considered failures for the school; they are not to be tolerated. Therefore, the school must make adjustments in its scope and its pedagogy in order to provide all students with an appropriate education. It is axiomatic in the graded school that in most, if not all, of the course offerings some percentage of students will not pass. The punishment for this failure is a repetition of the entire course, which costs the taxpayers more money and reinforces the students' dislike for the subject and formal learning in general. The nongraded philosophy says "no" to this custom. No student will fail. All will find some measure of success.

The nongraded school provides a curriculum in motion, sensitive to the varieties of the young people who attend. The core of the nongraded process are the academic areas of communications, mathematics, history, and science, in that order. These areas take priority over all other programs in the school. The curriculum is one of ableness, for each student commences from whatever he happens to be and moves on from that point. The rate of progress varies with the differences within and among students, for no curriculum is student-proof.

The curricula in the academic subjects do not reflect the grade level in which they are taught, but more importantly, the student's ability to grasp a particular activity and throw his weight into it. Reluctant learners often lack the background to deal with a subject when it is offered only at a singular level of operation. Much of what have been named learning difficulties are very much related to a youngster's environment and can be altered by a school that accepts the student on his own terms. The nongraded idea denotes a curriculum with opportunity. It says "yes" in an infinite number of ways. The curriculum itself is built on concepts and ideas to be learned, rather than facts to be memorized. Thinking activities take precedence over memorization.

The nongraded curriculum is developmental. It recognizes both the orderly structure of the disciplines and the orderly development of the youngsters. Whatever a youngster brings to school is accepted and built on. No one has to feel that he is not good enough. To accomplish this end, the standard textbook with its focus on the "normal" population of students is replaced by a multiplicity of materials for each area.

The Ingredients

The curriculum in the nongraded high school is founded on certain beliefs and assumptions about students, the nature of learning, and the role of the teacher. Curriculum is defined here as an all-encompassing entity, which embodies students, teachers, and materials. It is a course of action, a way to bring desirable goals to fruition. The following assumptions are the substance from which the nongraded model is constructed:

1. The learner should be assisted to understand the total educational requirements in each of the academic disciplines before he is asked to learn single units or ideas. He must have the totality in view so that he can see the relationship between what he is doing now and what he will be expected to do at the termination of the course. The teacher's role is to know the scope of the program so that he can assist the students in making the connection between the present and the ultimate. Both students and teachers must know where they are going in order to map the necessary steps to get there, otherwise the curriculum becomes an accumulation of unrelated events.

2. Each subject is valid in its own right. It has a structure and a process for discovering truth. As students inquire into the nature of the subject they know it more intimately. However, students have various readiness levels for confronting each subject, which are not necessarily related to their chronological age. Their readiness to tackle a subject is determined by their skills and their need to rely on concrete experiences, as opposed to more abstract forms. Learning is a process of developing a student's ability to function when no one else is around. The less he has to have an object present or a model of that object before him, the more mature he is becoming intellectually.

3. The curriculum should be organized so that the student can learn the ways of the specialists in the various disciplines. He should actually be able to do history, do mathematics, do science and do English as if he were a scholar seeking answers in these fields. Considered in this context, the processes are more important than the products. By placing the

student in the role of the scientist or the historian, he becomes a practicing scholar in each of these disciplines.

4. Every youngster has a natural curiosity for understanding his environment. The school can build on this inquisitiveness and offer experiences by which he can begin to control its unpolished nature. At the secondary school level, the activity is frequently a matter of reawakening the curiosity that formal education has repressed.

5. Learning activities should have meaning for the student. *He* must see the relationship between what he is doing in school to his own life. It does no good for the teacher to have a lofty idea of what the student ought to do, if the student does not prize it also.

6. If learning is based on intrinsic rewards it will have a more lasting effect on the student. School should provide a locale where a youngster can learn to learn for learning's sake. There is a satisfaction to be gained from knowing that one is able to do a difficult task well, and as a student begins to understand a subject in depth he develops more zeal for learning. The end of formal education comes when a student is able to free himself from dependence on a teacher, and is able to assess his own learning process from a set of standards that he has internalized and is willing to re-assess in the light of new data.

7. Teaching is the art of planning appropriate learning environments for individual students. Learning occurs when students are able to perceive new environments as challenges and not threats. The role of the teacher therefore must shift from lecturer and presenter of information to one of preparing environments to which students make a response. Thus, the teacher becomes a manipulator, but a manipulator of activities and environments, not people.

8. Learning occurs best when students are active. They must make a response to an environment. Very often the best learning situations occur when the student is placed in an environment that is responsive to his very command. That is to say, when he acts in a given way, the environment reacts accordingly. He gets immediate feedback from the consequences of his acts.

Some Illustrations

In the preceding chapter, two modes of nongradedness were discussed—the phased program and the continuous progress model. In an endeavor to establish the importance of the relationship of the curriculum to the nongraded high school, an example of curriculum programs from each of these settings will be presented. These examples are just examples. No attempt will be made in this chapter to outline an overall schemata for nongrading a high school. The interested reader must dig this out for himself.

The first example is taken from the social studies program at Miami Springs Senior High School, Miami Springs, Florida. This school follows the phased model for the most part, and offers world history or world cultures, as it is labeled, at four different phases. The program is described as multi-phased. Each phase reflects not the grade level but the student's ability to deal with varying levels of sophistication.

The world cultures program is available to any student, regardless of his chronological age, and is not considered a course that is aligned with a specific grade level. It is not organized around a single textbook, but focuses on four big ideas in the history and culture of the world. Buttressing each of the larger ideas are innumerable secondary ideas, which will not be included here. Each concept is a unit of instruction comprised of ordered experiences. The units are presented at four levels of difficulty. The basic difference between phases or levels is the accomplishment expected of the students when they leave the course. The units as described in the 1969–70 edition of the school's curriculum bulletin are:

> *Harmony*: Harmony is interpreted as that state of social union in which people develop a sense of belonging—of living at peace with one's fellow man in perfect brotherhood. Throughout history man has proposed many paths to group consciousness—religions, social institutions, utopian societies, world organizations, treaties, pacts, and even wars. The whole concept of harmony will be treated from an investigation of those attempts by man to live in love and fellowship with those of divergent opinions and beliefs.
>
> *Change*: Change is the aspect of man's life through which he has the opportunity to modify the circumstances of his existence for his benefit. Too often throughout history man has been oblivious to change when it is sorely needed. The concept of change will be treated from an investigation of man's attempts to effect change, the nature and the need for change, the psychological transformations which it requires and the corresponding considerations which must be taken into account, and the means through which man can both reconcile his existence to change and use it as a vehicle for his best interests.

The Creative Society and the Good Life: Creativity is an original expression of man's imagination; of unique insight into the meaning of man's situation; the product of man's being and becoming.

What is the relationship between creativity and making "the good life" for man?

This aspect of the course will inquire into creative societies that have and do exist, why they existed, and whether they satisfy the requirements for "the good life."

Comparative Political and Economic Systems: It is difficult to respond rationally and confidently to situations within countries and to international events without understanding the fundamental ideologies and practical application of differing economic and political systems. How does communism differ in China from communism in Russia or communism in Yugoslavia? What does communism have in common in all three countries? Was Naziism a form of communism? Is a government which becomes socialistic automatically taking a step towards a communist form of government? Communism, socialism and facism will be studied not only in their theoretical forms, but as they have been and are being applied in specific countries throughout the world.[1]

Each unit contains exercises and activities to assist the students to uncover the intricacies and nuances of the respective concepts. Units contain a rationale, a set of behavioral objectives, and a variety of activities from which students can select optional paths. Each unit, no matter what the phase, emphasizes historical process. Students are expected to dig for information on their own, weigh alternative data, come to conclusions, and evaluate their accomplishments. Naturally, this type of curriculum requires many more materials than one has come to expect in the more conventional social studies program. History, in large measure, has been a single textbook-oriented course accompanied by a wide assortment of embellishments that depended on the nature of the teacher. Advanced students were given reports for extra credit or asked to chair a committee or complete a research paper. The emphasis was on enrichment. This is not the case in the nongraded program. Depth, not enrichment, is the order of the day. Students are led into more sophistication in both process and content. The ultimate goal is for the student to be able to create his own history. Accordingly, the student becomes less dependent on the teacher.

The four units or ideas presented in world cultures are important for all students, regardless of what background they bring to the course. An understanding of these ideas at some depth is required of all citizens in a democratic society. It is therefore necessary for the school to invent ways of meeting this task. The instructional units are constructed by the teachers and revised during the course of the year. If enrollment in each course permits (a phase is considered a course), a team of teachers is usually assigned the task of teaching world cultures. Each member of the team is made responsible for a specific idea. He writes the unit, isolates the objectives, locates the material, and appropriately alters both content and pedagogy as he works with the students. No special sequence is required. The units may be taken by a student in any order. Hence, the typical chronological approach to history is avoided. The idea of phases enables the reluctant learner, who brings poor background, interest, and motivation to the learning act, to have an environment especially developed for him. Reading materials are geared to his reading level, direct experiences are planned, and class sizes are smaller.

Considering the major idea, *Change,* the phase one student might conceivably be asked to demonstrate an understanding that change affects what people do; phase two students could be required to comprehend that technological change has been a deciding force in the history of the world; phase three students are expected to understand that changes in one aspect of an environment cause other factors in that environment to make necessary adjustments; and the phase four students should grasp the idea that change breeds revolution and not vice versa. Phrased differently, change may be viewed in terms of specific behavioral outcomes. For example: *Phase One*—Discuss why the acceptance of change often takes longer than the change itself. *Phase Two*—Analyze change as a process to identify and weigh its components. *Phase Three*—Given a trend to exemplify change, predict the position of that trend in a specified number of years. *Phase Four*—Relate the process of change to the instigation of revolution.

Each unit is nine weeks long and is developed in such a way that a student who makes rapid progress can move into an advanced phase, accept a depth unit, or work on independent study. The refinement of these units requires a commitment by the teachers and the administration to schedule time for teachers to read, reflect, and " 'rite."

The second example, a continuous progress variety, is taken from the program in science for the traditional grades 7–12 at Nova High School, Fort Lauderdale, Florida. The students are theoretically able to work through the science sequence at their own pace and depth. In the previous example a particular subject area was indicated, but the

Nova model does not do so. The science sequence is comprised of a series of sequentially arranged ideas taken from the areas of chemistry, biology, and physics. The subjects are interrelated and prerequisites may derive from any of the three. No order by subject is given, unlike the BSCS version of the biological sciences, especially the blue and yellow editions, a goodly portion of which presupposes that the student has some working knowledge of elementary chemistry.

The program is built on learning by discovery. The students are expected to participate as scientists—searching for answers, testing data, drawing tentative conclusions, and framing new hypotheses. The emphasis is on intrinsic rewards and ultimate student independence. Building on the idea that each member of the human species has an innate drive for competence, the science curriculum constructs new environments out of familiar "materials." The program is considered sequential in nature in that the students are required to master certain basic ideas before going on to more difficult undertakings. Laboratory activities are of prime importance and precede most of the discussion requirements. Laboratory experiences also follow the discussion to enable the students to verify their findings.

The design of the science sequence leads the student from simple ideas to more difficult ones. A student is pre-tested to determine his level of understanding before he enters the sequence. If he tests out at a level above the most elementary concept, he begins at that point. Less advanced students begin at the first concept on measurement. Student achievement is converted into more conventional records by equating the completion of a certain number of concepts with a Carnegie unit in science. Reports to parents show the student's level of competency in terms of the total science sequence. Students who are able to complete the science sequence in less than the "normal" six years are encouraged to go more deeply into any of the topics, by completing depth units or working on independent study. When one considers the Nova science sequence in terms of Bloom's *Taxonomy of Educational Objectives, Cognitive Domain*, it is the higher-level cognitive objectives that appear with greater frequency as one progresses through the sciences. This is not to say that students do not get a chance to approach scientific knowledge at several levels of cognition, no matter what their level of sophistication in science. It merely indicates that as students gain more independence they are able to function at a variety of cognitive levels without external stimulation and explanation.

The sequence from the seventh year to conclusion follows. Space does not permit an annotation of each unit, as was done in the previous example. A fuller explanation is given in a publication of Nova High School.[2]

LAP 1.[3] Measurement in Science—History, Methods, Metric Precision and Accuracy
      2. Simplification of materials into basic parts and the ideas of the elements
      3. Further study of the elements—The Periodic Table
      4. "Logos Bios"—The Science of Life
      5. Classification—Structural Differences
      6. The Physical World—Energy affects matter
      7. Further study of the forces between molecules and the energy they possess
      8. Search for beginnings—Techniques of Archeology
      9. Introduction to Oceanography
     10. Change—A Glance at the Past
     11. Fundamental Particles of Life
     12. Fundamental Particles—part 2
     13. Fundamental Particles—part 3
     14. Fundamental Particles—part 4
     15. Encountering the Physical World
     16. From Microcosm to Macrocosm
     17. Apollo Simulation (an investigation of qualitative and quantitative approximation)
     18. The Sequel to the Apollo Simulation (an investigation of quantitative measurement and precision)
     19. Significant Relationships (a study of density, extrapolation and time)
     20. The Large and the Small—part II (a study of shadows, density and mass of earth)
     21. The Large and the Small—part III
     22. The Grand Canyon of the Colorado
     23. Celestial Bodies: How big? How far?
     24. Fundamental Particles—part 5
     25. Fundamental Particles—part 6
     26. Models and Reasoning
     27. Probability I
     28. Probability II
     29. Producing Change
     30. Structure of Matter—atomic theory
     31. Chemical Reactions and Energy
     32. The Gas Phase—kinetic energy
     33. Solids and Liquids
     34. Cellular Chemistry
     35. Reproduction and Selection
     36. Genetics

37. Microbiology
38. The Evolution of Simple Plants
39. Photosynthesis and Vascular Plants
40. Animal Evolution
41. Comparative Evolution
42. Chemical Reactions—rates and equilibrium
43A. Aqueous Solutions and Equilibrium
43B. Aqueous Acids and Bases
44. Electrochemistry and Chemical Calculations
45. Concepts of Motion
46. Motion in the Heavens
47. Energy, Waves, and Conservation Laws
48. Electromagnetic Theory
49. Development of Atomic Theory
50. The Nucleus
Beyond 50
TRENDS IN SCIENCE

Independent Research

Oceanography

Pre-Engineering

Physiology

Advanced Physics

Advanced Chemistry

Advanced Biology

A Learning Activity Package (LAP) is developed for each idea. The LAP is the vehicle by which the instruction is individualized. Each package contains the primary idea and its secondary ideas, the behavioral outcomes, variegated materials, and student-teacher evaluations. Differences in reading levels, motivation, and interest are considered in the outcomes and materials sections of the LAPS. Once again, the thrust is toward delving more deeply *into* the subject. The less able student can deal with the idea at one level of attainment, the average student at another, and the more advanced student at yet another. Within each package levels of difficulty differentiate the work at levels of meaning. Some of the material is required of everyone, some is a little more challenging and is optional, while other material is even more difficult and is also optional.

The student may take as much time as he needs to complete any LAP. Experience shows, however, that some students lack the inner drive to activate the inquiry-centered sequence. These students require much individual attention. Occasionally teachers need to isolate a small group of students in tutorial sessions of about 8–10 students. These groups are characterized by high interaction. The request for tutorial groups can be initiated by the students or the teachers. Attendance at the tutorial group sessions is mostly optional; however, when a student is experiencing great difficulty he may be assigned to a specific session or sessions. Very often the reluctant learner requires a series of individual tutorial sessions. Individual prescriptions often follow this exchange. The fact that the learning packages usually involve a team of teachers who have some clerical and instructional assistance makes this type of individualized prescription an instructional option for the teachers.

Although these examples were derived from two somewhat different approaches to nongradedness, certain similarities are apparent:

1. Some type of inventory of prior student accomplishment is necessary in order to place the student in the curriculum alternative appropriate to his intellectual development.

2. On the basis of the results of the pre-test or student inventory, certain assumptions are made about what a student can do, and then he is helped to discover if these assumptions match his experience. If they do not he is re-assigned to a different aspect of the program. If they do he is assisted in completing the goals.

3. Each student is accepted for what he knows about a given subject and not for what he *ought* to know according to his chronological age or years in school.

4. The curriculum is designed to accept the *present* functional level of the student.

5. The curriculum is organized to treat major ideas and their subideas (primary and secondary ideas).

6. When commercial materials exist they are "plugged into" the unit where most appropriate. When commercial materials do not exist to help students gain concept mastery, materials are invented by the teachers.

Determining Curriculum Effectiveness

The nongraded high school is committed to the idea that change is self-evident and healthy. But change for the sake of change is neither sound nor economical. It should be reinforced by carefully collected data as to the effectiveness of the materials and the instruction. A number, but certainly not a conclusive list, of activities is presented to give the reader some feeling of the attitude that prevails in the nongraded school. Teachers and administrators are inclined to try new proposals, but are also constrained to evaluate any proposal for change.

Some nongraded schools have found it very effective in testing curriculum content and methodology to narrow the responsibility of the teacher. Rather than have him responsible for handling an entire course of study or a parallel number of learning activity packages, he is assigned one idea or cluster of packages for which he is solely responsible. By working with the same material more than once per academic year, he can see how the students respond to the materials and to his teaching. Adjustments are then made before the next time around. In the example of the world cultures course, the teacher would have three occasions after the first nine weeks to refine and modify the unit.

A second approach narrows the responsibility of the teacher even further. The teacher tests the material with smaller groups of students for shorter periods of time. This approach, sometimes called micro-teaching, mini-teaching or instructional interviewing, enables the teacher to get immediate feedback as to the appropriateness of a learning environment for a given group of students. Video-taping these sessions allows other members of the faculty or the teaching team to assist with the field testing. This type of evaluation frequently costs more because the teachers must be released from regular teaching duties. It should not be too much to ask, however, if individualization of instruction is a worthy goal.

Another form of action-evaluation occurs when the members of a teaching team face each other, every day, for the purpose of discussing ongoing programs. The sharing of ideas and the clarification of thinking that can result from this kind of activity cries out for the administrator to find a way to make it possible. Experience shows that some member of the administrative staff should be present to keep the group of teachers task-oriented and to show by deed that the school administration approves of the practice. As Plato so aptly stated, "What is honored in a country will be cultivated there."

Still another source of data can come from the observations of the principal and other internal supervisory personnel. Careful observation of teacher and student behavior is a must, and a primary responsibility of the principal. Moreover, all observations should be based on an understanding of the related antecedents. The data from the observations should be fed back to teachers as rapidly and as unthreateningly as possible. Nonetheless, the primary goal is the improvement of instruction. This end must take precedence over personal feelings. The day of the anonymous teacher is rapidly disappearing. Teachers are just going to have to be more open to constructive suggestions from their colleagues.

A final possibility involves the students directly. Teachers should be encouraged to enlist students as a matter of course in judging the effectiveness of their programs. At educational diagnostic sessions[4] students are asked how they feel about what is happening to them and what suggestions they can offer for improving the programs. Any teacher can be encouraged to utilize the diagnostic sessions, but some training is required. Faculty in-service programs can be employed to teach teachers how to use the diagnostic groups. Like most social groups, the diagnostic groups become more candid as the students realize that they are not going to get into difficulty by being honest, and that the teacher really wants the students to help him build a better course of study.

Most instructional units in the nongraded setting have student evaluations built into them. These evaluations or assessments help determine whether a student has internalized the concepts at a sufficient level of depth so that he can move on to more challenging endeavors. The student assessment can be applied as a test of the effectiveness of the program by calculating the percentage of students who have successfully met the performance criteria. Remember that the goal of the nongraded school is to have all the students achieve these ends. If the students do not learn, it is because the school fails to educate them. Certain generalizations can be made about the effectiveness of any curriculum when it is known how many students were able to benefit from it.

The quest for feedback has an interesting concomitant benefit. Very often teachers become models of identification for students. If inquiry is the basic thrust of the school, then teachers can demonstrate its value by practicing it themselves. An aspect of inquiry is search. As teachers search for more appropriate educational environments they silently teach the importance of inquiry-centered learning.

The Teacher in the Process

The role of the teacher acquires new dimensions in the nongraded high school. The teacher is no longer the intermediary between the scholar and the student, who imposes his own thinking and values on his charges. The lecture is no longer the primary instructional strategy, but merely a way to present information, another weapon in the arsenal of instruction. Inasmuch as the art of teaching involves the interaction of a teacher-created environment with a student-initiated response to that environment, teachers are required to become planners of appropriate environments. Through careful planning students are activated to manipulate, transform, shape, and reshape a whole series of environments. Their responses to these environments enable them to go on to higher learning activities. In this context, teachers do not have to say anything, but they must be expert in establishing the opportunities for learning. To be able to construct an optimal learning environment is an act of creation. It should not be undersold by sentimentalists who still perceive learning solely as a "warm" relationship between a teacher and his students. As Will Rogers used to say, "Schools ain't what they used to be, and maybe they never was."

The master teacher is a master planner. He comprehends the nature of the learning act, and he realizes that his job is more than the transmission of knowledge. He is often the one who influences the students' attitudes toward a subject. What he does and how he does it are more important than what he says. He can serve as a valuable model for his students. The nature of the nongraded curriculum places the teacher in a closer relationship with the students. He needs to sharpen his own tools of the trade. Planning environments, consulting with individual students, occasionally giving a talk to provide information not obtainable from other sources, screening and selecting materials, aiding his colleagues, looking for better ways of teaching, and counseling students are aspects of the teacher's role in the nongraded high school.

A Touch of Anarchy

Any good curriculum allows for some spontaneity from both students and teachers. For too many years educators have checked and rechecked teacher and student suggestions with higher-echelon officials before giving permission to proceed. The genesis of nongradedness has been in the need for change. The notion grew out of a desire to put into practice the idea that students were different. It has maintained its strength because it has continued to honor change and has been willing to take chances with new approaches and new courses of study. Institutions that become complacent only contribute to their own death. To assume, however, that the millenium has been reached in secondary education when one of the new models has been adopted is to commit the school to an inadvisable rigidity. While it is true that adopting many of the suggestions made by the proponents of the nongraded school could improve secondary education manyfold, one should not miss the attitude of search underlying the nongraded philosophy. In order to continue the forward direction of the nongraded high school a certain amount of anarchy must be inherent in the system.

By definition, an anarchist incites revolt; he attempts to overturn the established order. A little anarchy is healthy. It keeps the institution alive and viable. Any good curriculum requires just a twinge. Students need to be able to construct their own learning sequences if they are dissatisfied with the preconceived ones. Imaginative students can create learning environments out of the stuff of their own experience. Schools must let them try; moreover, they should help them accomplish it. Teachers should feel free to suggest courses and to implement ideas that are far ahead of the data. The outcomes of these endeavors will not always be auspicious, but such is the nature of change. However, out of this spontaneity comes a new synthesis, a fortunate mix of the new with the established, and frequently the result of a new approach that is better than its predecessors. If the role of the school is literally to reawaken the students to the joys of learning, then it must be accomplished in an environment conducive to excitement. Placing new ideas into a dull atmosphere will dull the finish. Placing new ideas in an environment that resounds with change will give them added luster and viability.

The variegated curriculum of the nongraded high school provides many paths to truth. Each is valid for a given student or group of students. What is a challenge for one is a threat for another. If the school is to remain a vital force in American life it must take seriously the charge of individual differences and accommodate these differences. A curriculum that accepts students on their terms and invites them to go further is a step in the right direction. The nongraded high school provides just such a direction.

Notes

1. Miami Springs Senior High School, "A Courage of a Different Order," *Curriculum Bulletin 1969–70*, V, no. 1 (Spring, 1969).

2. Paul Bethune, Patricia Jackson, and W. O. Viens, "Science at Nova; Geared to Individual Progress" (Fort Lauderdale, Fla.: Nova High School, 1967).

3. "Sequence of Science Course Units at Nova High School," unpublished, Nova High School, Fort Lauderdale, Florida.

4. For a more thorough discussion of the educational diagnostic session, see William Glasser, *Schools Without Failure* (New York: Harper and Row, 1969).

PART II

A LOOK TO THE FUTURE

CHAPTER 9

Research Has a Word: Some Generalizations

by

HENRY J. OTTO

Dr. Otto has been a professor of educational administration at the University of Texas at Austin since 1942. He is the author of numerous books, monographs, and journal articles, among them Elementary School Organization and Administration *(with David Sanders) and* Value Orientations in Four Elementary Schools *(with Thomas Foster and W. K. Katz). He has also served as Director of Education of the W. K. Kellogg Foundation.*

THIS CHAPTER summarizes the research studies whose findings have become available in the literature, appraises the quality of the completed studies, interprets the findings, and suggests new directions for research in the area of nongraded elementary school organization and instruction.

The Research Studies

THE McLOUGHLIN ANALYSIS

In 1967 William R. McLoughlin published an analysis and critical assessment of 34 research reports that were available at that time[1] (see list of research reports at the end of this chapter). He found that 48% of the studies gave a comparison of children's achievement in reading, 26% in arithmetic, 11% in language arts, 9% in total achievement, 3%

in work-study skills, 1% in social studies, and 1% in science. Only eight of the 34 studies dealt with a comparison of pupil adjustment and social relationships. One reason that reading and arithmetic were covered more frequently than the other curriculum areas is that most of the research was done in the primary grades. The above data make it clear that only a few of the goals of a nongraded program were considered in evaluation reports. The reader should keep this fact in mind as he reads this chapter.

The following are McLoughlin's summary statements from each section of his analysis. In the area of reading (21 studies analyzed) he concluded, ". . . it cannot be claimed that nongrading makes a significant difference in the general reading attainment of children" (p. 16). About arithmetic (15 studies analyzed) he said, "Given these data, it would be difficult to develop an uncontestable argument for the positive influence of nongrading on the arithmetic attainments of children" (p. 18). In the language arts area (10 studies) he concluded, "These data hardly attest to the unquestioned superiority of either organizational pattern" (p. 18). Total achievement was considered in 8 reports; his concluding comment was, "Total achievement scores, too, fail to discern differences between the performance of graded and nongraded classes" (p. 18).

Eight studies included various measures of pupil adjustment; his summary statement here is, "But no matter how adjustment is defined or measured, there is scant evidence to support the contention that it is improved by attending a nongraded school" (p. 19). When comparisons of pupil achievement in graded and nongraded programs were made in terms of ability levels (6 studies made such comparisons), McLoughlin found, "The predominant finding of the research in this area is that there are no significant differences in the scholastic achievements of children of varying abilities resulting from attending nongraded schools. Where exceptions to this generalization occur the differences tend to favor the *average* and *below average* child from graded classes" (p. 24).

The Glenn R. Johnson Study

During the spring of 1967 Glenn R. Johnson studied classroom activities in 12 nongraded classrooms in Grades 4–5–6 in four schools located in two states and in three school systems.[2] Data were gathered from pupil diaries written during 20-minute periods at the ends of the morning and afternoon sessions on three consecutive days (864 diaries from 302 pupils), observations by the investigator (three 30-minute periods in each of the 12 classrooms during reading and arithmetic instruction, and three periods in each classroom in social studies, using the Flanders Interaction Analysis Technique), and individual interviews with the four principals and the 12 teachers.

Johnson summarized the data from the pupil diaries as follows:

    1.   The total number of *different* individualized activities during 3 days ranged from 118 in classroom No. 1 to 25 in classroom No. 9.

    2.   The total number of different *incidences* of individualized activities ranged from 430 in classroom No. 7 to 91 in classroom No. 5.

    3.   The time devoted to individualized instruction ranged from 86% in classroom No. 8 to 19% in classroom No. 5.

The observation records were summarized as follows:

    1.   The percentage of pupils receiving individualized instruction in arithmetic ranged from 0% (2 classrooms) to 100% (6 classrooms); in reading from 0% (1 classroom) to 100% (9 classrooms); in social studies from 0% (2 classrooms) to 100% (7 classrooms).

The following statements (pp. 109–11) are among Johnson's conclusions:

    1.   There was considerable variation in the amount of individualized instruction among the twelve nongraded classrooms. The inference seems to be that replacing grade labels with some other designation and expressing pupil growth as continuous pupil progress does not guarantee that all pupils will receive individualized instruction.

    2.   There did not seem to be a consistency between the extent of individualized instruction for a specific content area and the degree of direct or indirect teacher influence revealed during observations of specific content areas.

    3.   During the pilot study and throughout the major investigation, the pupil diaries revealed more information than did interviews or observations.

    4.   The findings did not appear to support the investigator's basic assumption that disregarding grade labels and viewing the child's growth as continuous pupil progress instead of graded advancement would influence the type and incidence of classroom related activities and the climate of the classroom. The great diversity among the twelve classrooms and within individual classrooms did not seem to support the assumption.

    5.   If one wishes to evaluate the effectiveness of nongraded classrooms in individualizing instruction, the researcher must go

beyond labels and what personnel espouse. Investigators should use instruments similar to those employed in the study to determine the degree of individualized instruction existing in nongraded schools.

As one reads Johnson's entire dissertation it becomes clear that teachers differ widely in how they teach children. These differences are evident in nongraded classes as well as in graded sections. It is also very clear that placing some teachers in a nongraded program does not mean that nongraded philosophy and practices will ensue.

The Dayton N. Ward Study

Ward's research involved 797 first- and second-grade pupils and 27 teachers in four schools in Fort Worth, Texas, and was conducted over a two-year period (1966–68).[3] Two of the schools had the experimental (nongraded) classes, while the other two schools were used as controls. Teacher qualifications, instructional resources, library service, the use of special teacher and service personnel, and the socio-economic status of the patrons was the same in each set of experimental and control schools. The data were treated separately for each pair of schools. System-wide policies, services, and financial support were the same for all the schools. Ward, therefore, protected himself against most of the uncontrolled variables that plague many studies done in public school settings.

Ward's study was planned as a companion to the Casis School study, which will be described later. In both of these evaluation efforts, careful records were kept of the time the teachers devoted to instruction in reading, arithmetic, and spelling, the time devoted to teaching the class as a whole and in subgroups, and the time devoted to helping individuals before and after school. Monthly records were kept of basal texts, supplementary texts, materials made by the teachers, and commercially published individualized learning materials used. Analyses were made of the number, size, and achievement ranges in subgroups taught by each teacher. The Metropolitan Achievement Test was given to all first- and second-register* pupils toward the end of April each year (1967 and 1968). The children's school anxiety was measured by

---

* The children were taught in nongraded groups, but for record-keeping purposes they are called first- and second-register pupils; i.e., a pupil normally enrolled in grade one is classified as a first-register student, and a pupil who would normally be in the second grade is classified as a second-register student.

analyses of The Draw a Man Test; these ratings were made independently of the judgments of two qualified psychologists, and an anxiety check sheet ratings by the teachers.

Ward found extensive differences in teaching practices among teachers in both his experimental classes and his control classes. His final report contained 501 comparisons, of which 386 were favorable to the nongraded program. Of the 108 comparisons that could be tested for statistical significance, 28 were favorable to nongraded classes, while two favored the graded program; the other 78 statistically tested differences showed no superiority for either plan of organization. The measures of children's school anxiety provided 64 comparisons, 36 favorable to the experimental and 28 favorable to the control classes. Sixteen comparisons could be tested for statistical significance of differences; only four resulted in a significant difference, two in favor of each plan of organization. All 72 of the achievement test differences could be tested for statistical significance; 16 proved to have statistical significance, all in favor of the nongraded classes.

Over all one would conclude that Ward's findings were predominantly favorable to the nongraded program during the first two years of school.

THE CASIS SCHOOL STUDY

The study to evaluate nongradedness in the Casis Elementary School in Austin, Texas, was begun in September 1965, and the last series of achievement tests was given in September 1968. Ward's study, which was planned as a supplement or companion to the Casis School project, included students in the first two years of school, while the Casis School nongraded program involved pupils in the third, fourth, and fifth years of school.

The instruments and data-gathering procedures were the same in the two studies, with certain exceptions. The Casis School project did not use a readiness test, and it measured school anxiety with a test developed and validated by Dr. Beeman N. Phillips. The testing program at the Casis School included the Metropolitan Achievement Test for grades 3, 4, and 5, which was administered each September, and the Iowa Every Pupil Test of Basic Skills, which was given each April in grades 3–6. The Casis School study also included an extensive analysis of children's use of the school library.

Each of Ward's four units were in different schools, but in the Casis School project the experimental and control classes were all in the same school; thus it was able to control certain variables that Ward could not, but at the same time it *added* the variable of communication between teachers.

The Casis School is a public school for pupils in a designated attendance zone. It was designed and built jointly by the Austin Independent School District and The University of Texas as a special center for research and demonstration in elementary education. It opened in January 1951. From the beginning and over the years the faculty has held professional or grade level meetings each Monday from 3:30 to 4:30 or 5:00 p.m. From 1951 through 1966 the faculty also spent three or four weeks in June working on curriculum improvement projects, several of which resulted in valuable publications. All of this shows that throughout its history its faculty has been immersed in professional growth activities. One of its publications dealt with curriculum enrichment for academically talented pupils in regular classes, another with meeting individual differences in arithmetic, while a third covered ways of dealing with special education pupils who are assigned part-time to regular classes.

Intraclass grouping by achievement levels, by interest, or by pupils' social needs has always prevailed.* In 1953 Mary Clare Petty published a monograph describing intraclass grouping in this school.[4] The Casis School also has an excellent school library, with more than 11,000 different titles, and each classroom from grade 3 up has its own complete set of encyclopedias. A comparative marking system has never been used. Individual parent-teacher conferences constitute the salient feature of the reporting plan. Sectionizing pupils within a grade level and promotion from grade to grade have always been based on the best group placement for each pupil. The school is located in a middle- to upper-middle-class neighborhood, with genuine and extensive parent interest in children's development. Pupil progress is viewed individually, on the basis of ability, effort, and background. Teachers find that not all able children work to capacity and parents are so informed in the conferences. The emphasis throughout has been to help each child make regular progress commensurate with his abilities and talents.

During 1964–65 three teachers at the Casis School became interested

---

* For an up-to-date research report on grouping by achievement see Glen Heathers' chapter in *Encyclopedia of Educational Research,* fourth edition (New York: Macmillan, 1970).

in nongradedness. They visited nongraded programs in California, and persuaded the principal to initiate a nongraded program in grades 3, 4, and 5, the grades represented by their respective teaching interests. The principal gave his permission and enthusiastic support. The three teachers then spent three weeks in June planning for the opening of the nongraded component in September 1965. It started with one section of about 25 pupils from each of the three grades. This three-teacher project came to be known as Component No. 1, and another similar unit was started in the fall of 1966. The first year, therefore, the nongraded project contained between 75 and 80 pupils, and each year thereafter the two components together contained 150 to 160 pupils out of about 700 pupils in the school. By 1968, when the pupils who had entered Component No. 1 at the third-register level reached the sixth grade, not enough of the original 25 were left to make a valid 3-year comparison of growth in achievement. Therefore only 1-year and 2-year comparisons were made.

The hypotheses that were tested in the Casis School study and the findings of this research are summarized in the following tabulation (E = Experimental group favored; C = control group favored; X = non difference in the comparison).

	Hypotheses	*Hypothesis* Accepted	*Rejected*
1.	There is no difference between experimental and control classes in the total number of minutes per week scheduled as the official period for instruction in:		
	a. Reading (Exp., 210 min; Control, 273 min.)	—	C
	b. Spelling	X	—
	c. Arithmetic (Exp., 250 min; Control, 282 min)	—	C
2.	Teachers in experimental classes devote a smaller percentage of instructional time to whole-class activities than do teachers of control classes in:		
	a. Reading (Exp., 5%; Control, 24%)	E	—
	b. Spelling (Exp., 28%; Control, 62%)	E	—
	c. Arithmetic (Exp., 56%; Control, 70%)	E	—
3.	Teachers in experimental classes devote less time to helping individuals before and after school than do teachers of control classes in:		
	a. Reading (Exp., 7 min.; Control, 0 min.)	—	E
	b. Spelling (Exp., 6 min.; Control, 22 min.)	C	—
	c. Arithmetic (Exp., 22 min.; Control, 37 min.)	C	—
4.	Experimental classes use a wider range of current state adopted texts than do control sections in:		

Hypotheses	Hypothesis Accepted	Rejected
a. Reading	—	C
b. Spelling	E	—
c. Arithmetic	E	—
5. In reading, experimental classes use a wider range of supplementary texts than do control classes.	—	C
6. Experimental classes use a wider variety of individualized learning materials than do control classes in:		
a. Reading	X	X
b. Spelling	X	X
c. Arithmetic	—	C
7. Experimental classes use more learning materials prepared by teachers than do control classes in:		
a. Reading	—	C
b. Spelling	—	C
c. Arithmetic	—	C
8. Children in experimental classes borrow more books from the school library than do children in control classes.	—	X
9. Children in experimental classes make more use of the school library for reference work than do children in control classes.	—	X
10. Teachers in experimental classes rely more heavily on achievement test data and less on personal-social needs data in forming sub-groups than do teachers of control classes in:		
a. Reading	—	E
b. Spelling	—	E
c. Arithmetic	—	E
11. There are more subgroups in the nongraded components than there are comparable contingents in control classes in:		
a. Reading	—	C
b. Spelling	—	X
c. Arithmetic	E	—
12. Subgroups in each nongraded component contain fewer pupils than do subgroups in control classes.	—	C
13. Subgroups in experimental classes represent a narrower range in achievement as measured by standardized tests than do subgroups of control classes in:		
a. Reading	—	C
b. Spelling	E	—
c. Arithmetic	—	X

Hypotheses	Hypothesis Accepted	Rejected
14. More pupils in experimental classes change subgroup placement each month than in control classes.	—	X
15. Children in a nongraded program for more than one year exhibit a decrease in school anxiety, while children in a graded program exhibit an increase as they progress through comparable years in school.	—	C
16. Children in the nongraded program achieve a greater mean gain each year in each subsection of the Metropolitan Achievement Test than do children in the graded classes.	—	X
17. Children in the nongraded program achieve a greater mean gain each year in the subsections of the Iowa Test of Basic Skills than do children in the graded classes.	—	X
18. The differential in mean achievement, favoring the pupils in nongraded classes as measured by the two standardized tests, is greater after two years in the program than it was after one year in the program.	—	X

From the above summary it would seem that this study resulted in a draw. The tabulation contains 31 comparisons, of which 11 favored the nongraded program, 16 favored the graded classes, and 8 resulted in identical ratings or were inconclusive. In comparing use of teachers' time, resources used, children's use of the library, and grouping practices one probably should not have expected important differences to appear in a school in which over the years teachers had made extensive efforts to adapt instruction to individual differences. These factors, plus the practice of reporting to parents and grouping, may also explain the lack of significant differences in pupil achievement gains. A complete monograph describing the Casis School study is available.[5]

Why Is the Research Inconclusive?

The McLoughlin analysis and the Johnson, Ward, and Casis School studies represent 37 of the 41 research reports listed. In reviewing these efforts to evaluate nongraded programs one cannot escape the thought that the results are conflicting and hence inconclusive. McLoughlin found some studies that reported the advantages of nongraded over graded programs, some that favored graded classes, and others that reported no difference in achievement. The Ward and Casis School studies, which were planned as companion studies, and probably attained the best control of variables and gathered the widest array of comparative data, ended with contradictory findings. What are the reasons for such diverse findings?

First, some of the studies were conducted for only six to nine months, which is too short a period for an organizational innovation to demonstrate its potential. If one allows for the errors of measurement in mental and achievement testing, one should hardly expect a statistically significant difference between pre- and post-tests. Secondly, some studies lacked adequate control over variables that could have exerted major influences. For example, when experimental and control classes are in different school systems there might be important differences in such factors as per-pupil expenditures, teacher qualifications, personnel policies, textbook management, budget allocations for library books and instructional supplies, supervisory services, the instructional leadership role of the principals, library programs, socio-economic status of patrons, home-school relations, and abilities and motivations of the pupils. Some of these variables could not be controlled even if the experimental and control groups were in the same school district but in different schools. The findings of research efforts can be meaningless unless *all other factors* are the same and the only difference is the experimental variable.

Third, some studies used group data taken before and after the experiment without specifying whether the membership of the groups was identical at each testing session. If there has been much pupil turnover between testing periods one cannot rely on the findings. The best way to compare pupil progress under two different instructional programs is to compare the gains made between testing periods by pupils in random assignment to experimental and control groups, but only if the same pupils' and only the same pupils' scores are used.

Fourth, most of the studies provide no description of the instructional practices in either the experimental or the control classes. Nor is any information given regarding the extent to which other organizational features were modified to give full support to the nongraded program. If the instructional program is about the same in the graded as in the nongraded classes one should not expect differences in pupil performance. The preceding comments lead to the fifth reason that the findings are inconclusive. For a nongraded program to flourish many of the usual features of a graded program must be modified. For example, teachers in nongraded programs should be able to use books that are normally assigned to higher grades. Pupil progress should be assessed on an individual basis and reported to parents in teacher-parent conferences. A comparative marking system is inconsistent with the philosophy of nongradedness. Grouping practices should be flexible and pupils should be assigned to subgroups and teachers according to their needs. Diagnostic procedures and extensive time to use them are necessary if a nongraded program is to have meaning.

The Ward and Casis School studies illustrate the importance of the above observations. Ward's experimental units made all the essential adaptations to support the nongraded experiment. His control schools "carried on as usual." Hence Ward's findings were favorable to the nongraded program. But for years the entire program in the Casis School had included all the features essential for the success of a nongraded program. Therefore the nongraded arrangement did not add enough to produce statistically significant differences.

Sixth, some nongraded programs were mandated by the administration on short notice, and teachers were assigned arbitrarily to the nongraded project. Such a procedure could not be expected to succeed. Nongradedness is an organizational arrangement that has a broad underlying educational concept. Unless the underlying theory and the essential accompanying practices are internalized by those who are to implement the organizational change one should not expect the change to produce anything particularly different.

Seventh, most people do not realize how complicated it is to conduct rigorous research in a natural setting like the public schools. Invariably some variables must be left uncontrolled, and then one cannot be sure whether the experimental or the uncontrolled variable caused a difference. The increasing mobility of pupil populations is an ever-present problem to the researcher. Teachers' personalities and teaching styles will still differ, even if all the other personnel criteria can be equated.

Whither Nongradedness?

Does the inconclusiveness of the findings and the difficulties encountered in doing rigorous research in public schools mean that nongradedness should be forgotten? Not at all. Although nongradedness is an organizational means of deploying pupils and teachers in particular ways, its philosophy embodies ideas that educators have championed for more than 40 years. Like any other organizational innovation, nongradedness has basic educational ideas associated with it. If all that is implied by the nongraded philosophy were put into practice, schools would undoubtedly be better places for children.[6]

Should you initiate a nongraded program in your school? It depends. If you have a school like the Casis School, in which instruction is already adapted to individual differences, and slow learners and special education pupils are given special attention while academically talented students have every opportunity to keep their intellectual reins taut, you will probably gain very little by changing to a nongraded program. If, on the other hand, you have a school that approximates the Procrustean Bed described in the literature, you should probably proceed at once to rescue your pupils. Nongradedness might be one way to proceed, provided that the teachers have internalized the philosophy of a nongraded program and have the skills necessary to put that philosophy into practice, and provided that you are also willing and able to change other features of your school organization so that nongradedness can flourish. Administrators should realize that organizational innovations are empty shibboleths unless those who are to implement the innovations understand all the ramifications, and are willing and eager to find out whether the change has merit.

New Directions for Research

If research efforts to evaluate nongraded programs are to continue, as they should, researchers should benefit from the weaknesses of past studies and design more rigorous projects.

The research should be conducted over a period of four or more years to enable one to tell whether whatever advantages accrue to nongradedness take place during the first year and fade thereafter, or whether the advantages are cumulative and increase as pupils remain in the nongraded program. A special effort should be made to supplement group data with case studies to discover whether pupils with certain problems or different learning styles benefit more from one type of pro-

gram than from another. It is entirely possible that certain pupils benefit from a nongraded program while others do not.

Any new evaluation study should start out with enough pupils in the
lowest register of the nongraded program so that after four or more
years pupil mobility will not have reduced the number of original en-
tries to preclude comparative data on the same students. Although pupil
transfer rates vary from school to school, the initial group in the experimental classes should contain 300 to 400 pupils, with a comparable
number in the control classes. The research should not be attempted in
schools with a complete turnover of pupils in four years or less. This
condition makes it particularly difficult to find suitable public school
situations for such research.

The goals of the educational program should be stated explicitly at
the outset, in such language that research procedures, gathering of data,
and the formulation and testing of hypotheses can be done in an orderly
way. This criterion has seldom been met in the studies reviewed.

Before an evaluation program is begun a comprehensive description
should be prepared of the practices that are to prevail in the experimental as well as in the control units. It is imperative to have such a
description and a thorough follow-through on it so that at the end the
researcher will know exactly what is being compared, in order to interpret comparative data. Teaching styles should be equated as nearly
as possible, even though each teacher is conscientious about implementing the descriptive pattern in which he or she chooses to work. Many
of the elements that should be covered in the comprehensive descriptions were named earlier. It should be remembered that in systems theory language a school program is a type of system, and that the various
facets of the organization, the pupil population, and the faculty are
subsystems within the larger system, which represents the school in
operation. Each subsystem affects other subsystems or the program as
a whole, and unless all the elements are recognized and harmonized it
may be one or more facets of the organization rather than the nongradedness that cause differences in pupil performance to appear. The Casis
School study is the only one reported so far in which all subsystems
were controlled, since they were identical for control and experimental
classes.

Another question that should be studied carefully is "What happens
to the curriculum?" Do content areas become more isolated in a non-

graded arrangement? Is there more correlation of subject matter in the graded program? Even though every teacher in the nongraded sections teaches every subject and pupils are assigned to classes according to instructional readiness or social needs, the period for teaching a given subject must be the same for all the pupils. This tends to produce rigid time schedules. How does this affect the organization of the curriculum and teaching procedures? What differences occur if the graded sections are partly or completely departmentalized? A related problem deals with curriculum organization and the cooperative efforts of teachers in a nongraded unit. Are the resulting curriculum variations different from those that arise from team teaching in a graded program?

Notes

1. William P. McLoughlin, *The Nongraded School: A Critical Assessment* (Albany: The University of the State of New York, State Education Department, 1967).

2. Glenn R. Johnson, "Nongraded Schools and Individualized Instruction" (Ed. D. diss., Teachers College, Columbia University, 1968).

3. Dayton N. Ward, "An Evaluation of a Nongraded School Program in Grades One and Two" (Ed. D. diss., The University of Texas at Austin, 1969).

4. Mary Clare Petty, *Intraclass Grouping in the Elementary School*, Bureau of Laboratory School Monograph no. 1. (Austin: The University of Texas Press, 1953). Available at $2.00 per copy from The University of Texas Press, 120 West 20th Street, Austin, Texas, 78712.

5. Henry J. Otto and others, *Nongradedness: An Elementary School Evaluation*, Bureau of Laboratory Schools Monograph no. 21 (Austin: The University of Texas Press, 1969). Available at $3.00 per copy from The University of Texas Press, 120 West 20th Street, Austin, Texas, 78712.

6. William P. McLoughlin, "Continuous Pupil Progress in the Non-graded School: Hope or Hoax?" *Elementary School Journal*, 71 (Nov. 1970), pp. 90-96.

Research Reports

Appleton Public Schools. "A Report of a Three-Year Study of Mixed Group Classes at Huntley School." Appleton, Wisconsin: The Schools, 1963.

Austin, Kent C. "The Ungraded Primary Unit in Public Elementary Schools of the United States." Ed. D. dissertation, University of Colorado, 1957.

Blackstock, Cecelia R. "A Field Study to Initiate an Ungraded Primary School in Brazosport." Ed. D. dissertation, University of Houston, 1961.

Bockrath, Sister M. Bernarda. "An Evaluation of the Ungraded Primary and an Organizational Device for Improving Learning in St. Louis Archdiocesan Schools." Ed. D. dissertation, St. Louis University, 1959.

Buffie, E. G. "A Comparison of Mental Health and Academic Achievement: The Nongraded vs. the Graded School." Ed. D. dissertation, Indiana University, 1962.

Carbone, R. F. "Comparison of Graded and Nongraded Elementary Schools." *Elementary School Journal* 62 (Nov. 1961): pp. 82-88.

Chance, Stanley E. "An Analysis of Some of the Effects of Multi-Grade Grouping in Elementary Schools." Ed. D. dissertation, University of Tennessee, 1961.

Chastain, Clarence S. "An Experimental Study of the Gains in Achievement in Arithmetic and Reading in Intermediate Grades in Traditional Classrooms, in Achievement Platoons, and in Nongraded Classes." Ed. D. dissertation, Colorado State University, 1961.

Cocklin, Warren. "A Study of an Ungraded Primary School." Dissertation, University of Pennsylvania, 1950.

Cushenberg, D. C. "The Intergrade Plan of Grouping for Reading Instruction as Used in the Public Schools of Joplin, Missouri." Ed. D. dissertation, University of Missouri, 1964.

DeGraw, G. S. "A Study of the Effects of the Use of Vertical Reading Ability Four, Five and Six in the Port Huron Area Public Schools over a Three-Year Period." Dissertation, University of Michigan, 1963.

Delgado-Marcano, Maria T. "The Operation of Curriculum and Instruction in Twenty Nongraded Elementary Schools." Ed. D. dissertation, Indiana University, 1965.

Di Lorenzo, L. T., and Salter, Ruth. "Cooperative Research on the Nongraded Primary." *Elementary School Journal* 65 (Feb. 1965): pp. 269-77.

Dufay, F. R. "The Development of Procedures for the Implementation of the Nongraded Primary School in Central School District No. 4, Plainview-Old Bethpage, New York." Ed. D. dissertation, New York University, 1963.

Eldred, Donald M., and Hillson, Maurie. "The Nongraded School and Mental Health." *Elementary School Journal* 63 (Jan. 1963): pp. 218-23.

Ernatt, R. "A Survey of Pupils' Attitudes Toward Intergrade Ability Grouping for Reading Instruction." Ed. D. dissertation, Wayne State University, 1963.

Fielder, Edgar E. "A Study to Determine and Analyze Parental Opinion Concerning the Initiation of a Continuous Learning Program." Ed. D. dissertation, Colorado State University, 1963.

Foshay, Wellesley. "Intergrade Grouping in an Elementary School: A Study of Certain Effects Associated with an Age Range of Three Years in Two

Elementary School Classes." Dissertation, Teachers College, Columbia University, 1948.

Halliwell, Joseph W. "A Comparison of Pupil Achievement in Graded and Nongraded Primary Classrooms." *The Journal of Experimental Education* 32 (Fall 1963): pp. 59-64.

Hamilton, Warren, and Rehwoldt, Walter H. "An Analysis of Some of the Effects of an Interage and Intergrade Grouping in an Elementary School." Dissertation, University of Southern California, 1957.

Hart, R. H. "The Nongraded Primary School and Arithmetic." *Arithmetic Teacher* 9 (March 1962): pp. 130-33.

Hillson, Maurie, and others. "Controlled Experiment Evaluating the Effects of a Nongraded Organization on Pupil Achievement." *Journal of Educational Research* 57 (July 1964): pp. 548-50.

Holmes, Doris. "An Analysis of Continuous Progress in the Indianapolis Schools." Ed. D. dissertation, Teachers College, Columbia University, 1953.

Hopkins, K. D., and others. "An Empirical Comparison of Pupil Achievement and Other Variables in Graded and Ungraded Classes." *American Educational Research Journal* 2 (Nov. 1965): pp. 207-16.

Ingram, V. "Flint Evaluates Its Primary Cycle." *Elementary School Journal* 61 (Nov. 1960): pp. 76-80.

Jaquette, Fred C. "A Five-Year Study to Determine the Effect of the Ungraded Classroom Organization on Reading in Grand Junction, Colorado." Ed. D. dissertation, Colorado State University, 1959.

Johnson, Glenn R. "Nongraded Schools and Individualized Instruction." Ed. D. dissertation, Teachers College, Columbia University, 1968.

Kierstead, R. "A Comparison and Evaluation of Two Methods of Organization for the Teaching of Reading." *Journal of Educational Research* 56 (Feb. 1963): pp. 317-21.

Klurve, Mary J. "An Investigation of the Effects of an Integrated Kindergarten-Primary Program." Ed. D. dissertation, Wayne State University, 1957.

Lewin, David. "Go Slow on Non-grading." *Elementary School Journal* 67 (Dec. 1966): pp. 131-34.

Moore, D. L. "Pupil Achievement and Grouping Practice in Graded and Ungraded Primary School." Ed. D. dissertation, University of Michigan, 1963.

Muck, Ruth E. "Effect of Classroom Organization on Academic Achievement in Graded and Non-Graded Classes." Ed. D. dissertation, State University of New York at Buffalo, 1966.

Parker, James R. "Comparison of Organizational and Instructional Practices in Graded and Non-Graded Schools." Ed. D. dissertation, University of California at Berkeley, 1967.

Ritzenhein, Betty Ann. "Survey of Personnel Perceptions of Selected Factors in Nongraded Programs in Eight Detroit Elementary Schools." Ed. D. dissertation, Wayne State University, 1963.

Ross, Geneva A. "A Comparative Study of Pupil Progress in Ungraded and Graded Primary Programs." Ed. D. dissertation, Indiana University, 1967.

Roberts, G. W. "Case Studies of Two Nongraded Elementary School Programs." Ed. D. dissertation, University of Tennessee, 1964.

Russell, D. H. "Intergrade Grouping for Reading Instruction in the Intermediate Grades." *Journal of Educational Research* 39 (1946): pp. 462-70.

Smith, Howard. *A Comparison of the Reading Achievement of Ungraded and Graded Primary Students.* Hillsboro, Oregon: Hillsboro Public Schools, n.d.

Skapski, Mary K. "Ungraded Primary Reading Program: An Objective Evaluation." *Elementary School Journal* 41 (Oct. 1960): pp. 41–45.

Ward, Dayton N. "An Evaluation of a Nongraded School Program in Grades One and Two." Ed. D. dissertation, The University of Texas at Austin, 1969.

Williams, Wilmajean. "Academic Achievement in a Graded School and in a Non-Graded School." *Elementary School Journal* 67 (Dec. 1966): pp. 135–39.

CHAPTER 10

A Strategy for the Development of Nongraded Schools

by

Roy A. Larmee

Dr. Larmee is a professor and Chairman of the Academic Faculty at The Ohio State University. He has served as a teacher; an elementary, junior high school, and senior high school principal; and as Director of The University of Chicago Laboratory Schools.

T<small>HE CASUAL READER</small> might conclude from the literature in the field of education that change has been a major concern of American educators for a long time. It is true that if we were to compare the schools in 1900 with the schools of today we would see many changes in pupil population, curriculum, physical facilities, and even in methods of teaching. We would also observe some distinct similarities, especially in the areas of basic organization and administrative structure. Even though the literature reflects considerable concern over change on the American educational scene, the writers reflect little understanding of either the processes or the consequences of change. In fact, it is only very recently that serious consideration has been given to the idea of carefully planned change. Terms such as *change agents, change mechanisms, inhibiting forces,* and *facilitating forces* have been given some attention in rural sociology and other fields, but carefully developed research on change in the field of education is only a very recent proposal. Data that might help those who wish to inaugurate planned change in education is extremely limited.

Today education is under repeated and increasing pressure to change, and this pressure is coming from segments of society that were formerly willing to leave educational decision-making to the professional educator. The pressure for change has become so great in some cases that innovations have been introduced with little or no planning.

John W. Gardner reminds us that no society should invite change for the sake of change. "It must court the kinds of change that will enrich and strengthen it rather than the kinds that will fragment and destroy it."[1] On the other hand Mr. Gardner encourages the introduction of carefully planned change. He further states:

> A system that isn't innovating is dying. In the long run, the innovators are the ones who rescue all human ventures from death by decay. So value them. You don't have to be one yourself, but you should be a friend of the innovators around you. And if you don't have any around you, you had better import some.[2]

Consideration of the process by which an educational organization decides to make changes and implements them (such as the nongrading of a school) is of utmost importance, particularly for educators contemplating the introduction of some change in school organization. The development of educational goals and the adoption of a plan to achieve these goals is necessarily a cooperative effort for the teacher, principal, supervisor, superintendent, or other member of the educational team. While it is not difficult to identify the concerns of the various professional education personnel in the nongrading of schools, it is a more formidable task to plan the specific role each one will have in the investigation, pre-planning, decision-making, programming, implementation, and evaluation stages of the undertaking.

Recognition of the Problem

The development of a carefully designed plan to nongrade a school or schools must be preceded by systematic investigation, study, and planning. Probably one of the best ways to initiate a study of the nongraded school is to consider a series of problems related to the operation of a graded school, many of which we have been wrestling with for years.

Initiation or recognition of these problems may come from any point in the educational hierarchy. Concerns such as the following are not new, but in the context of the nongraded school they offer a new set of challenges as well as new points of attack for staff study.

1. How do we deal with the differences in readiness among children entering school?

2. In a graded school system do we make any special provision for children who have had one or two years of nursery school before entering school?

3. Do the initial differences in ability increase or decrease as formal education proceeds?

4. Is there a difference in a child's interest and achievement rate as he moves from one learning experience to another?

5. In what ways does the graded pattern of school organization place restrictions on a student's desirable uninterrupted sequential educational experience?

6. Does homogeneous grouping of students for all educational experiences at a given age level provide a solution for some of the problems inherent in a heterogeneous grouping?

7. How do we fit independent study programs into a graded or homogeneously grouped school organization?

8. Do these independent study programs present new problems within the graded structure of school organization?

9. How can our report to parents on pupil progress be made more meaningful?

10. How valid are student claims that the curriculum is inadequate and inappropriate to meet their needs?

11. Does equality of educational opportunity mean that every school in the system has the same program at each grade level?

This list of questions is not meant to be exhaustive, but is rather illustrative of the problems that could easily lead to the discussion of the nongraded school concept. It is also relatively easy to recognize the sources from which they come. Students, teachers, counselors, supervisors, administrators, and parents, at one time or another, have all raised these same kinds of questions.

A careful examination of these or related problems raises the question of whether the formally graded school system offers the best organizational pattern for dealing with them. Are there other patterns that hold some promise for meeting these differences in ability, interest, and rate of learning? What are some of these new patterns? Concern with organizational patterns will probably move quickly to the consideration of some fairly firm policy questions related to staffing, curriculum, promoting student involvement in educational decision-making, parent-school-community relationships, independent study areas, instructional materials centers, and team teaching.

The pattern of questions may vary, but it would be a rare school system indeed that has not considered a number of them. At this point in defining the problem the concept of the nongraded school might well be introduced, as considerable experience with this type of school organization has now been reported in the professional literature in education. Many teachers and administrators have had some contact with the idea from professional workshops or meetings and college and university courses. A proposal to study the concept of the nongraded school may emerge because members of the staff have previously worked on some of the problems noted above.

The Role of the Administrator as a Change Agent

At this point in the staff's consideration of the nongraded school the role of the administrator as an agent of change is crucial. In a study of the change process in New York, Brickell states that teachers alone can make only three types of instructional change in the absence of administrative initiative: (1) change of classroom practice, (2) relocation of existing curriculum content, and (3) introduction of single special courses at the high school level.[3] He also states:

> Instructional changes which call for significant new ways of using professional talent, drawing upon instructional resources, allocating physical facilities, scheduling instructional time or altering physical space—rearrangements of the structural elements of the institution —depend almost exclusively upon administrative initiative.[4]

Basic change, such as nongrading a school, has far-reaching implications for staff members at the investigation, decision-making, programming, implementation, and evaluation levels. From his unique vantage point in the educational enterprise, the administrator has a critical role to play as planner, decision-maker, facilitator, allocator of resources, stimulator, and appraiser.

As a profession, education has become increasingly committed to the involvement of teachers in the decision-making process, but we have been unable to agree on the specific form that this involvement should take. Some have argued the desirability and feasibility of teachers' sharing in all decisions, while others argue that the area in which teachers can be effective is limited. In one of the most comprehensive investigations in this area, in a study involving more than 2,000 teachers in forty-three states, Chase found that teachers who report opportunity to participate regularly and actively in making policies are much more likely to be enthusiastic about their school systems than those who report limited opportunity to participate.[5]

Clearly, the collective negotiations movement has drastically changed the decision-making role of the teacher in public schools. Moskow and Lieberman take issue with those who argue that collective negotiations downgrade the role of administrators. They argue that "Nothing could be more erroneous. Collective negotiations puts a higher premium on effective administration than the traditional relationships between teachers and administrators ever did."[6]

Consideration of the implementation of the nongraded organization provides an excellent opportunity for the administrator to act as a change agent and for the other members of the teaching staff to be involved in the study. Fortunately many administrators have intentionally recruited teachers with varied abilities, skills, special preparations, and experiences that are invaluable in the consideration of a program as broad as that of the nongraded school. An essential element of administrative leadership is the ability to identify this diversity of talent and utilize these talents effectively. The administrator must couple this knowledge of his staff with a careful assessment of the scope of the investigation being undertaken, and he must assign the resources necessary so that all alternatives can be considered carefully before a plan of action is adopted.

A new dimension has been added to the decision-making process—the day when we could include students as our obedient clients appears to be past. Nystrand argues for meaningful involvement of students in educational decision-making when he states, "It seems likely that the educational world is on the threshold of a student power movement which could have at least as much impact as teacher militancy."[7]

We are only beginning to learn how to plan with students, to listen to them, and to include them in planning and evaluation. In an organizational scheme like the nongraded school it is imperative that we develop close, sensitive, sincere, and meaningful relationships with students at all levels and stages of planning.

Provision of the Proper Climate for Decision-Making

In the initial stages of the investigation many decisions will be made that will affect the final outcome of the study. The administrator must decide, first of all, whether the study can be undertaken within the regular framework of faculty meetings, curriculum studies, and professional conferences and workshops. The scope of the problem may demand a greater commitment of resources. There are a number of alternatives that might be considered, which would undoubtedly vary from school system to school system. In some schools a portion of the regular school day is allocated for studies and professional concerns of the students and staff. Some schools send teams to visit schools where interesting new practices are in operation. In other school systems a limited number of teachers receive extended contracts for the summer months to make careful studies and preparations for projects of potential benefit to the school system. A growing number of school systems provide leaves of absence so that teachers may have a year of uninterrupted study. Partial release from teaching responsibilities is another means of providing personnel resources commensurate with the task undertaken. Which of these alternatives will be necessary depends on the magnitude of the task of nongrading the school.

The attitude of the staff is greatly influenced by the work that is done during the planning, investigating, and decision-making stages. Teachers vary tremendously in their reaction to an undertaking such as the nongraded school. Initially their attitudes will probably range from enthusiastic support to open opposition. Recognition of these varied attitudes is important in selecting those persons who will be most active in the investigating and planning stages; it also assures those who raise serious objections that their concerns will be sincerely and conscientiously recognized and investigated. Those who offer serious objections can often offer appropriate dimensions that can be included in the evaluation and appraisal phases, which must be a part of the initial decision and of the plan that is inaugurated. It is also important to point out that all possible alternatives will be investigated impartially.

There will be many discussions of the new plan by the informal organization of the school, and as the plan progresses there will be many questions from students and from adult members of the community. Questions will not always be asked of those best qualified to answer them. In these cases it is important that the attitude encountered by the questioning parent or student is one sympathetic to the project being undertaken. Administrators have learned from the National Science Foundation projects that parents are very willing to have their children participate in a project that is clearly labeled experimental, if they can be assured that it has been carefully planned by competent persons who will thoroughly appraise the results.

Some teachers will have fairly well-established opinions that may be in opposition to the total study being undertaken. These opinions are often more apparent at the initiation stages of the study. Here again the role of the administrator is important and difficult, since he must be completely honest and straightforward in his presentation of the problem and of the proposal.

Staff members vary a great deal in their respect for the leadership ability of the administrator. One of the frequent causes for disappointment on the part of the staff is the introduction of serious limitations after the undertaking has been under way for some time. This is especially disastrous to morale, satisfaction, and productivity if it is discovered that these limitations existed since the beginning of the study but were not identified in the investigating, planning, and decision-making stages. For example, are there budget limitations? If so, have they been clearly specified? Is there a time limit on the study because the administrator has promised reports to the board of education? Probably the most devastating of all possible developments is the discovery by the students and staff that although the administrator has given assurance that all possible alternatives will be investigated and that the decision will be based on these investigations, he had a proposal in mind from the very beginning and has skillfully manipulated the study to reach this outcome. This kind of approach will not succeed and is very likely to be sabotaged.

Involvement of the Board of Education and the Community at the Planning Stage

Initial investigations of problem areas and possible alternate solutions should be planned with the full knowledge of the board of education and the total administrative staff of the school system. This stage should not be confused with later stages in the process when carefully developed plans are ready for explanation and dissemination to the communication media and to the community. In the early study phase, the board of education should be made aware of the care, the scope, and the thoroughness of the study to be undertaken; and those who make the presentation to the board should be careful not to make premature statements or implications of desired outcomes.

The board of education should also be made fully aware of the nature of the study, and should receive periodic reports as the investigation progresses. Members of the board should have the opportunity to raise questions and to offer constructive criticism of the proposed plan. Support of the board is crucial to any new plan devised by the professional school staff, and this support can best be gained from an involved, informed, and sympathetic board of education. Basic board policies should make provision for this type of investigation, and care should be exercised so that all programs of study are carried out in line with established board policies.

Some school systems have found it very desirable to include members of the lay community in the initial study groups. Active members of the Parent Teacher Association are often sincerely interested in studies of this type and they provide a parent's point of view, which can be invaluable in developing and implementing a decision, when it is finally reached. Community support can also often be gained by involving persons from public and private community agencies concerned with the health, education, and welfare of children. Their views are expressed from another vantage point, and they often make suggestions that prove to be very effective. The role of the administrator is again a key one as his contacts with the various agencies and groups in the community are often broad and at some depth. Indeed, one of the most recent challenges for the school administrator is to develop closer relationships with various community agencies, and to assist the board of education in finding ways of involving these agencies in educational decision-making.

Consideration of Alternate Plans of Action

After the initial investigation has been completed and all the alternatives have been examined closely, a choice must be made between a single plan or a combination of approaches to nongrading. Typically, one of the first decisions to be made is whether to experiment in the entire system or in one or two schools. Each approach has its problems.

If the nongraded organization is to be inaugurated in only one school, the original plan should include logical, carefully developed reasons for choosing this particular school, and an adequate explanation should be given to the parents and students. This task is much easier now that schools have undertaken limited experimentation in many other areas, such as the use of educational television, team teaching, and programmed instruction. Parents have learned to respect carefully planned experimentation if it is thoroughly evaluated and if the results of this evaluation are included in further expansion of the innovation throughout the school system.

An innovation like the nongraded school should be introduced system-wide only after a complete assessment is made of the personnel and material resources available in the school system because the first year of a new idea is usually its most expensive, even if it is evaluated and modified as it is put into practice. Many of the costs associated with its introduction will disappear as the experimentation is perfected, in-service training programs completed, and consultant services dispensed with.

Introducing the nongraded concept in a single school or in a small number of schools provides many advantages. Initially, teachers may vary considerably in their attitude toward the nongraded school and in their knowledge and understanding of the concept. It is important that those who carry out the initial introduction be thoroughly familiar with the idea and disposed to giving it a fair and objective trial. They should be selected with great care and given the advantages of a thorough in-service training program by persons who are familiar with the concept and experienced in using the plan. Reading the literature on the nongraded school and discussing it is not enough. The teachers must understand the change thoroughly in order to deal adequately with some of the new learning situations. However, in the initial planning stages it is important to think beyond the original introductory situation. If nongrading is introduced in only one or two schools, or in only part of a school (such as the first three grades) consideration must be given to the situation that will exist following the experimental period, assuming, of course, that the experiment will be successful, even though it may be modified in some ways as a result of the appraisal process. One or several groups of boys and girls will have had a completely new and, hopefully, a largely successful experience. Are they to be returned to the traditional type of graded organization? If so, there will be some fairly knotty problems of pupil, parent, and teacher reaction. Plans for dealing with this eventuality cannot await the completion of the experimental period. They must be made at the time the original investigation is undertaken. There may well be modifications at the end of the experimental period, but basic planning should have been included in the original master plan for the innovation.

Some schools have experimented with a very limited introduction of the nongraded concept. This decision too, depends greatly on each local school situation. Sometimes the introduction is in a specific curriculum area, such as reading or arithmetic. Again, assessment of local personnel resources is important. If the school system has some highly motivated teachers who are well-prepared in their fields and who are thoroughly familiar with and trained to introduce nongrading, these limited curriculum areas might be the best point of entry. If this nongrading effort is successful it may provide the stimulation needed to encourage nongrading in other areas of the curriculum. It can be a very convincing demonstration, for teachers responsible for other phases of the curriculum can study and observe the program at close range.

Programming the Change

Immediately following the major decision to attempt some form of nongrading in a school system, a series of implementing decisions must be made to make certain that adequate resources are available to give the new undertaking a fair trial. Visitation to other schools using the new plan may need to be scheduled. In-service programs for staff will need to be developed, staffed, and carried out. Careful job descriptions outlining the duties and responsibilities should be developed for each staff position, and these descriptions should be used in turn to determine the qualifications necessary for each position. If the present staff does not include persons with the necessary qualifications, additional staff may need to be recruited or additional training provided for those already on the staff.

Attention should also be given to adequate housing of the new program. One of the desirable by-products of the accelerated school building program of the last two decades is the recognition of the magnitude of the school building and equipment market by manufacturers and designers. Through the efforts of both public and private agencies many new products have been designed specifically from educational specifications, rather than being adapted from materials used for other markets. More adequate flexible partitions, acoustical treatment of classrooms, furniture designed for new school uses, technical communication systems, data processing programs, climate control systems, and many other new products have helped to remove material handicaps that existed in the past. These new materials and techniques have created unique classroom arrangements, improved instructional possibilities, and led to better utilization of the teaching staff. In addition to changing and enriching instructional possibilities, these carefully engineered innovations have, in many cases, reduced initial construction and maintenance costs.

The decision to nongrade a school must also be reflected in the budget of the school system. A number of references have already been made to costs associated with the planning and decision-making stages of the process—costs such as released time for staff planning, consultant service, travel, in-service training, as well as costs associated with the appraisal of the new program. Many of these costs are not of a continuing nature and will therefore disappear as the initial experiment is completed. However, it is important that the funds for personnel, materials, and equipment are available at the time and place and in the right amounts to insure a fair trial of the new plan.

Programming should also include a time allocation for scheduling the various stages in the master plan, but care should be exercised to be sure it is adequate and flexible. Moving into any new or unknown area is usually accompanied by some unforeseen problems, regardless of how much care was exercised in devising the initial plan. The time schedule should allow for readjustments in the master plan as the experimental period progresses and as the evaluation processes reveal that changes are necessary.

The Role of the Administrator as Stimulator and Coordinator

A crucial point in the introduction of an innovation is often reached after the initial implementing decisions have been carried out and personnel and material resources have been allocated. The staff is usually very enthusiastic during the investigating, planning, and decision-making stages of the project, and a great deal of this enthusiasm will be carried forward to the experimental period. Occasionally, however, it is necessary for the administrator to assist during difficult or trying periods with a word of encouragement or additional resources, which were not anticipated during the planning period. In some cases the administrator must remind some members of the staff of commitments they have made and of their importance to the success of the entire undertaking. A face-to-face contact is usually most desirable for maximum stimulation. In relatively isolated cases it may even be necessary for the administrator to exert pressure on individuals to gain the desired results. If careful staffing procedures and planned involvement have been followed during the planning stages, very little of this kind of stimulation on the part of the administrator should be necessary.

The administrator is also responsible for the coordination of the entire undertaking. In programming the master plan he has made provision for budget, personnel, and material resources and a time schedule has been established for carrying out the total experiment. As the coordinator he must make certain that the resources are provided at the time and place at which they are needed. The unique vantage point of the administrator again affords him an excellent opportunity to observe how well the entire plan is moving toward the objectives established during the planning and decision-making periods. If the immediate goals of the project and the institutional goals of the school system are to be kept in proper perspective, the administrator will need to maintain an objective attitude toward the findings revealed in the periodic progress report and in the interim appraisal results. The administrator may find it necessary to suggest reorientation of the project in order to accomplish the agreed-upon goals of the undertaking and of the institution as a whole.

Appraisal of Innovation or Change

Probably the most frequent reason for failure of an experimental program is the failure to provide for its adequate appraisal. Appraisal must be part of all planning activities from the very outset of the undertaking, and it must be included in all phases of the project—from investigation to experimental testing period. Appraisal programs, devices, and techniques too must be related to the goals of the school system and to the goals of the immediate project. It is most discouraging to review an experimental project and learn that the only specific appraisal information available is that "the children feel very good about it," "the experiment has been of real value to the staff," or "our parents are most enthusiastic and are encouraging us to continue our efforts." These outcomes are healthy, but they do not provide the specific information needed to appraise the undertaking, to revise and improve it, or to respond to the critics, who are always present in any new undertaking. A proposal such as the nongrading of a school system has a direct relationship to the goals of an educational enterprise, and any plan considered must be examined in the light of these goals. Are we modifying them in any way? If we are, it is extremely important that these modifications be recognized and that those responsible for the operation of the school system are aware of these modifications and support them.

In the planning stages of the project intermediate objectives will be established for the specific nongraded project that is chosen. These objectives may be based on specifically documented facts, on values, or on assumptions, but in any event they must be explicitly stated. The philosophy of the school system will usually provide the general framework for the selection of specific objectives. However, the learning experiences that are chosen to attain these objectives must be carefully examined. As each new experience is included in the program, it must be examined to see if it accords with school philosophy and if it is suitable for the age level at which it is to be introduced. It must, in other words, be filtered through both a philosophical and a psychological screen. If the experience is termed sound in these two respects ways must be found to measure the degree to which the pupil attains the objective for which the experience was selected. Some of the new National Science Foundation Course Content Improvement Programs sought the assistance of a major national testing agency to determine whether the new programs were better than the traditional programs being used by most schools. In each case the testing agency indicated that this question is not one that tests can answer. However, they offered assistance in determining whether certain experiences and objectives were suitable for children of specified age groups, and they assisted in the preparation of achievement tests to determine how well established objectives for the new program were being attained.[8]

The selection of procedures, tests, and other devices to be used in appraising the objectives of the new program is, of course, an integral part of the investigating, planning, and decision-making stages of the project. In many cases testing programs appropriate for use in the project are readily available. Alternate testing programs should be carefully examined to determine their suitability for the experimental program that has been planned. Standardized testing programs are valuable tools for use in appraising a project, but other devices must also be developed in line with the objectives of the school and of the immediate project. School communities differ in their composition and in the goals they have set for themselves. Appraisal devices and techniques must be chosen to reflect these differences. Paper-and-pencil tests, case studies, anecdotal records, interview schedules, as well as skilled observations by qualified consultants are additional evaluation devices that may be used in the appraisal of the new program. As each of the objectives and each of the stages of the experiment are examined and appraised, modifications of the original plan may be necessary. In this sense the process is a cyclical one and will lead to new decisions, which will modify the experiment.

Orienting Parents to the Change

Earlier in this chapter a word of caution was offered about premature public release of information about a nongrading plan under consideration. It seemed advisable that the board of education be involved at an early stage, and the inclusion of students, selected parents, and uniquely qualified representatives of community agencies was also recommended. The total plan should also make provision for the orientation of all the children and their parents. Since American schools belong to the people, the schools have been fortunate that most parents maintain a close interest in the schools. Parents are always interested in improving educational opportunities for their children, but they will also try to make certain that departures from traditional patterns of action are carefully planned, executed, and appraised. They have also insisted on being informed of changes and innovations.

One of the most difficult problems in nongrading a school is making parents aware of the variation in children's abilities. The differences in their rate of achievement was discovered some time ago, but the schools have not made adequate provision for these differences in their organization and operation. The graded system in many schools seems to deny these differences. If administrators and teachers subscribe to the basic concept of the nongraded school, they must also recognize these differences, plan for them, and modify the traditional program with respect to enrichment and achievement rate. Some teachers and administrators find it extremely difficult to convey this idea to parents who have lived through years of operation under the graded concept. However, this question must be faced and dealt with adequately if the necessary parent support for nongrading is to be obtained.

Specific techniques for parent orientation programs depend on local school situations. In some school systems school-community relations machinery is well established, and the orientation of parents can follow the general pattern that has been used for previous orientation activities. In some communities, agencies such as the Parent-Teacher Association handle parent orientation activities; in others it may be necessary to establish the orientation procedures. A carefully planned orientation program should include materials that can be utilized by the newspapers, radio, television, community forums, and other media available at the local level.

Presentations and materials for parent orientation programs should reflect the care with which the innovation has been considered. They should include a discussion of the planning process, consideration of some of the problems that stimulated the original investigation, the alternatives considered during the planning process, specific reasons for the alternative that was chosen, and the range of personnel involved in the planning process (students, staff, the board of education, consultants, and members of the community). Parents should also be familiarized with the objectives established for the program and the way in which these objectives are related to the goals of the school system. Finally, the operation of the program must be thoroughly described and illustrated, and plans for appraisal of the experimental program should be described. Future plans for expansion of the program should also be discussed, including possible alternatives that might result from the appraisal process. Whenever possible there should be time for questions.

All the pupils should be oriented to the new program, even if only a part of the school is affected. Those who are not to be included should be acquainted with the change, and they should be told the reasons for the limited introduction. Future plans to expand the experiment may also be shared with these pupils.

It is probably advisable to plan for parent and pupil orientation at approximately the same time. Pupils will find it easier to discuss the new program with their parents, and inadequate or erroneous interpretation of the program by pupils can be avoided. Obviously the pupil orientation program will differ from the parent program, but selected information from each stage of the introductory process should be presented to the pupils. The content will vary with the levels at which the nongrading experiment is to be inaugurated. Again a question period should be provided to avoid misunderstanding and apprehension.

Conclusion

This chapter is concerned with the process by which a typical graded school may be nongraded by cooperative staff and community action. It begins with a recognition of the problems inherent in a graded school structure and continues through the stages of investigation, planning, decision-making, programming, introduction of the nongraded plan, and provision for appraisal during the experimental period. The process is designed to do much more than change the organization from a graded form to a nongraded one, for mere change of organization will accomplish little. A nongraded plan removes certain restrictions for students and teachers, but this is really only the beginning. The process described should also alert the teacher to the new possibilities that can be accomplished within the nongraded organizational framework. It is designed to develop understanding, to change attitudes, and to deal more effectively with some of the most difficult problems involved in the education of children. It brings with it not only new opportunities but also new responsibilities, for the nongraded school offers a system of organization that is completely compatible with basic American educational values.

Notes

1. John W. Gardner, *No Easy Victories* (New York: Harper and Row, 1968), p. 48.

2. Ibid., p. 49.

3. Henry M. Brickell, *Organizing New York for Educational Change* (Albany, N.Y.: State Superintendent of Public Instruction, 1961), p. 24.

4. Ibid., p. 23.

5. Francis Chase, "The Teacher and Policy Making," *Administrator's Notebook*, I (May, 1952), p. 1.

6. Myron Lieberman and Michael H. Moskow, *Collective Negotiations For Teachers: An Approach to School Administration* (Chicago: Rand McNally, 1966), pp. 354–55.

7. Raphael O. Nystrand, "The Rights of Public High School Students to Make Demands," address before the American Association of School Administrators, Atlantic City, N.J., Feb. 1969.

8. Frederick L. Ferris, Jr., "Testing in the New Curriculum: Numerology, 'Tyranny,' or Common Sense?" *School Review*, LXX, no. 1 (Spring 1952), pp. 342–47.

PART III

THE PROCESS OF BECOMING

Exemplary Centers for Continuous Progress Education

by

EDWIN A. READ

As Director of Brigham Young University's Laboratory Schools Dr. Read successfully implemented the concept of continuous pupil progress in elementary and secondary schools. He was influential in securing federal aid for the establishment of the exemplary schools referred to in this chapter. His most recent major contribution is an individualized spelling program with Allred and Baird, "Continuous Progress in Spelling."

Formerly a public school teacher, a principal, a consultant, and director of three different campus laboratory schools, Dr. Read is currently a professor and Associate Dean of the Graduate School of Education at the University of Utah.

A MAJOR ESEA Title III Project in the state of Utah is in the process of designing elementary schools that are consistent in every feature (curriculum, instruction, learning resources, organization, reporting procedures and philosophy) with the theory of continuous pupil progress. Many of the innovative practices in this project's exemplary schools are comparable to those in schools across the nation since most major innovations in the public schools of the United States are founded on the same theory. This is true of such reforms as genuine nongrading of the organization, some forms of team organization, individualization of instruction, auto-instructional media and other educational materials designed to accommodate individual differences, differentiated curricula, and new information recording-retrieval practices that permit the teacher to monitor the progress of each child with greater precision and regularity. Many forward-looking teachers and principals are attempting to introduce some of these reforms, others, including those in the schools participating in Utah's Title III Project, "Establishing Exemplary Centers for Continuous Progress Education," are making a more total effort, and are working toward the complete implementation of the theory of continuous pupil progress.

One of the unique features of this project has been the cooperation of five major school districts ever since the initial planning stages. Teachers, principals, and central office personnel representing the five districts worked with me in planning the project and in formulating the operational grant proposal; and since the beginning of this three-year funded project there has been a united effort to establish several exemplary centers for continuous progress education in each district. Another distinguishing characteristic of this project and its principal participants has been the total conceptualization of a school designed in accordance with the theory of continuous pupil progress. The theory itself has been analyzed and refined, a model has been conceptualized, and the program for implementing the model in existing schools is now almost three years along and nearing its goal.

The Theory of Continuous Pupil Progress

The theory of continuous pupil progress derives from the theory of equal educational opportunity, which was first enunciated in the early twentieth century by educational spokesmen like Strayer and Mort.[1] Its early origin is deceiving, however, for it is more timely today and far more widely espoused than it was 40 years ago. Its acceptance and application are now clearly visible in the numerous Goodlad-inspired nongraded schools, in the widely acclaimed team teaching organizations, and in such projects as Individually Prescribed Instruction, all of which claim to meet children where they are and promote their continuous development.

As recently as 1960, the philosophical tenets of this theory received national recognition when the renowned John Gardner, on behalf of the President's Commission on National Goals, wrote:

> Our deepest convictions impel us to foster individual fulfillment. We wish each one to achieve that promise that is in him.
>
> Our devotion to equality does not ignore the fact that individuals differ greatly in their talents and motivations. It simply asserts that each should be able to develop to the full, in his own style and to his own limits.
>
> Each is worthy of respect as a human being. This means that there must be diverse programs within the educational system to take care of the diversity of individuals. No child should be required to fit a pace and pattern of education designed for children of other capacities.[2]

The fundamental assumption of this theory is that the function of the school is to promote and facilitate the optimum growth and development of each child in relation to his own potentiality and growth timetable and in relation to the goals of American education.

This assumption is in harmony with the dominant philosophy of American education, with our determination to provide equal educational opportunity for all, and with research findings about individual variability. It is, however, in sharp contrast with the Grade-Standard Theory of pupil progress, which perceives the function of the school as being that of teaching a body of essential knowledge that can be parceled out according to some kind of sequence and dispensed to all children in accordance with a predetermined timetable.[3] One finds it difficult to believe that this century-old assumption still reigns supreme in many graded schools.

Modern proponents of the theory of continuous pupil progress supplement this assumption with the proposition that America's future prosperity, the freedom of its people, and perhaps the very survival of our nation as a significant force in the world depends in large measure on the preservation of a sense of individuality among its citizens. Many of today's Americans, especially the youth, are sensing the stifling effects that automation, computerization, and urbanization are having on their individuality. There is a mounting reaction to what is perceived as a drift toward a controlled society, where conformity to institutional standards and the search for security are principal characteristics. Big business, big labor, and big government bureaucracies are perceived as contributing significantly to this end. So, also, are the mass communication media, such as television, which, whether commercial or educational, can exert an influence toward common denominators. The school, too, is seen as making its contribution to a creeping conformity whenever it rewards conformity, to the neglect of individual initiative and creativity. Hence, modern proponents of this theory talk as much about self-actualization as they do about optimum growth and development, and stress the importance of developing wholesome self-concepts, creativity, and a sense of individuality.

Postulate One

One of the original postulates of this theory, which has now become a proven fact (an illustration of the evolutionary nature of this theory), pertains to individual variability. We now have accumulated a wealth of evidence supporting the postulate that individuals differ widely in all aspects of their personalities. Our knowledge of inner-individual differences (learners differ from one another) and intra-individual differences (each learner differs in his aptitude and achievement from one learning area to another) rules out any logical support for the Grade-Standard notion that "standards of achievement can be established for each grade and that educators can parcel out the essentials in knowledge and skills in harmony with the grade norms thus established." We know, for example, that there is no such child as a fourth grader or a seventh grader in terms of achievement. Walter W. Cook concluded in 1941, after extensive research on individual variability, that "in any grade above the fourth a teacher may expect that almost the complete range of elementary-school achievement will be represented. The only thing we can say with assurance regarding a seventh grade pupil is that he is in the seventh grade."[4]

It therefore follows that a continuous progress school will be free of arbitrary grade standards that must apply to all children in a given class. Its curriculum and organization will be open and flexible, nongraded if you like, and one in which children are met on their own levels of achievement and encouraged to progress continuously in their own best style. The school will have replaced competitive Grade-Standard marking and reporting systems with individual records of growth and achievement gain. The instructional materials and media available in each classroom will correspond to the wide range of intra- and inter-individual variability among and within class members.

POSTULATE TWO

A second postulate holds that learners differ not only in their stages of development, but also in the way they acquire knowledge most efficiently. Some writers have referred to these differences in terms of "learning styles." Others have acknowledged them by encouraging teachers to employ a variety of "teaching strategies" in their classrooms. Cronbach holds that "teaching different pupils by different methods presents the greatest promise for meeting individual differences."[5]

Hypotheses adduced from this postulate have been the subject of several research projects in recent years, and although the findings are not altogether consistent, there is some evidence to support the notion that certain methods of instruction are more effective with some children than with others. This seems to be the implication of a study reported by G. I. Andersen, who found that a combination of a child's general ability and his past achievement in arithmetic tended to predict whether he would learn arithmetic better by the "drill method" of instruction or the "meaning method."

The findings of other studies seem to imply that defensive, anxious pupils, who feel compelled to avoid failure, achieve better under instructional conditions of a more structured and dependent form than do learners who might be described as self-assured or constructive in their makeup. Some of this research tends to suggest that the dependency-anxiety levels of a learner's personality will influence the way he responds to the motivation-reinforcement strategies of the teacher. Some learners respond with vigor (and with some anxiety) to a perceived risk of failure; others look for ways to avoid the related activity. Some seem to be most easily motivated by a direct assignment with a time limitation; others respond better when given an invitation to learn.

POSTULATE THREE

A third postulate of the continuous progress theory is that individual differences among learners cannot be organized away. This statement might be thought of as a modern addendum to the theory, arising out of the countless informal and formal experimental attempts to accomplish this end. Literature is replete with reports of formal experimentation and research that have investigated the effects of grouping and other forms of organization on learning. Comparisons in achievement gain and in student attitudes have been made between heterogeneous grouping and homogeneous grouping, between nongrading and grading, between team organization and self-contained classroom organization, etc., and although the findings are by no means consistent or conclusive, many authorities agree that present evidence supports the position expressed earlier—individual differences cannot be organized away.

Therefore if students are to progress continuously according to their own growth timetables, the teacher must accommodate their differences in the instructional dimension rather than in the organizational dimension of the school. It does not suggest, however, that organization is inconsequential. One hundred and fifteen years of experience with the graded school have surely taught us something about the obstructive effects of an organization that erects arbitrary barriers to progress. Hence, the increasing popularity of the nongraded school, which by virtue of its open vertical structure facilitates continuous pupil progress.

POSTULATE FOUR

Finally, the theory of continuous pupil progress postulates that all children and youth can learn and do so with enjoyment and satisfaction if the following conditions are met: (1) the learner has developed appropriate readiness for the particular learning act; (2) the verbal and nonverbal contents of the learning experience are geared to his level of development; and (3) the time factors permit him to conceptualize and develop skills, habits, and values at his own best pace.

This postulate was restated as a proposition by Bruner in his popular publication, *The Process of Education,* in 1962. In the introduction Bruner presents "the proposition that the foundations of any subject may be taught to anybody at any age in some form."[6] He goes on to explain that "it is only when such basic ideas are put in formalized terms and as equations or elaborate verbal concepts that they are out of reach of young children. . . ."

Bruner's proposition lends support to our postulate and its three conditions, and if research has not yet fully substantiated them, then experience surely has. Those who have had close association with the teachers and students in bonafide nongraded or continuous progress schools have witnessed the educational and human dividends that accrue from meeting children where they are, and allowing them to progress at their own best paces. In the pioneer Continuous Progress Plan at the Laboratory Schools at Brigham Young University, it was discovered, for example, that students who had consistently failed in mathematics were able to succeed when allowed to progress at their own rates. Their foreign language laboratory demonstrated, too, that students who "couldn't learn a foreign language" actually could when methods and pacing were adapted to accommodate individual differences. Any teacher of reading who has made a serious and sincere effort to individualize reading instruction has made a similar "discovery."

Conceptual Model of the Continuous Progress School

Theories present man with an irresistible temptation to test them in some real or simulated environment. To do so he commonly designs models and eventually constructs real environments according to the patterns he has created for examining the validity of his theories. Here is one such attempt, a paradigm of the continuous progress school. It attempts to describe, in abbreviated form, the major elements of an educational system based on the theory of continuous pupil progress, namely, its chief function, its curriculum, instruction, organization, instructional media and learning resources, the learner and the teacher, and evaluation.

SCHOOL FUNCTION

The school promotes and facilitates the optimum development of learners in relation to their individual potentialities, and the goals of American education.

CURRICULUM

The curriculum is two-dimensional: the personal dimension, through which individual interests and talents are cultivated; and the societal dimension, consisting of those broad concepts, modes of inquiry, attitudes, skills, and habits that society regards as fundamental. The open design of this curriculum (free of grade or other arbitrary barriers) facilitates continuous, cumulative learning with children working at different levels in each area of the curriculum.

INSTRUCTION

Instruction is individualized and personalized with respect to content, methods, achievement requirements, and pacing. Content is determined by the learner's needs, interests, and achievement; method, by an assessment of his stage of development and his personal makeup; achievement requirements, by an assessment of the learner's potentialities and abilities; and pacing, by an estimate of his rate of development and demonstrated rate of learning.

ORGANIZATION

The school is organized to facilitate continuous upward progress through the educational program from entrance to graduation. It contrasts with the traditional graded school in that its vertical structure is open and free from arbitrary barriers to student progress. It is, in a very real sense, a nongraded school.

In the horizontal dimension of the organization, there are alternate teacher-pupil affiliations and learning environments, and opportunities within each for individuals to work at different levels in each area of the curriculum and to progress at their own best paces. These affiliations have enough stability to insure that each learner is known well by those who guide his development.

INSTRUCTIONAL MEDIA AND LEARNING RESOURCES

A wide range and variety of learning resources are available to accommodate differences in ability, in prescribed learning activities, and interests. Instructional media are varied in nature for similar reasons and are designed for use by students and teachers in individual and group settings.

THE LEARNER AND THE TEACHER

The learner is perceived as an active partner in identifying academic and personal needs and interests, in establishing learning objectives, and in determining appropriate learning experiences. He is viewed as a principal partner in a developmental venture, accepting responsibility for his own progress.

The teacher is viewed as a growth counselor and facilitator of learning, one who identifies the learning needs and interests of individuals, prescribes educational treatment, sets the stage for learning, guides the learning act, motivates, provides learning resources, and measures and evaluates growth.

EVALUATION

Teachers evaluate continuously, keeping daily or weekly records of the progress being made by individual learners in all areas of the curriculum. Achievement is measured in terms of behavioral change. Decisions about the adequacy of these changes are made in relation to estimates of the learner's potentialities.

Curriculum and Instruction

Schools that exemplify the continuous progress theory are characterized by a curriculum containing both structured and unstructured components, both of which are designed to foster the unhampered progress of learners. Such a curriculum must have two major sources of its instructional objectives—the learner and the society that supports the educational system.

The learner must be a chief source of instructional objectives for the simple reason that he is the one seeking self-actualization; and he is the one whom we wish to become aware of the rewards of an independent pursuit of knowledge.

This component of the curriculum has been labeled variously as the pupil-centered dimension, the personal dimension, or the self-selected dimension of the curriculum. It consists of those learning and developmental activities in which the student chooses to engage, which may range all the way from rock collecting to creative art. Very often, perhaps more often than not, these personal interests furnish the best means by which the established educational goals of society are achieved. They are sometimes stimulated by student and/or teacher-designed displays, such as an insect collection surrounded with colorful references. At other times, they grow out of units of study, and lead to individual projects of undetermined length and complexity; for example, a boy whose interest in astronomy is stimulated by a short unit on the universe, embarks on an intensive investigation of this subject, or a girl, whose short encounter with water colors in an art class fails to quench her thirst for art expression, pursues an almost feverish encounter with other art media.

Some self-selected learning activities have their origins outside the school—in the home, in the scout patrol, or in some other community activity. In such cases, the student turns to the school for additional information, like the boy whose small home chemistry set leads him to explore intensively the school's more completely equipped chemistry laboratory.

Some self-selected learning activities are hardly distinguishable from those initiated by the teacher. In schools that operate under the continuous progress theory students are often challenged by the academic achievement of their peers and choose to engage in silent or open competition with them. We have seen children spend unusual amounts of time with the spelling program in order to match or excel the achievement of others. Similar learning sprees are to be found in reading library books or writing lengthy, highly creative stories or poems.

Learning, of course, takes time, and if the personal dimension of the curriculum is valued, time must be budgeted for it. Though some teachers find this hard to do, others see it as the most genuine and effective way to individualize instruction. Furthermore, it promises to be one of the most feasible strategies for achieving two of the most valued educational objectives of the modern school: a thirst and respect for knowledge, and the ability and tendency to seek and acquire knowledge.

The Committee on Economic Development gave top priority to these educational goals in a 1969 publication entitled, *Innovation in Education: New Directions for the American School.*

> The end result of competent instruction should be a desire and respect for knowledge and possession of the skills essential to getting and using knowledge. . . . It is more important to generate intellectual curiosity and a passion for knowledge and to cultivate good habits of thought and inquiry, than to concentrate on learning countless detailed facts which may soon be forgotten or abandoned.[7]

The second major source of instructional objectives is the society that gives its support to the educational enterprise. Often referred to as the "societal dimension," these objectives reflect the expectations of society and the content of established subject matter. This aspect of the curriculum is somewhat more structured and sequenced than the personalized dimension. Here individualization takes the form of variations in the way each learner progresses through sequences of objectives and related curriculum elements (concepts, skills, etc.).

There are two major approaches to the individualization of instruction in this structured component. In one, the instructional objectives and the learning resources are the same for all the pupils, but at different rates of progress. In a second approach, the educational objectives and their related curriculum elements are the common requirements, and individual variability is accommodated through differentiated learning experiences and instructional materials. A variation of this approach permits students to achieve objectives out of order, in accordance with their present needs and interests, or to skip certain objectives altogether when it seems educationally defensible.

These approaches to individualizing instruction will be discussed and illustrated below, but first let it be noted that the curriculum in all of them and in all the many possible variations has some form of structure. It is this structure that facilitates continuous pupil progress from one planned and purposeful instructional objective to another. It has six elements designed to individualize instruction:

1. A sequence of instructional objectives and related curriculum elements (concepts, skills, etc.)

2. Inventory and diagnostic instruments and procedures for determining appropriate placement of learners in each area of the curriculum and for identifying specific and general instructional needs

3. A wide range of instructional materials designed for individual use

4. Procedural steps to be followed by pupils in their independent study and evaluative activities

5. Teaching strategies that are effective in small group- and individual instructional settings

6. Instruments and records for evaluating and monitoring student progress.

APPROACH I

In one of the approaches to individualization referred to above, pupils progress through essentially the same structured content, starting at their own levels of achievement and progressing at their own best paces. In the spelling program (*Continuous Progress in Spelling*),[8] for example, placement tests are administered to determine on which of the sixteen sequenced spelling lists a pupil should begin his formal study. Then, through a procedural pattern of partner testing, independent study, delayed-recall testing, and record keeping, the learner progresses at his own best pace from one level list to another. One might say that the content is also differentiated to the extent that each pupil studies only those words in each spelling list that he cannot spell. These words are identified through pre-tests administered by another pupil, a partner with whom the child cooperates in administering both pre- and post-tests. Content is also individualized in the functional spelling phase of the program, which requires that pupils learn selected words that they have misspelled in daily writing activities.

To a certain extent arithmetic falls in this instructional approach, especially in those schools in which a major arithmetic series is employed. In such cases, inventory tests or "criterion tests" made by the teachers are employed to establish student placement in the series and to identify specific skill and concept deficiencies. The student is then given help with these deficiencies, either individually or in small common-need groups. Additional explanations and practice activities are provided in the basic instructional materials. The learner assumes appropriate responsibility for his own progress through these materials by following study guides, taking unit achievement tests, correcting his work, keeping accurate records of his progress, and reporting to the teacher.

Figure one shows a sample record form that has been used to check off the arithmetic skills and concepts as they are learned in the sequence. In the columns on the right, the several teachers who have taught the child during his elementary school education indicate (in whatever way they prefer) the skills and concepts that the pupil has acquired. Some will use a simple check mark, others might indicate the date on which the achievement was recognized and recorded.

INDIVIDUAL RECORD OF ACHIEVEMENT—ARITHMETIC

	Meaning and Use of Whole Numbers					
1	Concepts of Addition					
2	Concepts of Subtraction					
3	Concepts of Multiplication					
4	Concepts of Division					
5	Inverse Operations					
	Meaning and Use of Common Fractions					
6	Concepts of Addition					

7	Concepts of Subtraction						
8	Concepts of Multiplication						
9	Concepts of Division						
	Meaning and Use of Decimal Fractions						
10	Concepts of Addition						
11	Concepts of Subtraction						
12	Concepts of Multiplication						
13	Concepts of Division						
	Geometry						
14	Constructions						
15	Measurement						
16	Plane Figures						
17	Solid Figures						
	Numeration Systems						
18	Concepts of Base						
19	Operations						
	Measurement						
20	Linear						
21	Liquid						
22	Volume						
23	Weight						
24	Time						
	Graphs						
25	Interpretation						
26	Preparation						
27	Statistical Idea						
	Ratio and Proportion						
28	Meaning and Use						
	Percent						
29	Meaning and Use						
	Meaning and Use of Number Properties						
30	Commutative and Associative						
31	Distributive						

FIGURE ONE

APPROACH II

The goal of the other major approach to individualization of instruction is for all pupils to achieve common instructional objectives and their related concepts and skills, each accomplishing them in his own way, through learning activities that are most meaningful and productive for him, and through the use of instructional resources that are individually appropriate. The rationale for this approach to curriculum and instruction is cogently expressed by Wilhelms:

> The goal is essential; the particular means are optional. Similarly, to every important human goal there are many roads and, if not all of them are royal, neither are all of us kings. The fundamental error in curriculum-thinking has been to equate content with goal; or worse, to redouble our zeal as to content just because we have forgotten the goal.[9]

Pacing, then, is a less dynamic variable in Approach II than in Approach I. Individualization is accomplished here by (1) differentiation of learning experiences, (2) differentiation of learning resources, (3) differentiation of specific learning content, and (4) differentiation in achievement expectations, that is, not all learners are expected to attain the same level of conceptualization.

The science program in schools that follow the theory of continuous pupil progress illustrates Approach II. One of the science units used at the primary level in the Title III Exemplary Centers for Continuous Progress Education deals with the concept of gravity. It was prepared by Mrs. Maureen Jones, who introduces the unit by explaining that "it is designed to meet individual needs through the Choice of Learning Activities Approach."[10] The behavioral objective of the unit is to have each child involved and participating by:

> making his own choices of learning activities and problems
> identifying and selecting materials he wants or needs to use
> diagnosing and checking his own progress
> choosing and utilizing one of the art forms to express his creativity
> keeping his own retrieval system
> evaluating his participation and work in the unit.[11]

The following is an excerpt from the Teacher's Guide to the Gravity Unit. It illustrates how the concept, the supporting concept and the behavioral objective are identified for the teacher. The "group learning experiences" are examples of the kinds of activities children can select, according to their interests and capacities.

> *Major Concept #3:*
> Weight is a measure of the force of gravitation on an object.
> *Supporting Concept:*
> Scales measure the earth's pull of gravity.

Behavioral Objective:

The pupil will demonstrate, in a way of his choice, his knowledge of weight measure by accurately answering 2 out of 3 questions on quiz #1 and 3 out of 5 questions on quiz #2.

Group Learning Experiences:

1.   Select an applicable picture book or film to use and discuss. See bibliography.

2.   Have pupils take different objects in their hands and guess their weights. Then weigh them to see how close they came to guessing it. Try different materials so they get an idea of their different weights.

3.   Use a picture of a large super-market to start pupils thinking of all the things that are sold by the pound. Make a list on the chalkboard. Discuss why these items are sold by weight.

4.   Weigh pupils, see how many weigh the same and, therefore, are being pulled by the earth's gravity the same. See how many have different weights and, therefore, are being pulled by the earth's gravity differently.

5.   Get a small spring scale with a hook, a cardboard box about four inches square and a string or cord. Attach the cord to the box so that it can be hung on the scale. Select several articles to be weighed. Choose objects which are about the same size but have different weights. Select some large but light things and some small but heavy things such as a large pumice stone and a small piece of lead.

On the chalkboard write the headings LIGHT and HEAVY. Let someone keep the record. Ask pupils to point out the objects they believe to be light and the ones they believe to be heavy. Put the objects, one at a time, in the box attached to the scale. Observe that the spring on the scale stretches as an object is placed in the box. Explain that when we weigh something, we are actually measuring the force with which something is being attracted to the center of the earth.[12]

In a unit on "Matter and Change" prepared by Mildred A. Thornton,[13] a set of cards is prepared for each science concept to be learned. Each set consists of a key card containing the concept statement, several cards containing supporting concepts, and others on which experiments, research activities, and creative activities are described. Kits of materials are provided for each experiment, research activity, and creative activity, and the students assume the responsibility for independently acquiring an understanding of the concepts by conducting the prescribed experiments and other activities. Figure Two shows the statements that are found on Cards 1 through 5 for Concept 1: "A new material is formed when a chemical reaction takes place."

CARD STATEMENTS SHOWING CONCEPTS AND DIFFERENTIATED LEARNING ACTIVITIES[14]

Card 1   1–1
Concept 1: A new material is formed when a chemical reaction takes place.

Card 2   1–1
Supporting Concept: Some materials change in shape or form but do not change into a new material.

Card 3   1–1
Experiment 1
Experiment with the three states of matter.
     a.   Place several ice cubes in a beaker or pan and let them melt.
     b.   Place the pan of melted ice on a hot plate and heat until a vapor is given off.
     c.   Show that the condensate can be collected from the vapor by holding a glass over the boiling water. Be careful not to burn yourself. Steam is dangerous and burns badly.
Answer the following questions:
     1.   What is an ice cube?
     2.   Is the water in an ice cube different than the water that is left after the ice cube has melted?
     3.   What happens when steam is cooled?
     4.   Through all these changes, has a new material been formed?

Card 4   1–1
Experiment 2
Place a block of wax in a pan and heat it. Observe as the wax becomes liquid. Pour the liquid wax into a small paper cup, or some other suitable container. Observe as the wax cools and becomes a solid again.
Does the wax change form again as it cools? Is this physical or chemical change? If you are not certain, perhaps this is a good time to do some more research.

Card 5   1–1
Research #1
List some physical changes. Explain what happens when a physical change takes place.

FIGURE TWO

Each student is required to keep record of his progress through the science unit on what is called a retrieval form. Figure Three shows the retrieval form that is used for the science unit on matter and change.

SCIENCE UNIT RECORD OF PROGRESS

Name ————————————————————

Individualized Science Unit

Matter and Change

Retrieval
E—Experiments
and Projects
R—Research
C—Creative Ideas,
Reports
T—Evaluation

Card	Code	Date Begun	Date Completed
3	E		
4	E		
5	R		
6	C		
8	R		
9	C		
10	E		
11	E		
12	E		
13	E		
14	C		
14–A	T		
17	R		
18	E		
20	R		
21	E		
22	E		
24	R		
25	E		
26	C		
28	R		
29	E		
30	E		
31	E		
32	E		
32–A	T		
35	R		
36	E		
37	E		
38	R		
38–A	T		

FIGURE THREE

The pupil reports on each experiment he has conducted (independently or with a partner) on a form illustrated in Figure Four. He describes the procedure used, the observations made, the conclusion he has reached, and the concept with which he has been dealing.

PUPIL REPORT (SCIENCE PROJECT)

Name _____   Date _____

Card Number _____   Concept Number _____

Procedure
This is what I/we did:

Observation
This is what I/we saw:

Conclusion:
This is what I/we now believe:

Review the concept.

Comment:

FIGURE FOUR

At the end of each unit of study, the pupil must demonstrate his understanding of the related concept by completing an evaluation project. The criterion used by the teacher in evaluating the student's performance is the behavioral objective for the unit. In the case of Concept 1—A new material is formed when a chemical reaction takes place—the criterion is:

The student will demonstrate his knowledge of a chemical reaction by correctly experimenting with a cube of sugar and properly evaluating the experiment by using Evaluation Sheet No. 1.[15]

Mathematics was used earlier to illustrate the first approach to individualization, in which pacing was the major instructional variable. A new variation in the individualization of mathematics in the continuous progress school provides an excellent illustration of Approach II, with its several instructional variables. This variation was developed by Raymond D. Stensrud and reported in "A Teacher's Guide to Continuous Progress in Mathematics Instruction."[16] By using this program, arithmetic can be nongraded in any classroom of the elementary school by allowing children to work at their own levels of conceptualization in each of the major concepts and processes of arithmetic from simple addition to the multiplication of fractions. The most common teaching strategy employed by teachers using this program consists of involving the entire class in the study of a given concept or arithmetic process. Individual variability is accommodated by permitting and guiding students to select learning activities, "investigations," and "side trips" that are compatible with their individual interests and abilities. The three problems that follow illustrate the wide range of abilities that are accommodated by "side trips" into the study of addition:

1. How many different ways can you add 78
   $+ 67$?

A	B	C	D
		10	1
78	70 + 8	70 + 8	78
67	60 + 7	60 + 7	67
15	130 + 15	+ 5	5
130			

2. *Pop the Balloons*

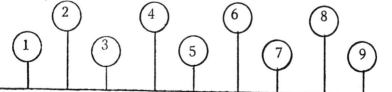

   Take three shots and score fifteen points.
   How many ways are possible?
   $3 + 5 + 7 = 15$
   $9 + 5 + 1 = 15$

3. Rearrange these fifteen numerals so that you have five columns with three numerals in each column and the same sum for each column.

1	2	3	4	5		6	4	1	3	2
10	9	8	7	6		8	5	11	7	9
11	12	13	14	15		10	15	12	14	13
22	23	24	25	26		24	24	24	24	24

(There is another way.)

Instructional Objectives and Related Curriculum Elements

Instructional objectives are fundamental to any educational enterprise, but the nature of the objective employed may vary greatly from one program to another. Educational objectives of the traditional graded school, for example, are typically general and long-range in nature. The relative usefulness of this type of instructional objective for defining the appropriate learning activities, lesson materials, and evaluative instruments have long been recognized. In a continuous progress school, where provisions are made for independent study and progress, objectives must be stated in terms that specifically describe the terminal behavior of the pupil who has achieved them. Once these behavioral objectives are specified, the curriculum developer can identify the concepts, understandings, proficiencies, and skills that are prerequisite to the behavior; the teacher can plan the most appropriate learning activities; and the evaluator can construct the most effective testing instrument.

Because of the common criticism of behavioral objectives, a word of explanation seems appropriate at this point. The careful specification of terminal behaviors and related concepts and skills does not mean that they represent the only learning opportunities of children. Actually, they define only the central core of the curriculum considered fundamental to all American education. In the process of their achievement, pupils acquire a wealth of facts, information, attitudes, and study skills. Furthermore, the doors are always open to research and exploration in fields introduced by core learnings.

Some people are also skeptical of structure within the curriculum, and for this reason it might be well to explain that the sequencing of objectives and related curriculum elements is merely an effort to introduce a framework to which pupils and teachers can relate when measuring and monitoring progress. The sequence is neither rigid nor universally applied. Teachers still have the option of introducing other learnings to individuals and groups, and pupils will still learn many things in addition to those specified. The personalized dimension of the curriculum provides adequately for this.

The nature of a sequenced curriculum of behavioral objectives is illustrated by the following segment of a reading program taken from "A Teacher's Guide to Continuous Progress in Reading Instruction."[17]

Sequenced Behavioral Objectives in Word Attack Skills

1. The child hears and identifies like and unlike beginning sounds.
2. The child identifies oral words with rhyming sounds.
3. The child hears and identifies ending sounds.
4. The child identifies the sound and names the beginning letter symbol in words beginning with single consonants.
5. The child identifies the sound and names the letter symbol in words ending with consonants.
6. The child identifies the sound and names the letter symbols in words containing consonant digraphs.

   ch   ck   gh   ng   sh   th   wh
7. The child identifies the sounds and names the letter symbols in words containing medial consonants.
8. The child identifies the sounds and names the letter symbols in words beginning with consonant blends.

   bl   br   cl   cr   dr   fl   fr   gr   pl   sl   sn   st   tr
9. The child identifies the sounds and names the letters of double consonants. Final and medial.
10. The child names the variant consonants and identifies their sounds in a word. Hard and soft c and g, gh, ph.
11. The child identifies silent consonants.

    gh   kn   wr
12. The child identifies the sound and names the letter symbol for the short vowels.
13. The child identifies the sounds and names the letter symbol for the long vowels.
14. The child identifies the sounds and names the letter symbol for the vowel digraphs.

    ai   ay   ea   ea   in   head   ee   oa   oo   oo   ui

This sequence of objectives does not dictate the exact ordering of instruction and progress for each pupil, but rather provides a useful organization through which the individual instruction and progress of learners can be facilitated. It furnishes a framework for determining the status of pupil achievement, and for planning and monitoring his future learning. Monitoring devices employed in such a program are illustrated in Figure Five, which shows one of the individual record forms used in the reading program.

Managing Pupil Performance Information

One of the major problems facing teachers who attempt to individualize instruction is finding time to keep records of their pupils' progress. These tasks, sometimes classified as student performance information management, include scoring tests, recording test results, analyzing evaluative instruments, retrieving and updating records, and storing and retrieving data on these records. Solving these problems was one of the principal objectives of the ESEA Title III Project.

One of the first, and still widely used, recording and retrieval devices is illustrated in Figure Six.[18] In its complete form, this chart lists the

INDIVIDUAL RECORD OF ACHIEVEMENT—READING

	1	Like and Unlike beginning Sounds						
	2	Rhyming Sounds						
	3	Ending Sounds						
	4	Beginning Consonants—Sound & Names						
	5	Ending Consonants—Sound & Names						
	6	Consonant Digraphs						
	7	Medial Consonants						
	8	Consonant Blends						
	9	Double Consonants						
	10	Variant Consonants						
	11	Silent Consonants						
	12	Short Vowels						
	13	Long Vowels						
	14	Vowel Digraphs						
	15	Diphthongs						
	16	Variant Vowels						
	17	Rules Governing Vowels						
	18	Phonograms						
	19	Rhyming Words						

Nongraded Reading Skills—Word Attack Skills

20	Rhyming Endings							
21	Plural and Possessives							
22	Compound Words							
23	Root Words							
24	Endings							
25	Contractions							
26	Prefixes and Suffixes							
27	Abbreviations							
28	Syllabication							
29	Alphabetical Order							
30	Dictionary							
1	Names specific Referents							
2	Geometric Shapes							
3	Identifies Own Name							
4	Uses Context Clues							
5	Basic Vocabulary Words							
6	Multiple Meanings							
7	Antonyms							
8	Synonyms							
9	Homonyms							

(Left margin labels: Vocabulary Skills — "Vocabulary" spanning items 20–30, "Skills" spanning items 1–9)

FIGURE FIVE

major reading skills along the top, and the names of all the pupils in the class down the left side. A mark of some type opposite the pupil's name indicates that he has achieved a particular skill or concept. The classroom teacher can see at a glance which pupils have common needs and can therefore be grouped for instruction in a particular concept and/or skill. In Figure Six, Fred, Louise, Bob, Mary, and Susan have not grasped the concept of diphthongs. If they have the prerequisite understandings, these five children could be grouped together for instruction in this concept.

The principal criticism of this device is that it requires a great deal of time to maintain, it must be updated constantly, and perhaps modified when a teacher discovers she has been too generous in crediting a student with understanding. Added to the time required for individualizing instruction and for administering and checking inventory and diagnostic tests, manual recording and retrieval devices such as this can become too burdensome for some teachers.

CLASS RECORD AND RETRIEVAL FORM—READING

	I. WORD ATTACK SKILLS																II. COMPREHENSION			
	Like-Unlike Begin. Sounds	Rhyming Sounds	Ending Sounds	Consonant Digraphs	Medial Consonants	Consonant Blends	Double Consonants	Variant Consonants	Silent Consonants	Short Vowels	Long Vowels	Vowel Digraphs	Diphthongs	Variant Vowels	Vowel Rules	Etc.	Noting Detail	Main Idea	Logical Sequence	Etc.
Fred	X																X			
Louise	X				X		X										X			
John	X				X		X				X						X	X	X	
Jeannie					X		X		X		X						X	X	X	
Helen					X		X		X		X						X	X	X	
Bob	X						X		X								X	X	X	
Mary	X				X				X								X	X		
Susan	X				X				X									X		

FIGURE SIX

The most promising solution to the problem of keeping records is to use a computer to perform many of the time-consuming tasks associated with "managing pupil performance information." A computer program was designed to the specifications of teachers who were individualizing instruction in the CPE Exemplary Centers. Robert Steffenson,[19] the developer, began by modeling the technique that is called individualized, personalized, or diagnostic instruction. Two models were produced —the Initial Process Flow Model (Figure Seven) and the Continuous Process Flow Model (Figure Eight).

Simply stated, these models depict the process of individualization as one that consists of the following steps: During the initial phase of the process the teacher:

1. Measures pupil readiness in a given area of the curriculum.

2. Interprets the results obtained from each child's response to the readiness instrument.

3. Develops a record (performance matrix) that provides the teacher with an overview of the readiness of class members for instruction in a specific area of the curriculum.

INITIAL PROCESS FLOW MODEL

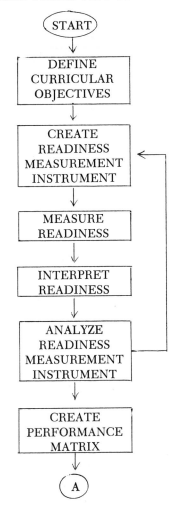

FIGURE SEVEN

4. Analyzes the test used in terms of student responses for the purpose of improving the validity and reliability of test items.

During the continuous phase of the process, the teacher:

1. Distributes or organizes students into common-need groups of various sizes for the purpose of instruction.

2. Defines the performance objectives for each group.

CONTINUOUS PROCESS FLOW MODEL

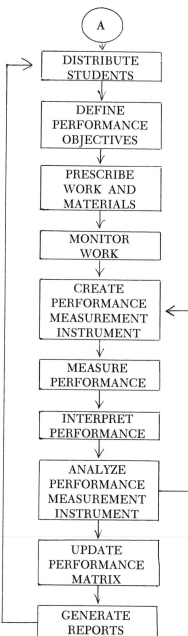

FIGURE EIGHT

3. Prescribes or assigns learning activities (with appropriate materials) to each child and group.

4. Monitors (supervises the students at work).

5. Tests (after procuring or developing an instrument) to determine growth and achievement as a result of instruction.

6. Interprets the results obtained for each student.

7. Analyzes the instrument used in terms of student responses and makes those revisions deemed essential for its improvement.

8. Updates or revises the record (performance matrix) in keeping with the latest measurement of achievement and readiness for further instruction.

9. Generates any reports which are necessary.

10. Regroups children for further instruction on the basis of the updated matrix.

The next undertaking was to abstract the basic steps or tasks that could be handled by the computer. These tasks can be classified as those relating to the management of student achievement or performance information:

1. Scoring tests

2. Analyzing tests (e.g., analyzing items as one aid to establishing the effectiveness of specific test items)

3. Loading the performance matrix

4. Updating the performance matrix

5. Identifying students with common needs and like readiness

6. Ready and rapid retrieval of achievement information about the group or any child.

With these tasks in mind the researcher then developed a program that would perform several of them for the teacher. The process of developing this computer program entailed the following steps:

1. Translating the abstracted teaching functions into a *procedural model*

2. Designing a *computer system* that simulates the procedural model

3. Designing a multi-routine *computer program* that performed the several functions of the procedural model, and that met the specifications of the computer system.

The Procedural Model in Figure Nine shows the functions that the

PROCEDURAL MODEL

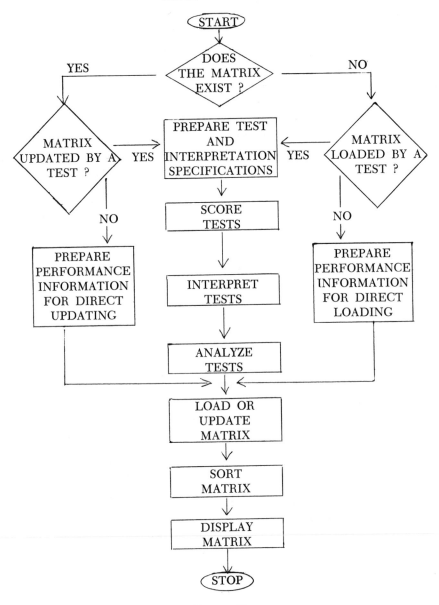

FIGURE NINE

computer performs. The student performance matrix or record that this
model prepares is represented in Figure Ten. The skills and concepts
related to a curriculum segment or an instructional objective are listed

across the top and the names of class members appear down the left side. For convenience in charting, each skill and concept is represented by a number. This matrix can be loaded and updated in two ways: directly, by a teacher or a clerk who has information about student achievement of each concept and skill; or by a test that can be scored, interpreted, and analyzed. The results are then loaded onto the matrix, sorted, and displayed on a cathode-ray tube by the computer.

Mastery of a concept or skill is represented on the matrix by a "1", non-mastery by a "0." Grouping of pupils on the basis of common needs is facilitated by calling on the computer to sort the matrix according to the sum of mastered concepts and skills. The teacher can tell at a glance which pupils should benefit from group instruction in a specific concept or skill; they will show a "0" in this concept, but a "1" in the prerequisite concepts. For example, Karen, David, Brian, Fred, Carla, and Harry, would appear to be ready for small-group instruction in concept #5.

PERFORMANCE MATRIX

Curriculum
Segment   *Skills and Concepts*

Math	1	2	3	4	5	6	7	8	9	10	11	12	13	14	15	16	17	18	19	20	Sum
Joe	1	1	1	1	1	1	1	1	1	1	1	1	1	0	1	0	0	0	0	0	14
Mary	1	1	1	1	1	1	1	1	1	1	1	1	1	1	0	0	0	0	0	0	14
Frank	1	1	1	1	1	1	1	1	1	1	1	1	1	0	0	0	0	0	0	0	13
Ellen	1	1	1	1	1	1	1	1	1	1	1	1	1	0	0	0	0	0	0	0	13
Mike	1	1	1	1	1	1	1	1	1	1	1	0	1	0	0	0	0	0	0	0	12
Henry	1	1	1	1	1	1	1	1	1	1	1	0	1	0	0	0	0	0	0	0	12
Robert	1	1	1	1	1	1	1	1	1	1	1	0	0	0	0	0	0	0	0	0	11
Jim	1	1	1	1	1	1	1	1	1	1	0	0	1	0	0	0	0	0	0	0	11
Kathy	1	1	1	1	1	1	1	0	1	0	1	0	0	0	0	0	0	0	0	0	9
Arlene	1	1	1	1	1	1	1	0	1	1	0	0	0	0	0	0	0	0	0	0	9
Alan	1	1	1	1	1	1	1	0	1	1	0	0	0	0	0	0	0	0	0	0	9
Kay	1	1	1	1	1	1	1	0	1	0	0	0	0	0	0	0	0	0	0	0	8
Richard	1	1	1	1	1	1	1	1	0	0	0	0	0	0	0	0	0	0	0	0	8
Karen	1	1	1	1	0	1	1	1	0	0	0	0	0	0	0	0	0	0	0	0	7
David	1	1	1	1	0	1	0	0	0	0	0	0	0	0	0	0	0	0	0	0	5
Brian	1	1	1	1	0	1	0	0	0	0	0	0	0	0	0	0	0	0	0	0	5
Fred	1	1	1	1	0	1	0	0	0	0	0	0	0	0	0	0	0	0	0	0	5
Carla	1	1	1	1	0	0	0	0	0	0	0	0	0	0	0	0	0	0	0	0	4
Harry	1	1	1	1	0	0	0	0	0	0	0	0	0	0	0	0	0	0	0	0	4
John	1	1	1	0	0	1	0	0	0	0	0	0	0	0	0	0	0	0	0	0	4
Colleen	1	1	1	0	0	0	0	0	0	0	0	0	0	0	0	0	0	0	0	0	3

FIGURE TEN

Instruction in concept #8 would seem appropriate for Kathy, Arlene, Alan, and Kay. Mike, Henry, and Robert apparently need help with skill #12.

There is a certain amount of risk involved in describing management of pupil performance information by computer. The flow charts and terminology might make it appear more difficult than the conventional record system, but this is not the case. The loading, updating, and retrieval processes are simple and automatic. Loading and up-dating by the teacher, teacher-aid, or clerk requires little more than the ability to type numbers on a teletype machine. Retrieval is accomplished by the simple act of pushing keys to signal the computer, and calling for specific records. No more effort is required to instruct the computer to check pupil performance on a test and then up-date the records; the teacher, of course, must first define the performance objectives for a unit or concept and construct an appropriate test—tasks that he performs whether or not he uses computers.

Organization for Continuous Pupil Progress

The conceptual paradigm of the continuous progress school presented earlier in this chapter describes the vertical and horizontal dimensions of the organization. The vertical dimension provides for the upward movement of students from school entrance to graduation. Since the mid-19th century, American schools have typically been graded in this dimension. The horizontal dimension provides for the assignment of students and staff members to groups or classes, and brings pupils and teachers together to facilitate the progress of learners up through the vertical dimension. In this phase of the organization, American schools have been characterized by variety. Pupils have been grouped heterogeneously and homogeneously. In some schools they have been platooned in departmentalized curricula, while in others they have been assigned to self-contained classrooms in which the curriculum has been highly correlated. Since 1957, a new option—team organization—has been available.

The organizational model for the continuous progress school specifies a nongrading of the vertical dimension. The nongraded organizations in the Title III schools reported in this chapter represent two major variations of nongrading: the nongraded-curriculum model; and the school-function model. The horizontal dimension was not specified, though the importance of alternate teacher-pupil affiliations or placements was stressed. This requirement, together with that of providing opportunities within each class setting for pupils to work at different levels in each area of the curriculum, has tended to promote cooperative teaching in one form or another. The majority of the Exemplary Centers for Continuous Progress Education feature one variation or another of this horizontal organizational structure.

At first glance one might have difficulty in distinguishing between a graded school and one designed after the *nongraded-curriculum model* (Figure Eleven). In some instances, the latter will consist of self-con-

NONGRADED CURRICULUM MODEL OF NONGRADED VERTICAL ORGANIZATION

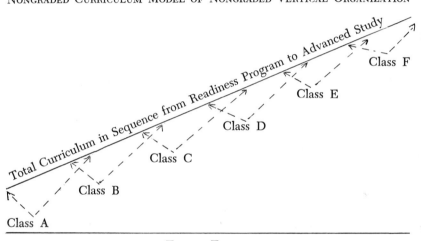

FIGURE ELEVEN

tained classes, and each class will be comprised of children of approximately the same age. In other instances this model of vertical organization will be used in conjunction with some form of cooperative teaching. Closer examination, however, will reveal that an unusually wide segment of the curriculum is represented in the instructional program of each class; and pupil placement and achievement will vary widely over this curriculum segment. The curriculum, in other words, will be nongraded, and instruction will be highly individualized. Thus in this nongraded school, the curriculum is employed as the basic organizational element. In contrast with the graded school, where the curriculum is organized into rigid graded packages, this school opens the entire curriculum to all teachers and pupils, and children are placed according to their achievement in each area of the curriculum. A particular pupil, for example, might be working at an advanced level of the elementary arithmetic program, but progressing very slowly at the lower end of the spelling program; a classmate of the same age might be in the reverse situation—hence the label: nongraded curriculum model.

As in all nongraded schools, there is no promotion or nonpromotion in the usual sense of these terms. Pupils simply advance through the curriculum at their own best paces. At the end of the school year, achievement levels in each subject field are recorded, and in the fall the pupils resume their studies where they left off. They continue their upward, continuous progress, uninterrupted by artificial barriers in the organization or the curriculum.

The nongraded curriculum model has several notable advantages: (1) To the untrained observer, it looks like the graded school and hence it is not likely to disturb or confuse the public. (2) Its capacity to provide for individual differences is limited only by the teacher's ability to individualize instruction and to cope with wide ranges of achievement among his pupils. (3) It is equally compatible with team organization and the self-contained classroom. (4) It makes no artificial attempt to organize children into classes on the basis of their homogeneity. Children can be assigned to classrooms at random or according to some plan, and then grouped within each classroom in ways that facilitate the individualization of instruction.

Thus, all individual differences are accommodated within the classroom by means of the nongraded curriculum and individualized teaching procedures and materials. The demands that such a system make on a teacher are often great, sometimes too great for teachers who lack the requisite training and organizational abilities. Some educators think that these heavy demands can be reduced through team effort, hence the trend in some schools toward cooperative teaching of the nongraded curriculum model.

The *School-functions model* receives its name from the fact that the organizational element in its vertical dimension is the school function. In other words, upward pupil progress is made through a curriculum that is organized vertically around the school's major functions. Each function has some vertical or sequential relationship to the others, one being defined as the first major function of the school, another as the second, still another as the third, and so on. Goodlad reports on one nongraded elementary school that has three functions in its vertical structure—Function I: The development of a sturdy, wholesome self-concept. Function II: The progressive development of the fundamental skills of self-directed learning. Function III: The development of the ability to understand and use man's approaches to understanding social and natural phenomena, and the development of initiative and independence in learning.[20]

An attempt to diagram this variation of the nongraded school appears in Figure Twelve. Note that some classes or clusters of pupils are self-

SCHOOL-FUNCTIONS MODEL OF NONGRADED VERTICAL ORGANIZATION

Vertically Structured Curriculum Organized According to Designated Functions of the School

FIGURE TWELVE

contained, while others are taught by teams. This provision is designed to accommodate the preferences of individual children and teachers for either large or small groups. The instructional program in each of these classes cuts across the functional lines of the organization. The teachers are free to serve more than one function, especially as the achievement and advancement of children in the curriculum calls for the introduction of the school's next function.

Unlike the nongraded-curriculum model, in which children are often assigned to classes on the basis of age, this model pays relatively little attention to age. Children may differ by as much as three years in age in the classrooms of the school-functions model; class assignments are made by the professional staff after carefully considering peer compatibility, teacher-pupil compatibility, and appropriateness of the curriculum and teaching style.

The school-functions model is the most daring, and at the same time, the most promising of all nongraded models (a third model, the curriculum-levels model, has not been discussed here). It has all except one of the advantages ascribed to the other models, and this aspect may represent its major disadvantage, at least in communities where changes in the schools are vigorously resisted. It looks nothing like the graded school; it is obviously different in its organization and in the way it assigns pupils to classes. Conservative communities that are not properly prepared for such a radical change might conceivably look with suspicion on a school designed after this model. Progressive communities, properly educated in advance, should find the answer to many public school ills in a school-functions model of the nongraded school. It is because of the apparent advantages of the school-functions variation of the nongraded school that several "exemplary centers" have selected this model as an ultimate organizational objective. Time will be required, of course, but there is evidence of careful planning and thoughtful preparation.

Summary

Across the nation a new type of school is being developed, as educators, boards of education, and other supporters of educational reform unite in their efforts to establish schools that will lift every learner from his beginning point and carry him to the point of self-realization. This is certainly the case in Utah's exemplary centers for continuous progress education. Founded on the theory of continuous pupil progress, these schools are developing curricula and instructional practices that meet learners where they are and help them realize their fullest potentialities. They are gradually and systematically abandoning the traditional, century-old graded organization in preference to one model or another of the more accommodating nongraded organizations. In some schools teachers are working in teams; in others they prefer a modified self-contained classroom organization. In all of these schools, teachers are using instructional resources, recording and retrieval systems, and reporting strategies consistent with the philosophy of equal educational opportunity, and the magnification of the individual.

Notes

1. Paul R. Mort, *The Individual Pupil* (New York: American Book Company, 1928).

2. John W. Gardner, "National Goals in Education," *Goals for America* (The Report of the President's Commission on National Goals, Prentice-Hall, Inc., 1960), p. 61.

3. Willard S. Elsbree, *Pupil Progress in the Elementary School*, Practical Suggestions for Teaching #5, ed. by Hollis L. Caswell (New York: Bureau of Publications, Teachers College, Columbia University, 1943), pp. 2–30.

4. National Society for the Study of Education, *Individualizing Instruction* (Chicago: University of Chicago Press, 1962), p. 164.

5. Robert M. Gagne, *Learning and Individual Differences* (Columbus, Ohio: Charles E. Merrill Publishing Co., 1967), Chap. 2.

6. Jerome S. Bruner, *The Process of Education* (Cambridge: Harvard University Press, 1962).

7. Committee on Economic Development, *Innovation in Education: New Directions for the American School*, A Statement on National Policy by the Research and Policy Committee of the Committee for Economic Development, July 1968.

8. Edwin A. Read, Ruel A. Allred, and Louise O. Baird, "Continuous Progress in Spelling," unpublished, 1968.

9. Fred T. Wilhelms, "The Curriculum and Individual Differences," *Individualizing Instruction*, ed. by Nelson B. Henry (Chicago: University of Chicago Press, 1962), p. 68.

10. Maureen Jones, "Gravity: An Individualized Unit of Work in Science," Continuous Progress Education Title III Project, 1969, p. 4, mimeographed.

11. Ibid.

12. Ibid., p. 16.

13. Mildred Thornton, "Matter and Change: An Individualized Unit of Work in Science," Continuous Progress Education Title III Project, 1969, mimeographed.

14. Ibid., pp. 3–4.

15. Ibid., p. 1.

16. Raymond B. Stensrud, "A Teacher's Guide to Continuous Progress in Mathematics Instruction," Continuous Progress Education Title III Project, 1969.

17. Carma J. Hales, Dorothy O. Wardrop, and James R. Young, "A Teacher's Guide to Continuous Progress in Reading Instruction," Continuous Progress Education Title III Project, 1967, p. 10.

18. Continuous Progress Education, "A Teacher's Guide to Retrieval and Reporting Practices," Continuous Progress Education Title III Project, 1969, p. 12.

19. Robert Steffenson, "A Computer Program for Management of Student Performance Information" (Diss., University of Utah, 1969).

20. John I. Goodlad, "Meeting Children Where They Are," *Saturday Review* (March 20, 1965), p. 72.

CHAPTER 12

The Development Research Center
by
WARREN G. SMITH

Mr. Smith has been a teacher, coordinator, supervisor, and director in the educational field for twenty-two years. He was the coordinator of Technical Science when Nova opened in 1963, has been a supervisor, and is presently the Director of the Nova Schools. Because of his program experience, he has done extensive consulting, especially in the areas of individualized education and technical science.

NOVA BLANCHE FORMAN and Dwight D. Eisenhower Elementary Schools, together with Nova High School, make up the Developmental Research Center of the Broward County, Florida, School District. In these schools some 4,000 students progress through a sequence of learning experiences in a systematic manner at a pace best suited for each individual.

Many different patterns of scheduling, teaming, and grouping have been employed in an attempt to provide students with the best possible climate for learning. The facilities provided by the district are modern and flexible. The search for proper materials and tools has been thorough. A talented and dedicated staff and a fine student body have cooperated to make Nova the great school it is today, seven years after its inception.

At Nova each student is recognized as an individual who has the right and the ability to make decisions—decisions that affect his membership in the student body, his learning, his appearance, his participation in school activities, and his role in the world he is preparing to enter. His right to make these decisions was given to him when he was born in the United States or became a naturalized citizen.

The State of Florida is organized into county school districts, of which Broward County is the third largest in school population. It lies just north of Miami and south of Palm Beach. The largest cities are Fort Lauderdale, Hollywood, and Pompano Beach. About 600,000 people live in the county, of which about 110,000 attend the public schools.

The three Nova Schools make up the Developmental Research Complex of the district. Enrollment is voluntary from anywhere in the district. Students are selected from the list of applicants in a systematic manner that will insure a cross-sectional distribution. A perfect curve of student characteristics is not possible or desired; a curve similar to the student population of the district is the goal. At present there are 3,200 secondary students in a facility for grades 7–12, and 1,400 elementary students in the two lower schools.

The physical plant is of the campus type at Nova High School. The two elementary schools are in separate buildings. Every possible configuration of classroom space is represented—from the single classroom to the completely open Dwight D. Eisenhower School, which has no partitions in an instructional area designed for 720 students. Some uniquely designed areas are the teaching auditoriums for 200 students; the test center, in which 80 students from the various disciplines may be served simultaneously; a science laboratory, in which 100 high school students may perform experiments in biology, chemistry, physics, or earth science; four separate learning resource centers; an outdoor cafeteria; and classrooms that may be opened' to include up to six rooms. Because Nova requires each student to take some "salable skill" courses nearly every year, there are also extensive technical and business laboratories.

Every student is required to pay fees for expendable supplies and for school bus transportation. Some students travel a great distance, creating problems for participation in extra-curricular and social activities, and lengthening the school day.

Yearly course requirements and the resulting Nova graduation requirements are well above normal. All the standard skill development programs of the elementary school are included in the student's day, as well as many unique additions that we deem necessary for the growth of every child. In addition, he is constantly being faced with the necessity of making decisions about his education, a responsibility usually assigned to the teacher. All secondary students are enrolled in six subjects, a situation that taxes both the student's and the teacher's stamina. The secondary student is also confronted with many (more specific) decision points, a condition much sought by the adolescent but, for many, a frustration when the moment of truth arrives.

In light of the conditions and demands made on both students and parents at Nova, why is there such a demand for enrollment in the schools? What are the advantages that overshadow the problems of attending such a school?

At the expense of seeming repetitious, I can only state that at the Nova Schools each student is respected as an individual and is given many opportunities to express his preferences. Even first-year students are not tied to one group or one teacher, but move from center to center as the need arises. As would be expected, the amount and direction of their choices are carefully planned and monitored.

As the Nova student progresses through the continuum of concepts, he is given more and more opportunity to make choices. He can choose the learning media with which he feels the most comfortable. He can choose the learning activities that most nearly meet his personal interests and that will allow him to perform as expected when his progress is evaluated. He can even determine the time and, in some cases, the mode of such assessment.

Before the reader labels our program as "progressive education" or "permissive," let me state that: (1) each choice by a student must fit into an overall system of learning, which was very carefully planned so that the student can meet the objectives; and (2) the Nova student knows the intent of the system and is constantly helped in his decisions to insure progress towards his goals.

The system, which permits a wide latitude of choice but insures the meeting of performance objectives, was devised by a group of educators representing the Nova Schools, Nova University, and Florida State University. After much discussion of the learning habits of children as found in research reports, a model was designed that met the requirements. It included a rationale, a set of behavioral objectives, a set of self-assessment devices, a set of learning activities, and a final evaluation. This model was called the Learning Activities Package, or LAP, an acronym that suggests the original seat of individual learning.

Because the LAP is a system, a learner may enter, cycle, and recycle according to his needs. Each LAP is designed around a model flow chart or P.E.R.T., as shown in Figure One.

The first section of the LAP that the student sees is a simple orienta-

246

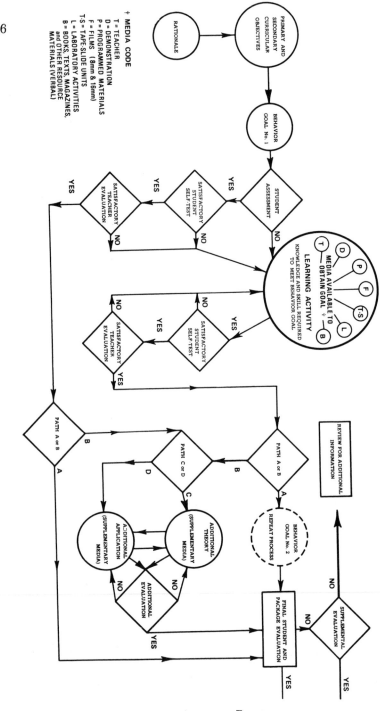

LEARNING ACTIVITY PACKAGE

FIGURE ONE

tion statement called a *rationale*. In it the relevancy of the LAP is explained in relation to a planned sequence of learning experiences. Special instructions and suggestions that will aid and, hopefully, motivate the individual, make up the balance of the rationale.

The objectives of the LAP, stated in behavioral terms, usually come second—the theory being that the student must have clearly stated assignments available in order to make certain self-assessment and procedural decisions. These objectives must be written in such a manner that the student can and will read them. Stereotyped formats, which may appeal to educators, tend to "turn off" the young learner and be ignored.

Not all the objectives need be reached by each individual. In order to meet the needs of a heterogeneous group of learners, objectives on several levels of the taxonomies are included in each LAP. After the student has read the objectives, he may have a conference with his teacher to determine his progress through the LAP. This usually occurs when a pupil feels that he cannot perform as expected and therefore must follow the sequence of events provided.

When there is doubt in the scholar's mind about his ability to prove his mastery of some of the objectives, he proceeds to the self-assessment phase of the LAP. This section contains sample questions or tasks that are related to and coded for each objective. Acceptable responses or performances are included so the learner can not only determine the correctness of his answers but also identify the objective to be re-studied if he has given an incorrect response.

Because of the varied interests and abilities of our charges, a number of learning experiences are included in the LAP in the *Activities* section. There is also a provision for student initiated *activities*. At this point a student-teacher conference is necessary to determine the activities in which the pupil will participate. Decisions are also necessary about time limits, materials, and media to be employed. If properly conducted, this meeting becomes a diagnostic-prescription conference.

Our learner now proceeds through the *activities* as planned with his teacher. In several subject areas he is in a laboratory, where the teacher, the materials, the audio and visual media, the reference books, and the equipment and supplies are all available when needed. Although other students in the lab are working on different LAPs, there are usually enough classmates working on identical material to provide the necessary group interactions. However, he is not confined to the lab. If some other resource areas of the campus can provide needed help, he is free to take advantage of them. His movements are monitored only for administrative purposes.

Another pupil-teacher conference is held when the student feels he is ready to be evaluated. Pre- and post-tests, as well as self-evaluation devices, are available in the LAP to help him decide. At this conference the mode of assessment is determined. As might be expected, this assessment is usually in the form of written objective tests, but some performance and oral testing is done when appropriate.

A unique part of the Nova assessment program is that the student leaves the learning labs and goes to the testing center to be evaluated. He presents a card indicating the specific device to be administered. The tests are issued, monitored, and corrected by the center personnel. If the results meet the performance criteria, the next or succeeding LAP is given to the student and the learning process continues. On request, content area teachers interpret test results in a conference with the student. Errors are related to specific objectives and a prescription for further study is developed.

Progress is reported to the parents in stanine terms at regular intervals. Instead of a single letter grade for each course, student progress is stated for test results, class participation, oral contribution, class assignment, lab work, and quantity. Each category is weighted and a final number grade is determined by computer. Depth study grades are added to this final grade.

Several innovative schools in the country are developing programs and curricula in order to reach a predetermined goal or prototype. At some time they will reach their goal and become operational. Nova is a developmental center and, therefore, has no single fixed image to reach. Rather, the Nova Schools continually set new long-range goals and constantly strive to reach them. A realistic look at the problems confronting us today can be used to predict the type of education necessary for the student of tomorrow.

A Trilogy

The startling increase in knowledge first brought to the public's attention by Sputnik has created a serious problem for today's educator.

There is no way we can evade the issue—we must provide an ever-increasing number of learning experiences for our youth and we must do it without a longer school day—or a longer school year. One or more of these alternatives might prove to be feasible, but with a taxpayers' revolt as a distinct possibility, we must review other solutions.

The Nova Schools have been experimenting with several systems that make learning more relevant, more interesting, and more efficient. The fact that each individual is encouraged to move through sequences of experiences at his best rate, and therefore, may reach advanced concepts at an earlier age than is traditional, partially resolves the problem. The time and energy of about two hundred teachers are bent on perfecting these systems. Present goals of individualized education will be achieved in the near future.

Because the Nova Schools are research oriented, the staff accepted the problem and are searching for a possible solution. One big assumption has been accepted—if the student's school time cannot be increased then economies must be made in the use of that time.

Flexible scheduling; use of technology, facilities, differentiated staffing, and team teaching; and multi-media, multi-mode, and independent study are all being implemented and evaluated in various degrees in the innovative schools in the United States. Each one has merit. Each one improves efficiency in education when it is employed by experienced people. However, the big problem will not be solved by these variations alone.

Another obvious answer is to remove those experiences that are no longer considered essential. This process is continuous but difficult because each traditional bit of content has many supporters. Such deletion is a threat to those whose entire careers embrace these obsolete areas. Even though it is unpopular, this step is essential.

Repetition of learning experiences must be eliminated. Re-learning of concepts in several disciplines cannot be condoned if educators are to meet the needs of the adults of tomorrow.

Every step towards more efficient use of school time is valuable. If the school of tomorrow were to have a curriculum that evolved after application of all of these steps it would provide an environment for learning that almost meets the needs of today. But what about tomorrow?

The dramatic technological advance is providing our world with conveniences and necessities to meet nearly every physical need—the space program, medical science, the communications media, transportation, and food production—to cite a few. This force (technology) is doing its job with a gusto never before witnessed. This very gain, however, is not without loss. Because of technological gain, we are despoiling our environment. Our rivers and lakes are the dumping ground for industrial wastes. Our land is scarred, robbed of its minerals, and then left. The very air we breathe is saturated with the waste from industrial combustion—from blast furnaces, electrical generating plants, and automobile exhausts.

We must now learn to reap the benefits of technological progress without paying the penalties. Every individual must become competent in all manners of preventing the pollution of our environment and the people who inhabit it. Conservation of resources, physical and human, must be made an important part of the student's world. Every concept related to preservation and rejuvenation of our environment and its inhabitants should be grouped into a discipline to which every child is exposed, just as he is exposed to the other basic skills. The ecology of our world is everyone's responsibility, and only by emphasizing it throughout the public school years will we ever achieve security. Ecological thinking must be a natural and involuntary response.

If we advance only in technology and ecology, we will have a healthy and comfortable place to live, but one more ingredient must be added to make life have meaning and beauty—the humanities. Aesthetic concepts seem to be a natural division to add to technology and ecology, making a trilogy of disciplines for the school of the future.

Nova has taken the first steps to reach this ambitious, long-range goal. Since conservation of the pupils' and the teachers' time is a pressing need, the staff has begun to interrelate some of the disciplines. LAPs that treat common concepts are being written in mathematics and science in order to establish a relevance. Many technical science activities are becoming a part of English LAPs. Art and music are integrated into science, literature, home economics, and social studies.

A reorganization of teaching teams across discipline lines for planning and curriculum development will move the plan another step forward. Study groups will identify common areas in the courses of study and will negotiate changes to eliminate redundancy. Several other subtle attempts will be made to advance the schools toward their goal.

Even though it is painful, innovation is necessary. Ideas must become experiments and then, if feasible, pilot programs. Every program must be investigated for its ultimate value to the education of our youth. These steps can best be done in a school complex that is staffed and equipped for the process and in an environment in which both success and failure are accepted as valuable.

CHAPTER 13

The House Plan

by

PETER TELFER, JR.

Mr. Telfer has worked at the middle school, high school, and college levels. He has been a teacher, a guidance counselor, a director of guidance, and a college admissions director. He was principal of Fox Lane Middle School, Director of Middle Schools in Broward County, Fla., and is now Assistant Superintendent for Instruction at the Scotia-Glenville Central Schools, Scotia, N.Y. Mr. Telfer is an educational consultant on middle schools and innovation, and is the author of articles on the middle school to be published in the Encyclopedia of Education *(Macmillan) and in* How to Organize and Operate an Ungraded Middle School *(by McCarthy).*

THE OPENING of the Fox Lane Middle School in September 1966 marked a major reorganization of the educational system in the Bedford (N.Y.) Public Schools. Until that time, each of the four elementary schools in the district housed students in grades K–6, and there was a single junior-senior high school for grades 7–12. The Fox Lane Middle School was built for a maximum of 1,050 students in grades 6, 7, and 8. The elementary schools were then organized for grades K–5, high school for grades 9–12.

Planning the educational program and designing the physical facilities began in 1961, although the school did not open until September 1966. The first step was taken by a committee made up of staff members, and was followed by a two-day conference of seventeen persons representing fifteen disciplines. A second conference of local staff members and four members of the first conference was held to translate the ideas developed during the first conference into a more precise definition of the requirements of the educational program and physical facilities.

As a result of the two conferences it was decided to organize the Fox Lane Middle School for instruction that would enable the individual student to become more self-educating. The program would be organized around teaching teams and would eventually lead to nongradedness. In its fourth year of operation it is still geared to a grade-level basis, but with the thought that in the near future multi-age grouping would not only be a possibility but a reality.

Academic House Plan

Since the four elementary schools that send youngsters to the middle school are small, there was a great deal of concern about the transition to a school built for 1,050 pupils. Therefore it was decided to organize the school on an academic house plan. Three separate academic houses, each built for 350 students and each containing sixth, seventh, and eighth graders, make it possible to have multi-age grouping and enable the teaching staff to get to know the students better.

The concern for the individual student begins in grade 6, with the assignment to an academic house. Each house has a full-time guidance counselor. The three counselors visit the elementary schools to discuss each individual youngster with his teachers. A color-coded 5×8 articulation card is completed for each student (the color identifies which of the four elementary schools the student comes from). The counselor gathers information about the youngster's achievement and academic potential from standardized test results and teachers' recommendations. He also tries to find out about special talents and interests and whether any special consideration should be given to placement in one of the three academic houses. For example, if a shy, dependent student had finally developed a friendship with another student, the teachers might recommend that they be kept together in order to make the transition to a new school easier.

The assignment of students is planned so that each house will have a heterogeneous range of abilities and a geographic distribution from all four communities. The sociological backgrounds of the students vary greatly according to the community they live in, from the exceptionally privileged to the most deprived. Therefore it is essential that there be an even geographical distribution in each academic house. The students remain in the same academic house throughout the three years they are at the middle school.

Staffing

The staff within each academic house is organized as an interdisciplinary team. Each of the three grade levels has a team consisting of four teachers, one each for language arts, social studies, mathematics, and science. In addition, each house has two foreign language teachers, a full-time guidance counselor, two teacher aides, and a house secretary. One teacher is designated as the head teacher. He has a half-time teaching assignment and is responsible for coordinating the instructional program and supervising the teachers in the house.

The central facility building, which all the houses share, has five full-time and one half-time teacher in unified arts, four physical education teachers, three general music and two instrumental teachers, two librarians, one language arts reading consultant, a nurse, a psychologist, a director of educational communications, a graphics artist, and two technicians. The school is administered by a principal and an assistant principal, who work very closely with the head teachers and staff members.

Program

The framework within which the educational program operates lends itself to flexibility and decision-making at the teacher level. All the students are scheduled for language arts, social studies, mathematics, science, music, physical education, and unified arts. In addition to these subjects more than seventy-five percent of the students take French or Spanish. Although the students do not have a choice of the subjects they take, except for foreign language, they do make choices and decisions within the various subject areas.

The day is divided into twelve half-hour modules. Each interdisciplinary team in the academic houses is allotted seven modules for their programs. The teams have forty-five minutes each day for team plan-

ning, during which time they make decisions about scheduling, grouping, and coordination of the curriculum. There is also additional time
for individual planning.

The teachers organize the youngsters into heterogeneous groups with
the intent that the learning activity will dictate the nature of new
groups. Since the teachers are trying to individualize instruction and
have the authority to re-group youngsters when they want to, there is
very little concern about which group a student is in. The teachers can
plan for large- or small-group instruction, according to the need.

The day of the single textbook approach is a thing of the past, and the
use of the lecture method is more the exception than the rule. Teachers
are very much aware of the individual differences among their students
and take them into account in planning the learning activities. Many
teachers are using the contract system and learning activity packets. In
the contract system the youngster makes decisions and choices with the
assistance of the teachers. The types of activities are varied and most
often take into consideration the individual's interests. Since the students do not have unscheduled time in their daily program, the teachers
must provide them with time from the seven modules to pursue independent study activities. Much of their time is spent in the library or in
the educational communications center. Students may select a teacher
to serve as their advisor for independent study. If a student is on independent study, he may plan his own schedule and activities with the
assistance of his advisor, and is not required to attend classes unless he
chooses to do so.

The Fox Lane Middle School has a school-wide dial access retrieval
system of sixty stations, which allows students or teachers immediate
use of audio or video programs. There are thirty group viewing stations
throughout the school, each equipped with twenty-three-inch monitors
and speakers and dial plates. In addition there are thirty electrically
wired carrels with seven-inch monitors and earphones. The carrels can
accommodate one or two students at a time. A specific program can be
selected by dialing a pre-arranged three-digit number on an attached
telephone dial in either a group viewing station or from a carrel.

One hundred twenty different programs can be stored in the system.
The programs originate from video-tape recorders, film chains, multi-
plex film strips and slide projectors, audio tape decks, and a live cam-
era. UHF and VHF television and AM-FM radio programs are available directly off the air. In addition to materials prepared commercially

or by the teachers, it is not uncommon for students to prepare their own video tapes, films, transparencies, and slides. The youngsters are very conscious of what is available on various subjects in printed as well as non-printed materials.

The most drastic departure from a traditional curriculum is in the area of unified arts. In lieu of separate home economics, art, and industrial arts departments, there is a unified arts team, which operates a specially designed, open facility containing equipment for work in textiles, foods, design, ceramics, graphics, crafts, wood, and metal. The program is divided into three phases: the orientation phase, in which the student is introduced to each of the eight areas; the pre-independent phase, in which the students learn problem-solving methods; and the independent phase, in which the student works as an independent researcher on projects he himself has selected, with the teacher available as a consultant and resource person. The students develop an understanding of the interrelationship of design, technique, and materials. The program is planned and executed by the unified arts team with one person designated as a coordinator.

The Fox Lane Middle School program is constantly being looked at to see what the needs of individual youngsters are. The program is flexible because many decisions that used to lie within the domain of the administration are made by the teachers. Since the teachers can decide how much time they require for instruction and what is the most appropriate grouping pattern, they can readily involve the students in decisions about their learning activities.

Hopefully, the students at the Fox Lane Middle School will become more self-directed, and self-educating individuals, who are able to meet new challenges. After the first four years of operation this appears to be the case, and the program has met with community support.

CHAPTER 14

Student Responsibility for Learning
by

MAURICE BLUM

*Mr. Blum was a teacher, vice principal, and principal at Mead-
owbrook Junior High School. He has held teaching posts in the
United States and in Mexico, where he served as Director of
the English Department at the University of Guadalajara and
as Director of a private school with a Mexican program, K–6.
He is currently headmaster of the American School in Madrid,
Spain, a private, college preparatory school, K–12. Mr. Blum
has been a consultant to school systems in many sections of the
United States, and was State Chairman of the Title III Advi-
sory Committee for Massachusetts.*

MEADOWBROOK JUNIOR HIGH SCHOOL is one of five junior high schools
in Newton, Mass. In 1962, a summer study committee of the faculty
established a set of objectives for Meadowbrook, which have served as
a basis for the program that has since evolved. The continuing sense of
development for improvement is one that has characterized the atmosphere of the school and has helped make continued progress possible.
Reassessment of the program never ends; continued progress towards
an ideal is still the goal.

The quality of the statements made by the faculty committee in 1962
has to a great extent determined the structure and operation of the
school since that time. The two items expressed as philosophical ideals
indicate the position and direction of that committee: "Inherent in
man's existence is the right to develop his individual potential," and

"Given the opportunity, man will select goals which are beneficial to both self and society."

Along with these ideals, the following basic assumptions and premises underlie the program.

THE LEARNING PROCESS

1. Learning is evidenced by a change in perception and behavior; the most meaningful learning takes place through the process of inquiry and discovery for oneself.

2. Relationships are uniquely drawn from an experience by each individual.

3. There are similarities and differences between individuals.

4. Learning can best take place when the individual has freedom of choice.

5. The individual reacts to a stimulus, initiates action, and progresses at a rate and depth that may be independent of other members of a group.

6. Learning takes place best when an individual makes a personal commitment to and becomes involved in his own education and its selective use.

THE CHILD

1. The child is in the continual process of individual growth, and learns in a transactional process between his own goals and the goals set by society.

2. The child has rights and responsibilities as an individual and as a member of groups.

THE ENVIRONMENT

1. The environment must provide for integration of experiences, offering a daily opportunity to meet in a situation that encourages a feeling of belonging and security.

2. The student must have the chance to think and work as an individual and as a member of a small group composed of various age levels, in a situation that is free from the pressures of subject content.

3. A daily opportunity must also be provided for learning to take place through the process of inquiry and discovery by a personal commitment to a task.

The Teacher

1. The teacher has the primary task of contributing to a change in the perception and behavior of the student.

2. By providing opportunities for freedom of choice, the teacher helps the student accept the responsibility for his own education.

3. In fulfilling this task, the relationship between the teacher and pupil should be viewed as a transactional one in which the teacher acts as a resource person.

The School

The school should be considered an institution that is specifically designed to provide a setting within which the child may prepare for the place he will make for himself in society.

Much of the above has been summarized in the statement of the school's objectives: "It is the purpose of the Meadowbrook Junior High School to help each student learn how to take charge of the development of his own potential, and to understand that only he, in the long run, is responsible for his learning."

We have called this objective agency development because the student is the primary agent in the educational process. Our objective is to have the student recognize that it is he who should be the initiator, the seeker, the determinant of what happens to him. The other objectives are related to motivation, creativity, and scholarship:

to help each student become personally involved in his learning—to be free to actively explore his own resources and those of the school and the larger environment.

to help each student develop enough confidence in himself and in others to be able to think imaginatively and explore openly ideas, values and relationships.

to help each student find true satisfaction in learning, and to understand that the subject matter skills acquired are not only useful in themselves, but are tools with which to meet situations and solve problems.

These statements indicate rather clearly that the school has an underlying faith in the individual as being good, competent, able and eager to learn, and responsive to opportunity. It recognizes as its charge the creation of a school that will maximize the development of these characteristics.

The Agency Development and Decision-Making

At Meadowbrook, we expect our students to be active decision-makers in the areas in which they can and should be active. All of us make decisions all the time. Too frequently we find ourselves making decisions in response to others' decisions that seriously limit our alternatives. We either obey or not.

We want our students to be aware of the decision-making process, to know the full range of decisions, those made for them, those that limit alternatives, those they are making themselves, those they should be making, those they can make, and finally, those they cannot control. Decision-making is a process that can be learned. It is never too early to learn it. Some of our students come to us quite skilled in this area. They can consider alternatives for both long- and short-range goals, and have enough trust in themselves and society to make decisions. Other students are far less able. It is the school's task to accept the students as they are and to go on from there. The school must provide the kind of opportunity for which the individual is ready; it must also provide the kind of protection for the individual so that he "trusts" enough to be able to risk making decisions. To provide this kind of positive, protecting, supportive, "trusting" atmosphere calls for close, sensitive personal relations between everyone in the school—administrators, teachers, students, and parents.

School Structure

During the seven years of developing the program at Meadowbrook, the structure of the school has been modified to allow for closer personal relations. We divided the approximately 900 students into four units or schools within the school, each of which is exactly like the others, and heterogeneous in all respects. For the sake of convenience they are named Alpha, Beta, Gamma, and Sigma. Each unit consists of 220–225 students, almost equally divided between 7th, 8th, and 9th grades. There are bright students, slow students, active students, and passive students, and students with all varieties of talents in each unit.

Each unit is further divided into 12 "houses" of 17–20 students. Each house is heterogeneously composed of five to seven students from each grade. One of the teachers in the unit is in charge of the house as a house advisor, and the house bears his name. Table One shows a typical house plan.

TABLE ONE

MEADOWBROOK HOUSE PLAN

1968–1969

Beta Team		*220 7th, 8th, and 9th Graders*
Dooley House	(SSE	17
Barclay House	(SSE)	18
Buchanan House	(SSE)	20
Wolf House	(SSE)	19
Nierintz House	(SSE)	18
Roberts House	(SSE)	19
Sarmiento House	(Science)	17
Brunke House	(Science)	19
Doyle House	(Math)	18
Humphrey House	(Math)	19
Teel House	(Foreign Language)	18
McCallie House	(Foreign Language)	17
Guidance Counselor		

During the three years the team of teachers and students assigned to a unit become a very close group, and spend most of their school time working together. In case of difficulties, house advisors or students may request that a student be changed from one house to another.

Each teacher of a major academic subject area—math, English, social studies, second language, and science—is assigned to a unit and serves as a house advisor. Each unit, therefore, is composed of 3 social studies teachers, 3 English teachers, 2 math teachers, 2 science teachers, 2 second language teachers. Each unit also has a guidance counselor. The 13 faculty members assigned to a unit work almost exclusively with the children of that unit. A number of teachers of fine and applied arts serve all four units. The complete organization appears in Table Two.

TABLE TWO

MEADOWBROOK ORGANIZATION

UNIT (*each unit and each house contains 7th, 8th, and 9th graders*)

	Alpha	Beta	Gamma	Sigma
No. of students	220	216	218	211
No. of houses	12	12	12	12

School Population

7th grade	281
8th grade	277
9th grade	308
Total	865

STAFF

A Unit Team	*Teachers Serving the Entire School*	*Other Personnel*
6 SSE teachers	2 Art teachers	3 Administrators
2 Math teachers	1 Audio-visual specialist	1 Administrative assistant
2 Science teachers	2 Home economics teachers	8 Paraprofessionals
2 Foreign language teachers	3 Industrial art teachers	3 Title III staff
1 Guidance counselor	1 Librarian	1 Research assistant
	2 Music teachers	7 Secretaries
	4 Physical education teachers	6 Custodians
	1 Reading specialist	1 Matron
	1 Typing teacher	

The cross-discipline team of teachers, which deals almost exclusively with the same students, meets a minimum of twice a week to discuss the operation of the unit and the children's progress. The house advisors maintain the cumulative records of the students in their house, and meet almost daily with the house for a minimum of 30 minutes. The agenda consists of matters that concern the house as a group or the individuals in the house.

The Schedule

The schedule at Meadowbrook has been designed to support the objectives of the school. Each year it has been revised to be more effective.

Currently the schedule is based on multiples of 10-minute modules. Each unit (Alpha, Beta, Gamma, Sigma) has its own schedule and particular offerings, but the categories of offerings for every student in the school are the same. Every student has six major academic courses, two electives, and physical education. He has one unscheduled period of 50 to 70 minutes, lunch, and a 30-minute house period daily.

Each academic class meets four times per week, but total time in class for each subject is reduced to permit the variety of experiences available each week for the students. To be able to take six major academic classes when the school has only five major academic areas means that the students must double up in one subject area. Although most students take two courses in either English or social studies, some take two science courses, two math courses, or two foreign languages.

The fine and applied arts courses are available to all students, and meet twice a week for 60 minutes each. Included in these offerings are typing, music, art, physical education, industrial arts, and homemaking. The students may take two of these at a time. All courses run 12–15 weeks.

The unscheduled time available each day for each child is spent in the subject area learning centers. Meadowbrook has a learning center for math, English, social science, and foreign languages. The library and the language laboratory are considered part of the learning centers. Each center is staffed by an aide who holds a college degree in the subject area. At least one teacher of the subject is also available in the center during center time. In almost all instances, when the child is in the learning center, his teacher is available to him. Students decide a day in advance which learning center they will attend.

The Curriculum

Except for mathematics and, to a lesser extent, foreign languages, all classes at Meadowbrook are nongraded. Students of all three grades take courses together within their unit. Meadowbrook uses nationally prepared curricular materials, materials prepared in Newton, and materials prepared at Meadowbrook, much of which have been prepared by the Meadowbrook staff.

The knowledge explosion has forced a reconsideration of what should go into the curriculum. It is clearly impossible for any one person to hold in his mind all the knowledge in any given subject. It is equally clear that there is very little knowledge that *all* students should hold. There are, however, *skills* that all students should have. Skills can be learned and developed with a great variety of content materials.

Curriculum development at Meadowbrook is based on the particular interests and knowledge of the teachers responding to the expressed interests of the students. The developmental skills of the subject area remain more or less constant.

Since the focus of the school is on the individual, the materials that engage the students' minds are developed primarily for individual learning. Our students, like students in other schools, attend classes. At the beginning of each term, however, the individual students and the teacher discuss a plan of study for that term. The plan includes such items as the materials the student will cover, the extent and depth of his efforts, and the form of production the student will provide, such as papers, projects, and reports.

The agreement is written out and followed through the term with written comments by both teacher and student on the student's Study Plan. The Study Plan, therefore, provides a running commentary on the student's progress. In some instances the comments are judgmental, in others merely indications of work completed. The use of the forms varies with different teachers and students, but it does offer continuing indication of the work being done. The Study Plans are kept by the students during the term and filed by the house advisor thereafter. The constant availability of information on the progress of the student makes it possible for house advisors to follow the progress of advisees on a regular basis.

The Program in Operation

The school year at Meadowbrook is broken up into three terms of 12–15 weeks each. At the beginning of each term the students are offered a catalog of courses compiled by their unit team (Alpha, Beta, Gamma, Sigma). The catalog indicates in rather general terms the intent of the course, the materials and techniques that may be used, the extent of sophistication in the subject expected, the times and place that the class meets, and the teacher's name. A similar catalog for courses in fine and applied arts for the entire school is also given to the students. In consultation with his house advisor and his parents, the student selects the courses he wants and builds his schedule. To assist him, a profile is prepared of all standardized test scores the school has for the student. The test scores in the profile include general ability tests on a quartile basis. The sequence of courses in mathematics and foreign languages is generally pre-determined for the students by the staff. Ability grouping on a sequential continuum of knowledge generally results in graded classes. Since all other subjects, however, are primarily based on student interest they are nongraded.

In those instances in which the student has demonstrated an inability to make effective decisions or where the parents feel the students should not be involved in making decisions of this nature, placement in classes is done by the house advisor with the aid of the guidance counselor of the unit.

It is interesting to see how quickly students accept the responsibility of making such decisions about their school life. They very soon become adept at manipulating the schedule to serve their purposes. More importantly, they quickly accept the concept that the school exists to serve them, and it is in their own best interests to get the most out of the experience.

Scheduling all the students takes three days, and then classes begin. Students and teachers develop their study plans and the work goes forward.

A daily decision for the students is that of selecting the appropriate learning center for their needs. In an attendance room period with the house advisor at the beginning of the day, the student simply selects from his own personal deck of IBM cards the card for the center that he wishes to go to for his unscheduled period the next day. The cards are collected and sent to the data processing center. The same afternoon the school receives two print-outs showing where each student will be during his unscheduled period. One goes to the house advisor, the other to the learning center aide.

Reporting to Parents

In addition to the regular comments made by the teacher and the student on the individual study plan, students receive an evaluation of their efforts at the end of each term. This progress form scores the child in terms of the objectives of the school as well as the objectives of the class.

During the course of the school year parents are invited to two conferences with the student's house advisor at which the student's profile of standardized test scores and his progress to date are explained. The house advisor prepares for these conferences by consulting with the student's teachers in the unit team meeting. Ninth grade students receive letter grades at the end of each term, and 8th grade students may receive a letter grade upon parental request at the end of the year.

It is important for anyone involved in making significant decisions to have as much data as possible when considering alternatives. The current reporting procedures take a lot of time and effort, yet they are not enough. The staff is studying means for supplying more effective information more frequently.

Since the initiation of the program in 1962 under the leadership of the principal, Miss Bettina King, research and evaluation have been a continuing concern. The evaluation has served various purposes: first, it measured as well as possible the progress of the children, and second, it fed back data to the staff, which resulted in changes for improvement.

The program was initiated with a small group of 156 students. A control group, which matched in all measurable areas, remained in the more traditional program. The performance of the two groups was compared. From 1963 on, more students were added to the program each year, until 1966 when the entire school was placed on the continuous progress program.

Our evaluation has shown that academically our students do as well if not better than those not in the program. Follow-up studies in the high school and college support this judgment. In addition, our students generally have shown a strong tendency to be leaders in and outside of school.

In standardized tests, which are generally based on a traditional curriculum, our students do as well as they would if they had experienced a traditional program. All the ancillary information they acquire is not tested, and the traditional examinations do not test the skills that are so important for living successfully in tomorrow's world. Comparisons with other junior high schools in the city, again based on standardized tests, show no significant differences between students from the Meadowbrook program and the other junior high schools. Admissions to college are consistent with expectations for our students—they are very high, approximately 85%. Grade point averages in the somewhat more traditional setting of the high school have shown a clear superiority of students who were in the program over those in the more traditional portion of the school.

In addition our research has shown that students' attitudes towards themselves and school can be modified by the way the school treats them. That which we term "agency" can be developed in students. Characteristics of the high-agency student have been identified by Dr. Charles E. Goff, vice principal and researcher for the program, and serve as directions for further efforts of the school:

1. He establishes self-initiated goals.
2. He has a positive self-image.
3. He sees himself in relation to the environment in terms of self-determined alternatives.
4. He shows a feeling of hope and promise toward the future.
5. He indicates high need for satisfaction in achievement.
6. He has interest in society and a concern for the welfare of others.

The evaluation of growth in all these characteristics has been most difficult since satisfactory instruments are not available and must be developed. Enough has been done, however, to indicate directions for further efforts by the school.

The quality of the atmosphere in the school has not been measured, but it is certainly felt by all involved. The students are generally happy and purposeful in their efforts. Certainly they are involved. The teachers are most intensely and deeply involved as professional educators.

Clearly, there is much more to be done. Some of the present elements of the program must be changed. More curriculum materials consistent with the operation and objectives of the school must be developed. Training for faculty members in the many roles they serve must be intensified. With sufficient time and effort all this can be achieved. Since we are searching for the ideal, however, it is unlikely that we will ever be satisfied.

I wish to express my appreciation to Mrs. Ernestine McDonough, Mrs. Isa Zimmerman, and Mr. Robert Weiser for their assistance in writing this article.

CHAPTER 15

Secondary Continuous Advancement Program

by

MARTHA A. LEE

Dr. Lee has taught social studies and language arts in junior high schools for fifteen years. She has been a department chairman in social studies and a team leader for SCAP. As a visiting professor at Indiana University Dr. Lee has taught social studies methods to prospective teachers. She is a contributor to Curriculum Change and Innovation in the Junior High School, *published by the Curriculum Research and Development Center, Indiana State University, and* Common Learnings: Core and Interdisciplinary Team Approaches, *edited by Gordon F. Vars.*

Introduction

THE SECONDARY CONTINUOUS ADVANCEMENT PROGRAM, SCAP, at Binford Junior High School, Bloomington, Indiana, is a nongraded, interdisciplinary approach to instruction in social studies and language arts.

Four teachers, two in language arts and two in social studies, work with 230 students representing grades seven, eight, and nine. There are two 105-minute blocks of time, one in the morning and another in the afternoon. Approximately 115 students are assigned to each block. Social studies classes and language arts classes in each block of time may meet separately, may combine into one, two, three, or four groups, or may break down into many smaller groups. Within each block of time there are variable lengths of "periods," variable sequences or rotations of classes, variable groupings of students, variable meeting patterns, variable staffing, and variable times allocated for each subject.

Without major concern for chronological age or grade level, each pupil is assigned to variant instructional groups in which learning experiences are generally adapted to meet the needs, abilities, interests, aptitudes, and rates of progress of the individual. These learning experiences are designed to stimulate the emotional, social, and intellectual growth of the individual student. Furthermore, learning experiences are designed to aid each student to accept a part of the responsibility for his own learning.

This concept of complete nongradedness is designed to accommodate different rates of progress, and to allow for explorations of subject matter, concepts, and skills in varied depths of study according to the interests and abilities of pupils. In a nongraded SCAP classroom pupils work at their own pace, without having to wait several years to learn what they are capable of learning now, or without having to sit through classes that concentrate on learning experiences beyond their comprehension.

Sequence of Learning

The courses of study in social studies and language arts are based on a three-year cycle. The same team of teachers works with the same pupils throughout the three years. Hence, teachers and students are not restricted by the prevalent belief that a certain subject is only appropriate at a certain grade level or age. Each pupil in SCAP can study the same subject at the same time, but at his individual level of understanding, without regard to his chronological age or grade level. This type of curriculum keeps learning experiences for each pupil on a continuum, since each team member knows what the pupil has been taught in the program.

A semester is spent on each of the following areas: the Soviet Union, Europe, China, Southeast Asia, Africa, and South and Southwest Asia.

Each semester of the three-year cycle in social studies is based on the same general objectives. Although these objectives are similar for all levels of ability, the depth and degree to which they are examined vary considerably. The general objectives for social studies are as follows:

1.   Knowledge: to define and become familiar with a large number of terms which are related to and necessary for an understanding of the area being examined; to possess major facts about particular areas, and, to be aware of the ways of organizing, studying, judging, and criticizing such information; to possess knowledge of the ways of treating and presenting ideas through a conscious effort to use correct form and usage in speech and writing; to become familiar with criteria for judgment appropriate to the purpose for which materials are studied; to recall major generalizations about particular cultures.

2.   Intellectual abilities and skills: to understand what is being communicated about cultures; to interpret various types of data, to deal with conclusions and to determine implications; to apply general ideas and principles used in previous learnings; to recognize assumptions; to formulate, test, and evaluate hypotheses in light of new data; to judge logical fallacies in arguments and to analyze relationships.

3.   Attitudes, values: to show a willingness to receive and to respond to phenomena; to develop a sense of the worth of phenomena by deliberately examining a variety of viewpoints on controversial issues with a view to forming tentative opinions about them.

The curriculum in social studies is drawn from the following disciplines: geography, anthropology, sociology, psychology, history, political science, economics. The specific objectives for social studies in each area are as follows:

1.   Geography: to recognize the physical features of an area (land and water forms, climate, vegetation) and determine how and why these physical features affect the people.

2.   Anthropology, sociology, psychology: to explore differences and similarities between people (historical genesis, location, customs, physical appearance, language, religion, major and minority groups, social structure, leadership, communications, institutions), examine their nature (growth, development, attitudes, beliefs, knowledge, skills), and determine how and why these phenomena affect the people, the area as a whole, and the area's relationship with other areas.

3.   History: to become familiar with the historical sequence of events, cause and effect, and internal and external factors affecting

the area's stability and change, and determine why it is the kind of area it is today;

4. Political science: to examine the political organizations of the area (sources of power, governmental forms, political parties, law-making bodies, enforcement, interpretation, external and internal power groups, involvement in war and peace) and determine the effects of organization on the area as well as its relationships with other areas.

5. Economics: to explore the economies of the area (wealth, occupations, products, transportation, science, technology, natural resources) and determine the effects of such economies on the area as well as its degree of viability with other areas.

At the beginning of each year the language arts teachers make a cooperative outline of the year's study. The purpose of this outline is to determine when the skills suggested in the "SCAP Language Arts Curriculum Guide" for each level of the cycle will be taught. At this time the teachers decide which skills they feel they are most capable of teaching. English grammar is taught for a minimum of six weeks each semester, and is interspersed with the study of literature, writing, speech, and other language skills. The theories of "new" grammar are incorporated in the curriculum whenever possible.

Spelling is identified from both social studies and language arts materials, but it is treated in the language arts classes in whatever manner the teachers feel appropriate to each of the various levels. Throughout some semesters, all members of the SCAP team administer formal spelling tests.

"The Language Arts Curriculum Guide" provides for oral expression activities and written expression activities throughout each semester of the three-year curriculum. An example of the items studied in sentence structure during the three years is provided in Table One.

TABLE ONE

SENTENCE STRUCTURE SEQUENCE

Level I, Cycle 1:   kinds of sentences and end punctuation; parts: simple subject and predicate; variety in writing

Level I, Cycle 2:   kinds of sentences and end punctuation; parts: simple subject and predicate; four basic sentence patterns; variety in writing

Level I, Cycle 3:   kinds of sentences and end punctuation; parts: simple subject and predicate; compound subject and predicate; basic sentence patterns

Level II, Cycle 1:   fragments and run-ons; four types of sentences and end punctuation; parts: simple subject and predicate; agreement of subject and a verb; completers: direct and indirect objects; simple clauses: recognition of conjunction, distinguishing dependent and independent

Level II, Cycle 2:   fragments and run-ons; simple subject and predicate; compound subject and predicate; simple compound sentences; sentence patterns; capitalization and punctuation: in-depth uses of capital letters; end punctuation; commas; quotation marks; colon; hyphen; underlining; apostrophe

Level II, Cycle 3:   fragments and run-ons; simple subject and predicate; compound subject and predicate; simple clauses; review of agreement; sentence patterns; completers: predicate nouns and adjectives

Level III, Cycle 1:   review of basic subject and predicate; completers in-depth: objects, direct and indirect, related to study of transitive and intransitive verbs; predicate nouns and adjectives; fragments and run-ons; capitalization and punctuation, uses of capitals, end punctuation, commas, quotes, semicolon, colon, hyphen, underlining, apostrophe

Level III, Cycle 2:   fragments and run-ons; compound sentences agreement; simple complex sentences; variety in sentence structure

Level III, Cycle 3:   review of basic subject, predicate; fragments and run-ons; compound sentences; complex sentences: simple recognition and distinction of dependent and independent; phrases and use; variety of sentence structure

Level IV, Cycle 1:   review of basic parts; capitalization and punctuation in-depth: capitals and end punctuation, commas, quotes, semicolon, colon, hyphen, underlining, apostrophe; fragments and run-ons; completers in-depth:

direct and indirect objects, predicate adjective and noun; noun clauses; review of simple, compound, and complex sentences

Level IV, Cycle 2:   review of basic parts; fragments and run-ons; compound forms: subject and predicate, sentences in-depth: agreement; review of simple and complex sentences

Level IV, Cycle 3:   fragments and run-ons; review of compound forms; complex sentences: distinguishing dependent and independent clauses, distinguishing phrases and clauses, adjective and adverb clauses

SCAP is organized around both a correlated curriculum and a co-ordinated curriculum. It is correlated in that articulation and relationships between language arts and social studies exist without destroying the boundaries of each discipline. It is coordinated in that common guidelines have been established in both disciplines.

Correlated Curriculum

Language arts and social studies each have units of instruction on the same areas of study: Soviet Union, Europe, China-Korea-Japan, Southeast Asia, Africa, South and Southwest Asia. Tables Six and Seven show the common area in reading materials on Southeast Asia.

The degree of correlation goes much deeper than just having general areas of instruction in common. For example, within each semester of the three-year cycle the topic "People" arises. In social studies the students examine various sub-topics, such as education, local customs, social conditions, traditions, religion, and dress. At the same time they are studying folklore, myths, or biographies in language arts. Some of the correlated instructional experiences can be seen in spelling, independent study projects, correlated assignments, and correlated test schedules.

Not visible in the curriculum as such—but certainly an integral part of the correlated curriculum—is the concept of team teaching. It necessitates continuous inter-departmental communication to exchange information about individual problems, solve common teaching problems, discuss appropriate materials, correlate test schedules and homework assignments to ease the demands on the students' time, and eliminate strict departmentalization of subjects in order to produce a significant correlation between social studies and language arts. Furthermore, the team approach permits SCAP teachers to know each other better and to know the students better, since they continually share information. It further allows a pooling of ideas, encourages constructive professional criticism, permits team members to specialize in tasks they do best, provides more efficient use of teacher time, and gives new teachers the opportunity to observe experienced teachers and profit from their advice.

In SCAP it is difficult to separate completely the correlated curriculum from the coordinated curriculum. Table Two shows both correlation and coordination in one area, the Soviet Union.

The language arts curriculum is coordinated in that all the pupils examine folktales at the same time. These same pupils experience a correlated curriculum in social studies by examining the geographic setting of the folktales.

TABLE TWO

CORRELATION AND COORDINATION: SOVIET UNION

Instructional Level	Reading Level	Readings: Language Arts Coordination	Social Studies Correlation
I	3.0– 5.0	*Tales of Faraway Folk* (folktale)	geographic setting
II	4.0– 6.0	*Russian Folk Tales* (folktale)	geographic setting
III	6.0– 9.0	*Overcoat and Other Tales* (folktale)	geographic setting
IV	9.0–11.0	*Great Russian Tales* (folktale)	geographic setting
V	11.0–12.9	*Selected Tales* (folktale)	geographic setting

Coordinated Curriculum

SCAP's coordinated curriculum concentrates on cooperative teaching efforts. This intra-disciplinary approach affords coordination of learning experiences, common lectures and films, joint experiences with guest speakers, and common large- and small-group activities.

In the coordinated curriculum students study the same topic at the same time, but obviously at different levels of study. Table Three shows a typical schedule of topics in social studies and the approximate number of days in a semester to be spent on each.

TABLE THREE

A COORDINATED SOCIAL STUDIES SCHEDULE

Days	Topic
5	Review social studies skills
5	*Land*: surface structure, ecological factors, land masses, waterways, flora, fauna, soils, location of political divisions (cities, states, countries)
5	*Climate*: altitude, temperature, rainfall, winds, seasons, effects on population
15	*History*: sequence of events, cause and effect: factors affecting stability and change
10	*Government*: sources of power, governmental forms, political parties, law-making bodies, enforcement, interpretation, power groups (external and internal), involvement in war and peace
15	*People*: groupings, nationalities, dress, homes, language, customs, traditions, attitudes, family life (pre-revolution and today), general welfare, medicine, foods, standard of living social structure, religion, educational institutions
15	*Economics*: farming, grazing, natural resources, industry and manufacturing, handicrafts, wealth, occupations, products, commune, technology, trade
5	*Transportation and Communication*: types, uses, locations, degree of development
20	*Present Day*: Foreign Policy (U.S. to China and China to world), arts, reaction, military strength, science, festivals and holidays, cities

A schedule such as Table Three is planned cooperatively by the two social studies teachers well in advance of the semester in which the area is to be examined. It is, of course, only a tentative guideline and may be changed by them at any time.

Independent Study

Independent study in SCAP has three basic purposes: (1) to provide the student with experiences in using human and material resources within the school, (2) to develop a sense of responsibility for his own learning, and (3) to provide a student with opportunities to pursue his special interests and talents. All SCAP students have some continuous learning experiences in the first two. The SCAP experiences place the burden of learning directly on the individual, but it is obvious that one must first acquire the skills necessary to accept this responsibility of independence. The conditions for SCAP's independent study are:

1. A student submits a proposal to the SCAP teacher(s) he wishes to sponsor his project. Accepted proposals are placed in SCAP's central files. Table Four presents a sample proposal for independent study.

TABLE FOUR

SCAP INDEPENDENT STUDY PROPOSAL FORM
Name
Teacher Sponsoring Project
Proposed Topic:
Approximate Time for Project:
Materials and Facilities Needed:
Approved by librarian:
Method of Reporting Project:

2. Not all projects will be approved.

a. Approval depends on the sponsoring teacher's decision after conference with the SCAP team. That decision will be based on the interest of the student, the maturity and responsibility of the student, and the facilities and materials available for the project.

b. Use of the library conference room for study must be cleared through the librarian.

c. Use of the public library or Indiana University library facilities are possible only if the student brings a permission slip from his parents and clears it through the school office.

3. A project may be terminated at any time by the sponsoring teacher or by the librarian.

4. Choice of topic and method for reporting the project are decisions to be made by the student and the sponsoring teacher.

5. The sponsoring teacher will decide whether the student will be held responsible for the class work he misses while he works on the project or whether the project will serve in lieu of class work.

6. The decision to credit a student with a grade in more than one SCAP subject for one project (such as one project earning a grade in both social studies and language arts) is to be made by the teachers involved.

7. All SCAP teachers should be kept informed of the students working on independent study projects.

8. The number of students working at any one time on projects should be limited to the number that can comfortably and profitably work in the library.

9. Duplicates of written reports or notes of oral reports of study projects will be placed on file.

Procedures for Determining Pupil Position in the Sequence

Each fall SCAP has an extensive testing program to determine a tentative position for each pupil in the curriculum. Pupil placement is a team effort and is based on several criteria: the results of current standardized tests and teachers' tests, past performances, past records, and teachers' judgments about social maturity, emotional maturity, physical maturity, academic performances and accomplishments, attitudes (particularly toward school and peers), cooperation, and willingness to accept responsibilities.

The *Stanford Achievement—Advanced Battery, 7–8–9* is administered initially by SCAP teachers to all SCAP students. Certain portions of this test give an approximate grade equivalent measurement in each of the following areas: paragraph meaning, spelling, language (usage, punctuation, capitalization, dictionary skills, sentence sense), and social studies skills. These measurements serve as a base from which SCAP teachers determine a tentative position for each pupil in the curriculum.

Further information about each pupil is obtained from the tests given every fall as part of the school's regular testing program. The *Gates-Mac Ginitie Reading Tests, Survey E,* yield measurements and grade equivalents in speed, accuracy, vocabulary, and comprehension. *The Lorge-Thorndike Intelligence Tests Levels E* and *F* yield measurements and grade equivalents on verbal I.Q., nonverbal I.Q., and a total I.Q., which is an estimate of overall ability. After scoring, recording, and analyzing these results, the SCAP teachers reassign each pupil to a more permanent starting position in the curriculum.

It is at this point that social studies teachers administer their batteries of tests; specifically, they are interested in inquiry skills and basic social studies skills. Students whose abilities in reading fall between grades 9 and 12 are given the *Watson-Glaser Critical Thinking Appraisal, Form Ym* or *Zm.* This test measures critical thinking abilities in inference, assumptions (made–not made), conclusions (follow–do not follow), and argument (strong–weak). *The Sequential Tests of Educational Progress Social Studies, Form 3A* or *3B* are administered to students with reading levels 7–9. *Form 4A* or *4B* is administered to students whose reading level is grade 6 or below. These tests measure ability to think critically in identifying generalizations, in identifying values, in distinguishing fact from opinion, in comparing data, and in drawing conclusions, and in reading and interpreting social studies materials (maps, graphs, the printed word).

In addition to the standardized tests, SCAP social studies teachers administer their own tests, which are written at various levels of reading, and are designed to measure ability in the following map skill areas: recognition of land and water forms; location of places by using lines of longitude and latitude; use of direction finder, mileage scales, and map legend; recognition of surface features; recognition and interpretation of maps: political, distribution, topographical, weather, and ocean current.

The SCAP language arts teachers also administer the *Sequential Tests of Educational Progress: Writing, Form 2A* (levels 10–12), *Form 3A* (levels 7–9), and *Form 4A* (levels 6 and below) at the appropriate reading level. These tests are designed to measure ability to think critically in writing, to organize materials, to write material appropriate for a given purpose, to write effectively, and to observe conventional use in punctuation and grammar.

If abnormalities (such as an increase in several grade levels from the previous year, or any kind of decrease) appear at any time during the testing period, the student is retested with an equivalent test. The SCAP teachers then reevaluate each pupil's position in the curriculum, and changes that appear advisable are made at this time.

Since there are obvious variations in levels of skills, maturities, and abilities, each student is assigned to that sequence that approximates his own abilities and capabilities. He may be assigned to several different group levels at the same time. Table Five shows the assignments of an eighth grade student who has a wide range of language arts abilities.

TABLE FIVE

RANGES IN LANGUAGE ARTS ABILITIES
OF AN EIGHTH GRADE STUDENT, AND GROUP ASSIGNMENT

Ability	Grade Equivalent	Group Level
Comprehension	9.0	IV (8.0–9.9)
Speed	6.1	III (6.0–7.9)
Accuracy	7.5	III (6.0–7.9)
Vocabulary	10.8	V (10.0–11.9)
Spelling	4.3	II (4.0–5.9)
Writing: Organization	3.9	I (2.9–3.9)
Effectiveness	5.2	II (4.0–5.9)
Appropriateness	6.0	III (6.0–7.9)

Table Five not only shows the variety of group placements that are possible for an individual but also serves as an example for the multi-grouping concept, which is an integral part of SCAP. This concept is discussed later at greater length as a strategy for providing for individual differences.

It should be noted that the position in the curriculum to which any given student is assigned is not permanent. Regrouping is a part of the continuous procedure in SCAP. A student may be placed in another position in the sequence as soon as he demonstrates that he is ready to be moved.

In addition to the various tests administered each fall for pupil placement, further analysis is made on those students who have been in the program for one or two years. This phase of the evaluation is perhaps the most rewarding. When current measurements are compared to the previous year's, it is not at all unusual for a pupil to show a progress of two, three, or four grade levels. A few have even progressed five or six grade levels in some areas.

One interesting analysis compared SCAP students in grade 8 to non-SCAP students in grade 8 in the same school on the *Iowa Test for Basic Skills*. Both groups of students were similarly representative of the "averages" and the "extremes." Yet SCAP students scored higher than non-SCAP students in every area of language arts and social studies that this test measured.

Strategies to Provide for Individual Differences

MULTI-MATERIALS

SCAP has no textbooks in the usual sense, since no single text is relied on throughout any of the areas of study. Some hardback materials are used, but the major types of multi-materials are paperbacks and mimeographed handouts.

The levels and types of materials are made available to each student on the bases of ability, maturity, and interest. The use of multi-materials introduces the student to many different points of view, and provides learning experiences in which he can arrive at his own valid conclusions.

Most of the materials listed in Table Six are produced commercially. The mimeographed material, particularly what is provided to students in Level I, is composed in one of two ways: the teacher writes an original article on the needed topic at the desired reading level, or the teacher translates the major points of an already published article into appropriate reading levels. Thus, no matter when in the three-year cycle a pupil is exposed to the curriculum, materials and learning experiences are so varied in depth that each individual is permitted to examine the topics at the level of his own capabilities.

TABLE SIX

MULTI-MATERIALS FOR SOCIAL STUDIES, SOUTHEAST ASIA

Level I (3.0–6.0)
Southeast Asia (Fideler)
Book I: Workbook (Benefic)
My First World Atlas
(Hammond)
Project Book III (Scholastic)
Handouts prepared by teachers

Level II (6.0–9.0)
Southeast Asia (AEP)
Southeast Asia (Fideler)
My First World Atlas
(Hammond)
East and South Asia (Allen)
Story of Indonesia
(McCormick–Mathers)
Handouts prepared by teachers

Level III (9.0–11.0)
Asia: Focus on Southeast Asia
(Fideler)
Rim of Asia (Scholastic)
Southeast Asia (AEP)
Southeast Asia (Cambridge)
Comparative World Atlas
(Hammond)
People and Nations (Bete)
Handouts prepared by teachers
Current newspapers, magazines

Level IV (10.0–12.9+)
Asia: Focus on Southeast Asia
(Fideler)
Southeast Asia: A Policy
(Laidlaw)
Thailand (Van Nostrand)
Indonesia (Van Nostrand)
Philippines (Van Nostrand)
Comparative World Atlas
(Hammond)
Japan and Southeast Asia
(Harcourt)
Two Viet Nams (CES)
Current newspapers, magazines

MULTI-GROUPING

The flexibility of SCAP's organization is such that multi-grouping and regrouping are continuous operations. SCAP teachers do not assume that all the pupils must learn the same things, nor do they organize their learning experiences in order to accommodate the largest number of pupils in any one group. Grouping and continuous regrouping in SCAP are arranged for the instructional purposes as determined by the needs of pupils and teachers at any given time.

The placement of pupils into small groups is made in a variety of ways. Depending on the nature of the activity, the factors considered for group determination include reading levels, basic skills, skills of inquiry, levels of social and/or emotional maturity, common interests, speed, accuracy, writing skills, readiness for skills, special needs, and sometimes even physical maturity.

With SCAP's multi-grouping, a student is no longer forced to advance at a more rapid rate than his skills allow, nor is the individual forced to bide his time while waiting for others to catch up. Even large-group instruction provides for individual differences. While one teacher is involved with large-group instruction, three teachers can work with individual students, independent study projects, or small seminar groups.

TEAM TEACHING AND EVALUATION

Team teaching in SCAP is concerned primarily with eliminating duplication of small classroom tasks and repetitive materials, providing additional time for team members to work with individual students or small groups, providing opportunities for teachers and students to be involved together in independent study projects, making effective use of teachers' talents in various types of instructional approaches, and exposing students to a variety of instructional techniques and teachers' abilities. One basic reason for arranging the instructional staff in cooperative teams to group, instruct, and evaluate pupils and to plan is that no teacher can be all things to each student.

Since each team member is exposed to all the SCAP students, cooperative evaluation is essential. If, for example, a student is working with one team member in formal spelling, another member in language skills, and still another in literature, it should be obvious that cooperative evaluation is necessary in order to arrive at a "total" individualized evaluation of each pupil. This procedure, then, individualizes student evaluation. Team members, observing the student under varied circumstances, are in a better position than one single teacher to make judgments about a particular pupil.

CORRELATED AND COORDINATED CURRICULUM

SCAP's correlated curriculum can make social studies and language arts more meaningful experiences than they are when presented as single subjects. The literature used in the language arts classes is correlated with each area of study in social studies. Table Seven illustrates the correlation and the multi-material concept for the Southeast Asia area of study, and also indicates how the language arts literature pro-

TABLE SEVEN

A CORRELATED, MULTI-MATERIAL CONCEPT
IN LANGUAGE ARTS: SOUTHEAST ASIA

Level I (3.0–6.0)
    Novel:
        Shan's Lucky Knife
        Burma Boy
        Second Son
        Tino and the Typhoon
    Short Stories:
        Kantchill's Lime Pit
        Sunken City
        On the Threshold
        Cavalcades
    Biography:
        Dr. Tom Dooley, My Story

    Poetry:
        Handouts prepared by teachers

Level II (6.0–9.0)
    Novel:
        Pearl Lagoon
        Lost Kingdom

    Short Stories:
        Kantchill's Lime Pit
        Wide Wide World
        Adventures in Reading

    Biography:
        Tom Dooley
        Deliver Us From Evil
    Poetry:
        Handouts prepared by teachers

Level III (9.0–11.0)
    Novel:
        Anna and King of Siam
    Short Stories:
        Wide Wide World
        Adventures in Reading
    Biography:
        Edge of Tomorrow
        The Night They Burned the
            Mountain
    Poetry:
        Handouts prepared by teachers

Level IV (10.0–12.9+)
    Novel:
        The Ugly American
    Short Stories:
        Adventures in Reading

    Biography:
        Edge of Tomorrow
        The Night They Burned the
            Mountain
    Poetry:
        Handouts prepared by teachers

gram is coordinated. Common tasks, lectures, and units of instruction may be planned together about the novel, short stories, biography, and poetry. What is perhaps more important, Table Seven shows that individual differences in reading levels are recognized.

Since the curriculum in SCAP is coordinated, teachers can easily adapt the subject matter to the changing needs of the individual. Coordination and correlation allow team members to vary the learning experiences within the block of time and from day to day. They allow team members to control daily responsibilities assigned to each student, such as homework and tests, so that no student is burdened with more responsibilities than he is capable of handling.

CHAPTER 16

The Frontier of Change

by

SCOTT G. RICHARDSON

Scott G. Richardson is presently the Director of Secondary Curriculum of the Tulsa Public Schools, Tulsa, Oklahoma.

Mr. Richardson's experiences at Ridgewood High School began with its second year of operation. He served as a teacher on several teaching teams, and in the supervisory-administrative capacity of chairman of the math-science division. His last four years at Ridgewood were spent as Superintendent-Principal. Mr. Richardson has served as consultant to many school districts as they developed plans for change in their schools.

IN THE PERIOD between 1956 and 1959 there seemed to be a feeling that all was not as well as it might be in secondary education. Much of this uneasiness was generated by the pressures of increased student enrollment, shortage of competent staff, a demand for higher academic excellence, and what is generally referred to as the "knowledge explosion." The time was ripe for an assessment of the performance of the secondary school in the light of a society that was in an age of change.

At least some of the impetus for change in the high school was generated by the work of the Commission on the Experimental Study of the Utilization of the Staff in the Secondary School, under the direction of J. Lloyd Trump. This commission was appointed by the Secondary School Principal's Executive Committee in May 1956, and the report by Dr. Trump, *Images of the Future—A New Approach to the Secondary School,* was published in 1959. A subsequent and more comprehensive report was made by J. Lloyd Trump and Dorsey Baynham in *Guide to Better Schools.*

Organization of the Program

Since its opening in the fall of 1960, Ridgewood High School in Norridge, Ill., has been organized around some of the new practices being introduced into secondary schools at that time—large group, seminar, and independent study phases of instruction. Since then the use of a laboratory phase in all areas of instruction has generated what we now call a four-phase program, which is complemented by the use of team teaching in all subject areas, a modular computerized schedule, and a somewhat unique administrative and supervisory plan.

Philosophical Perspective

Much of the effectiveness of any organization depends on the declared or implied objectives of the organization. This is particularly true of schools because the end-product is not tangible, and cannot be measured in the relatively simple terms, "quality, sales, profit."

Unlike manufactured products, the obsolescence of a human being is unthinkable; therefore, the need for a philosophy and objectives is acute. Schools cannot serve the society that supports them if they do not attempt to identify those educational experiences that might be most useful to the individual. It is therefore imperative that schools declare the intent of the institution in the form of a philosophy and objectives, and then use these declarations as operational guidelines for the instructional program.

The essential parts of the Ridgewood philosophy are encapsulated in the following statements, called the "Nine Beliefs Basic to Decision Making":

 1. The unique purpose of education is the development of intellectual powers. Of special importance in a rapidly changing world is the development of the inquiring, creative mind and the self-directive individual.

2. Education in a democracy should be primarily an individual, not a mass, process.

3. An important aim of the school is to develop each individual's capacity to assume more and more responsibility for his own education. . . . Self-educability is an essential quality of good citizenship.

4. Every area of human knowledge has significant contributions to make to each student's intellectual growth.

5. Knowledge is by nature unified, rather than fragmented. . . . The concept centered approach to knowledge is a more realistic approach.

6. The rate of progress through the school should be determined by the readiness of the individual to move from one stage to the next.

7. The school is committed to providing worthwhile educational experiences for all the children of all the people.

8. The public school is only one of the fundamental educational institutions in our society.

9. Desirable change in education can be speeded up by the free exchange of ideas and by active participation.

Our objectives can be broadly defined as the individualization of instruction and the professionalization of teaching. We need not go into full detail of all the points of the objectives, but it would be useful to examine some of those that are most relevant to the operation of the program.

The key element of individualization of instruction is a curriculum (content and learning activities) that provides learning experiences that are significant, relevant, and appropriate to the capability and interest of the learner. It should provide for quest activities on the part of many, and encourage critical thinking, self-directiveness, and creativity. It should also provide for variations in pace and content in keeping with the individual's stage of development.

As to the concept of the professionalization of teaching, the following notions probably have the greatest impact on the organizational and operational procedures of the school:

1. Teachers' time and energy should be conserved by freeing them from non-professional tasks. This time should be reinvested in individual and small-group teaching, and in professional growth.

2. Teachers should assume decision-making responsibility in the development of curriculum, materials, and practices, consistent with the school's philosophical commitment. The assumption of this respon-

sibility would include the need to recommend scheduling parameters, resources for student and faculty use, and the development of the materials and methods necessary to encourage independent study on the part of the majority of the student body.

The Parameters of Instructional Grouping

The development of a workable scheme for the use of large-group, laboratory, seminar, and independent study requires a recognition by the staff that these practices are not solutions to educational problems, but are useful tools. Their value is limited by the ability of the staff to capitalize on the unique characteristics of each type of activity.

In general, the teaching teams must formulate a new set of questions and answers:

What kind of ideas, concepts, skills or understandings are basic to all students in this course, and consequently appropriate to large-group instruction?

What techniques—verbal, audio, or visual—are most likely to give the necessary "one-time" impact to a large group?

What kind of individual experiences—reading, writing, listening, or viewing—will be most appropriate to the expansion and rounding-out of the large-group experience, and consequently most appropriate to the laboratory setting that provides multiple resources as well as instructional help on an individual basis?

What kinds of ideas will best lend themselves to discussion and be most appropriate to the seminar group?

What kinds of options can be provided that will encourage individual students to engage in further learning activities on an independent basis?

The mechanics of large-group, seminar, laboratory, and independent study are probably not obvious to a teaching team until they have some experience with the effect these groups have on their schedules and those of their students. It cannot be over-emphasized that the choices or recommendations made by a teaching team must be based on the limitations of the staff and the schedule, as well as on the educational need.

Organizational Patterns and the Team Enterprise

Experimentation with team teaching over the past five years has generated many difficulties because of the various interpretations placed on the meaning. In some instances the adoption of team teaching without a well thought-out plan has led to lower efficiency and less effectiveness than the system it replaces. In other cases much higher efficiency and effectiveness have evolved through a careful and continuous analysis of intent before the adoption of team teaching and during the developmental stages.

A definition is in order here so that we may avoid any semantic difficulty that may arise from the reader's prior experience with team teaching. The characteristics of an effective teaching team are typical of many kinds of teams:

1. A common purpose exists within the membership of the team.
2. The team membership concentrates various talents by pooling those unique capabilities that are relevant to the purpose of the team.
3. The activity of the team is planned by the team and implemented by the team.
4. Team planning capitalizes on the unique talents of members of the group by undertaking appropriate activities and relegating appropriate responsibility to the members.
5. The team continually assesses individual and team performance in light of specific objectives.
6. The team enterprise encourages interpersonal relationships that foster professional growth and a consistently higher level of performance on the part of the individual.

The processes of making decisions and delegating leadership functions are often points of confusion with teaching teams when professional peer relationships actually exist. There are many arguments concerning the use of designated, versus emerging, leadership, but in either instance the leader needs to involve every team member in the process of making decisions that are consistent with team objectives.

The organization of teaching teams at Ridgewood is generally done on the basis of rather clear-cut instructional needs. As a general rule, all faculty members belong to two or more teams.

One of these teams will be rather like the departmental structure used in some schools, i.e., a math department made up of all math teachers. The functions of this team are to coordinate all the subject matter materials and furnish guidelines for the design and implementation of a curriculum that is consistent with the philosophy of the school. The most pertinent question that might be posed to a team is, "What in this discipline is most relevant and useful to the educational growth of each individual student?"

Each teacher is also a member of a second team, whose responsibility is the development of curriculum materials and activities that are in keeping with the established guidelines.

Other variations in team structure are worth noting because they illustrate the diversity of patterns that may exist. There is a remedial team, composed of mathematics, science, English, and history teachers. Its purpose is not a correlated curriculum, as one might suspect, but rather a working arrangement for identifying the problems of slow learners. Another example is a language team, composed of teachers of German, French, Spanish, and Latin. Here again the purpose is not content but the development of activities and procedures leading to the solution of problems common to language instruction. There are many other variations, such as a newly formed humanities team, encompassing English, social studies, art, and music. The point is that if purposes are identified and evaluated continuously, then effective team structures can be built and re-built at any time.

There seems to be a strong indication that the interpersonal relationships established through team interaction may generate a greater receptivity to, and concern for, students as individuals. In the process of evolving an educational setting to encourage self-direction and independent study, it seems likely that teachers who are encouraged to make decisions and to be independent learners themselves would probably encourage these same characteristics in their students.

The general principles that furnish guidelines for the formation of teaching teams are also applicable to the formation of leadership teams. It is difficult to imagine an administrator, supervisor, counselor, librarian, audio-visual director, or disciplinarian who does not have an effect on the educational program, even though in some instances contact with students is minimal. It is necessary to utilize the feelings and perceptions of various administrative personnel so that the decisions made by the administrative and supervisory personnel will be consistent with the philosophy. Leadership then changes from the usual hierarchical structure to one that places the various specialists in a peer relationship. An individual in an administrative team then functions much like a member of a teaching team in which decisions are coordinated by using established guidelines.

Ridgewood High School uses a flat administrative organizational plan. The group, called the Superintendent's Administrative Team, includes the superintendent-principal; the administrative assistants for Student Affairs, Math-Science, Humanities, and School and Community Relations; the Director of Guidance; the head Librarian; the Audio-Visual Director; and the Discipline and Attendance Officer.

Each individual in the group has considerable autonomy in his domain, as long as his decisions are consistent with the philosophy and objectives of the school. In order to assure this consistency considerable interaction is necessary on the administrative team level.

The Laboratory Phase and Independent Study

The laboratory phase of instruction is singled out for examination here because it is a highly appropriate setting for individualized learning activities. Historically, school laboratories have been considered as places where experimentation and manipulation of materials go on. This notion is still valid, but with a little imagination, it can easily be extended beyond the historical limitation of science, home economics, and the like. If we consider all the resources available in all subject areas, we can broaden the definition of laboratory to encompass experimentation, manipulation of materials, handling of data, and development of ideas and concepts. With this definition in mind it is not difficult to see the idea of a laboratory phase for most subject areas.

The development of the laboratory phase as a part of the general four-phase program at Ridgewood seems to have grown out of the combination of the usual science laboratory activities and the use of subject matter resource areas in science, mathematics, and English-history.

The approach in science was similar to most laboratory approaches in that generally all the students were involved with the same kind of activity at the same time. The first type of flexibility in the laboratory was a change in facilities to allow the use of the laboratory period for optional seminar discussion. As the teaching staff began to see the need for more flexibility, they realized that the right materials and the instructor were seldom available to the student in the science resource center at the time he needed them. The laboratory attempted to broaden the curriculum to incorporate new science materials, along with student use of audio-visual materials. It adopted a multi-experiential approach, using supplementary texts, references, filmstrips, slides, tapes, and program materials, as well as the usual manipulation of laboratory equipment.

As might be expected, questions arose about organizing the curriculum to help students learn how to use the available resources and to encourage them to initiate independent study projects. These questions were partially answered by producing an expanded syllabus of specific assignments, on a unit basis, in reading, viewing, listening, and experimenting. This syllabus also correlated the various phases—large-group, laboratory, and seminar—as an experience sequence distributed over a fixed time interval for all students, i.e., one week for unit one, etc. Options for individual differences were provided by allowing choices between the various kinds of experiments, reading, or viewing materials.

The applicability of this technique to other subjects became apparent to other staff members as they became more adept at producing various kinds of curriculum materials and more cognizant of the value of having pertinent resources immediately available in the laboratory. Considerable impetus was given to the development of the multi-resource approach by the concern and participation of a fine library staff and audio-visual director. Their skills in acquisition of materials were brought to bear time and again. They made a concerted effort to be in constant communication with the teaching teams as curriculum ideas developed.

The role of the teacher in this kind of laboratory setting began to change to one of being a learning strategist and a resource person rather than a disseminator of information. This change was not drastic for the teachers who ordinarily worked in a laboratory setting, but in some subject areas, it represented a radical departure from the teachers' usual lecture-recitation orientation.

Providing additional options for the students seemed to be the most reasonable step toward attaining the philosophical objectives of producing self-sustaining learners through independent study activities. Much of the pressure to provide more options for variation in pace, depth, and breadth came from the students' response to the materials available.

The implications of the kind of curriculum reorganization and development suggested here are difficult to imagine because this kind of change has two dimensions: It poses new questions about the teaching-learning processes, as well as new kinds of organizational problems.

The Learning Package and Individualized Learning

The development of the learning laboratory approach generates a flexible setting that is vital to independent study. This flexibility occurs in time and content. Modular scheduling, which allows the students to use unscheduled time as laboratory time, furnishing the laboratories with pertinent content material, and having appropriate teachers available reduce the physical problems.

Many teaching teams and individual teachers are faced with the problem of providing curriculum materials that will be useful to students on an individual basis. The expanded syllabus, mentioned earlier, proved to be one of the most useful techniques to emerge from the staff. Later, learning packages in physics were developed around a few basic concepts so that a student could utilize these packets as individual units. the general composition of this kind of packet included some basic explanatory material written by the staff, reading assignments from standard textbooks, viewing filmstrips, prescribed laboratory experiences, some related problems, and a post-test. The variety of activities depended on the kinds of materials available. Materials—books, filmstrips, etc.—were stored in the laboratory and checked out by clerks, thus leaving the instructors free to help individual students or groups of students.

Basic concepts, for all the students, were presented in large-group meetings, thus providing a thread of continuity. Students then had the options of working on units directly related to the large-group topic, on units of special interest, or of pursuing a topic of special interest to themselves. Eventually the students' schedules were altered so they could assign themselves laboratory time that best fit their needs. A minimum time was required, and additional laboratory time was left to the discretion of the student.

Class performance was found to be on a par with classes previously conducted by a lock-step technique. However, many more students became involved with individual projects and learning activities that took them well beyond the usual expectations of the course.

The general organization of the learning packet was also used in other subject areas. Model building, drawing, painting, and creative writing became substitutes for the experimentation part of the package. For example, historical documents were reproduced for the students to analyze so that history would take on the perspective of a living discipline. These techniques, with variations, appropriate modifications, and available resources, may be used in many areas of instruction.

Other approaches in special areas are worthy of note, although the highly developed learning package was not used. The procedure used in shorthand gradually allowed students to accelerate out of the group activities by using dictation tapes. These tapes, run from a console similar to the type used in language laboratories, enabled the individual students to pace themselves, increase speed, and develop listening skills necessary for mastering shorthand. This technique made it possible for some students to complete two years' of work in one, while others were able to extend one year's work over a longer period of time.

In the development of curriculum packages it is important to consider the behavioral objectives. The most prevalent problem is the inconsistency between the stated purpose of the learning activity, the activity itself, and the evaluation of the activity. Much of this difficulty can be eliminated by careful development of a statement of behavioral objectives. This method is basically a logical attack on a learning problem by asking three questions:

1. What do I expect the student to be able to do as a result of this learning experience?
2. What subject matter content and experiences are most likely to produce a change in student performance?
3. How is the performance to be evaluated?

Perspective for the Future

In the growth of programs oriented toward the individualization of learning activities on a school-wide basis, the most critical factor is the human one. It is most important that the perspective of the teaching and administrative staff be altered considerably with respect to the utilization of time, space, and talent. Receptiveness to change and a strong awareness of the need to change not only organizational but also behavior patterns is most necessary. A professional role other than that of the omnipotent disseminator of information is essential if the tools are to be utilized to best advantage.

New questions need to be asked so that the functions and responsibilities of students, teachers, supervisors, specialists, and administrators are properly defined. These persons must be firmly committed to a continual refinement and assessment of procedures that will generate an atmosphere that encourages the individual, both student and professional, to become a better self-sustained learner.

CHAPTER 17

New Dimensions

by

SISTER M. PACIS ROTH, O.S.F.

Sister Pacis has been at Archbishop Ryan Memorial High School since 1960, as chairman of the English Department, assistant principal, and, for the last seven years, as principal. In 1964 she initiated and implemented a modular schedule that has evolved into a nongraded or progressive learning school. Ryan was the first such school in Nebraska, and it has since become a resource center for educators from all over the country. Sister Pacis is a consultant for innovative high schools, and also conducts summer workshops at Creighton University for high school administrators.

WHEN GERTRUDE STEIN lay dying in Paris, her good friend Alice Toklas hovered over her, pen and tablet poised, ready to record for posterity the last words of that literary giant. Gertrude's eyelids fluttered and Alice waited: "Yes, Gertrude? Yes?" Gertrude looked at Alice and asked, not without anxiety, "Alice? Alice, did we get the answer?" Alice, hovering, said, "Yes, Gertrude, yes, we got the answer." Gertrude relaxed and said, "Good. What was the question?" And she died.

Whether or not the facts of the Stein anecdote have been embellished over the years, the point for educators is stark. Educators over the decades have had many right answers, but we have not carefully related the answers to questions. When we begin to do this, we are forced off the very dead center of performance teaching and impoverished learning. This is what we discovered at Archbishop Ryan Memorial High School in Omaha, Nebraska.

Education Questions

Here are questions we asked and answered and implemented. "What is the object of the high school game?" To get the student to learn. "What is the easiest way to learn?" To teach. "Who, then, should do the teaching?" Student-learners to a great extent. "How do we avoid having groups of students merely exchanging ignorances?" Have the staff create 1. a learning climate, and 2. learning tools to direct, activate, and evaluate student performance. "How can teachers have time to do this?" Take away from them the non-teacher tasks that absorb their time and energy but do not use their professional competence—like cafeteria supervision, clerical tasks, disciplinary tasks, test supervision, study hall proctoring "What does this leave for the teacher to do?" To be a professional researcher and educational consultant.

Then we recapped, refined, and redefined. The school is a learning center. A differentiated staff releases the maximum professional expertise of all persons concerned. Learning is really an individualized project, which should permit each student to learn at his own rate of speed and to learn those things best suited to himself as he plans to live in society. Learning should have as an essential by-product the facility of educated decision-making on the part of the learner. How can educators assure this unless the student is faced with multitudes of options: selection of his educational consultants (teachers), selection of his own study groups (Digression: when schools group students, they group by talent whether the students get along with each other or not; when students group themselves, they group on the basis of compatibility, which is humane and motivational), selection of what he will study, where he will do it, for how long, whether he has completed it to his satisfaction and wishes to test out into a new segment of learning, whether he needs to come to school five days a week to get the job done, whether he will master all the objectives and earn all the credit or part of the objectives and gain partial credit. These choices are made in the midst of a professional staff, eminently equipped to challenge the decisions, help a learner reconsider if he makes wrong decisions, evaluate, consult, lead, urge, and sometimes coerce.

Education Fallacies

For too long we have burned incense before false educational idols. Educators have been like comic sleuths looking over their shoulders and following their own footprints. It is time that we fix our educational sights on the 1980s. That is when the students we have now will be functioning in society and taking over the decision-making positions that will shape our geriatric years.

We must begin to be concerned that the climate we create at school is educationally nonpollutant, that it is an evolving, nonstatic, person-oriented, learner-responsible milieu. This means that we must train staff to untie the apron strings they have knotted around students. Too many teachers think: my room, my chalk, my kids, my mop. The student who is still so dependent on a teacher that he needs to be told to take out his book, take out his paper, take out his pencil, put his name on the paper, open the book, turn to page 261, answer questions one through five, is a rather weary prospect as a citizen after graduation.

Change Rationale

The educational change syndrome is fortunately petering out. Educators who have been involved in viable new programs must be impatient with schools that change what they have been doing only for the sake of changing—like refashioning their lock-step time schedule to the more fashionable modular time schedule without changing what happens in the new time structure.

We should be outgrowing the time when structure of any kind dictates what happens in a school. Staffs must begin to use structure as it is needed, and not let structure abuse learning. Generally, structure in a school dictates when something happens, for how long, and with whom. It facilitates life for the administrators of the school, for the staff, and for the students—in that order. Traditional schools, after all, are organized for the convenience of the adults who work in them. This need not be so and, indeed, cannot be so if the school is learner-oriented.

We advocate that students who need structure use it as a tool for learning. When the tool interferes with learning, it must be set aside. The inhibiting thing about following a precise computerized schedule of classes is that the meetings always magnetize everyone to the same starting position each time the class meets. What is the point of a student moving more or less quickly through work according to his need if he has to keep reporting for information or discussion at set intervals?

There are principals who get nervous at the thought that they will not know where everyone is at every moment. It seems a small value to be able to tell Mrs. Jones when she phones to inquire about her son, "Oh yes. He is in room 210 with Teacher X and 29 other students for 13 more minutes." If Mrs. Jones says, "Oh, what a good school you run," on the basis of custodial-care values, then the education work of PTA meetings is cut out for the school. If a student really needs to be located, and this may happen once or twice a day, the PA is available. All major businesses today use this locator system.

Appointment Learning

Once the schedule is not seen as an end but as a means, students must have something to direct them in their use of time. It can be a tool like a learning activities package (LAP) or a contract, something specific to help the student determine how to learn what he needs to learn to earn credit in a course. With some general orientation about procedure, the students then can group themselves, make appointments with their consultants, and set themselves to the task of learning. A teacher's schedule is reshaped daily by the needs of the students who make appointments with him or those appointments the teacher initiates because some students have been remiss in learning, much as a principal's day is shaped each day by the people who need to see him or whom he needs to see.

Students can determine the length of time a course should take them, given their talent and motivation. In effect, they can determine how long high school should be for them—three, four, five years, or any point in between. Calendars cannot dictate when a subject is mastered.

Our School

Education based on the principles cited in this paper is viable, exciting, successful. We know this at Ryan High School. Endorsements? Evaluations? We have them on file, but probably the timid or questing educators must come and see. One thousand to 1,500 educators a year visit and examine our operation. Most of the 50 states and some foreign countries have had representatives in the school, talking to staff and students. (We take visitors now by appointment only, and one group per day.) We have teacher applications from all over the country, as well as from foreign countries.

We are not selective in our enrollment; the admission policy states simply that a student who wishes to enroll any day from any area must be warm and still breathing. We will work with him from there and keep him as long as he needs to be with us to satisfy the requirements for a diploma.

We resist publishing *what* we do. We have hundreds of Learning Activities Packages created by the staff. Our current curriculum has 363 unique course offerings and 1,006 semester hours of credit with no grades (just credit issued or no credit issued). We hold three graduation ceremonies a year for the sake of the parents (though students can get diplomas any time their work is completed). We have no set schedule, with structure-on-demand only. As soon as something works, of course, it is obsolete; and we cannot be bothered recording where we have been.

Ryan, and schools like it, are exciting places to be. Not the least of the excitement comes from stories like this: One day in March a student told a visitor to the school that he would finish his math course that day. The visitor asked the boy what he would do when he finished the course. The options are numerous. The boy looked at the visitor and said simply: "Why, I'll help my friends with *their* math, of course." Isn't that what it's all about?

CHAPTER 18

A School That Cares

by

KENNETH D. JENKINS

Dr. Jenkins is currently the principal of North Miami Beach Senior High School, a new nongraded high school in suburban Dade County (Miami), Florida. Prior to this appointment he served as Director of Student Activities, and later, as Director of Curriculum for Miami Springs Senior High School, Miami Springs, Florida. He has also served as NASSP Administrative Intern at Melbourne (Florida) High School. Dr. Jenkins did his undergraduate work at the University of Florida and his graduate work at the University of Miami.

THE CURRENT educational vogue for the nongraded school is too frequently expressed in organizational schemes that succeed only in redistributing the same old problems and conditions, improving none of them. Principals take students, regroup them within their established structures, and then sit back, glowing with the warmth of accomplishment. Combs expressed it so well when he said:

> We know what we ought to eat, but we don't eat that. We know we ought not to be prejudiced, but we are. Most of us need more information about these things like we need a hole in the head. Yet, whenever we want to improve education, we go right back to the thing we know so well how to do. We provide still more information in the hope that if a little is good, surely a whole lot more would be better.[1]

Schools must provide for different kinds of information as they move beyond organizational patterns to the realities of human problems and processes. Such schools will tend to stress involvement rather than mere attendance, participation rather than regurgitation, and learning rather than absorbing. Miami Springs Senior High School, Miami Springs, Florida, demonstrates ways in which one school has operated to implement these goals.

The Plan

Miami Springs bases its program and operation on three philosophic tenets: responsibility, inquiry, and humanity. It is obvious that these concepts must extend well beyond mere administrative or curricular contrivance. This school not only dispenses knowledge, but exemplifies values, none of which it considers more vital than responsibility.

At Springs, responsibility, as a value, is built into the program. Students are able to exercise responsible behavior by being given real choices, and having made them, they must live with these choices. If the decision proves to be a mistake, then the school will counsel to help ameliorate the difficulty. By making these real choices, students practice responsible behaviors in areas important to them and their lives. For instance, every student at Miami Springs has the opportunity of choosing every aspect of his schedule, including his teachers. Once his schedule is made, he assumes the responsibility for his educational placement. In this manner young people are told that they are trusted to make these decisions. This trust forms the nucleus for the student's assumption of responsibility.

The notion of inquiry and discovery is quite prominent in contemporary education, but little is really done to implement its use. In order for students to want to inquire, it is necessary that they feel free to question, to search, and to discover answers not handed them by the pat statements of a textbook. A school that accepts and promotes divergence, as Springs does, will engender the kind of faith needed to get below the epidermis of knowledge to the skeletal processes of learning. The presence of inquiry and questing is symptomatic of a desire to learn. Every school must strive for this quality.

The third aspect, humanity, is little more than practicing and gaining respect for one's fellow man. Miami Springs respects its students, their opinions, and the choices they make. If a student feels that he needs to change his placement in a course, his decision is respected. Open communication is given credence rather than lip service, from the principal on. When students make their schedule choices in the fall, the most remarkable aspect of the scheduling process is the amount of "help talk" among all concerned. It is not accidental that this phenomenon occurs. The students have real identities; they are known by their names, and are not given a number, even for minute identification purposes. Moreover, this kind of atmosphere implies a tacit demand for reciprocity, and Springs students reciprocate, because they know the school wants to know, understand, and help them.

This philosophical tripod forms the basis from which procedures at Miami Springs have emerged. To implement them the school curriculum has been organized into a series of achievement plateaus or phases. Each subject discipline is arranged so as to provide as much structural flexibility as possible. Placement into these phases is based on several criteria: achievement, both in class and on standardized instruments; aptitude indexes; staff recommendation; and student preference (another way to show trust). But these plateaus are only devices. Their presence demands several concomitant considerations, which, if absent, render any program ineffective and sterile. First, each phase level in each discipline must be treated as a separate course of study, complete with differentiated objectives, expectations, content, activities, and materials. Second, each plateau must be a *temporary* step from which a student can move up or down, depending on the appropriateness of the direction. If a student feels his position is frozen, it is doubtful that he will take any risks; without risks there can be little inquiry; without inquiry, little discovery, and, alas, little real learning. Third, and closely related, provisions for student mobility must be built in, in case a placement is obviously inappropriate. Not only must the student be allowed to re-phase at any time but the decision must also be largely his responsibility. Heretical as this may sound, it works. The rationale of a nongraded school is to make the student feel successful and worthy, even when he is taking chances. To oversimplify—this is how he grows, and learns to enjoy growing. Unless these factors are present, a phasing system is nothing more than an administrative "gimmick."

The nongraded school exists, in large measure, to guide students towards learning, rather than berate them for not learning. If problems in learning arise (as they do in any school), this school gives help by seeking the causes of the problem and dealing with them as humanely and effectively as possible. Punishment only treats symptoms; help tries to root out causes. Miami Springs Senior High is committed to helping. Punishing irresponsible behavior does not change the causes of the behavior any more than taking aspirin eradicates the causes of fever from the body.

The Humanistic Thrust

The school exists not only to perpetuate the culture, but to impart the concept of helping others. It is hoped that students will become subsequent helpers of people. The school places its premium on people learning (to paraphrase Emerson), rather than on the static dissemination of knowledge. How does a school move from complacency to involvement? Is there, or must there be, a relationship between having a nongraded school and concentrating on humanistic endeavors? We think so.

Miami Springs High School believes firmly that one of the fundamental reasons for nongrading a school is to personalize and humanize it, in order to bring children and their learning closer together. It is not accomplished by administrative manipulation, but by the creation of an invigorating, vibrant school atmosphere, physical, aesthetical, and interpersonal. When one walks into the school, he finds himself literally surrounded by examples of student and professional art. The school is a virtual gallery for student artistic endeavors. The physical presence of aesthetic sensitivity lends overwhelming credence to the school's faith in involving students in their learning process. Students come to know that the school cares for them, not as bodies to justify jobs, but as people with needs, talents, expectations, and achievements. They, in turn, treat others in much the same manner. While the situation might seem to promise chaos, in reality it achieves a loose, but very real, sense of order. The school is still standing, and functioning.

Atmosphere is also created by the kind of program a school offers. A rather standard, non-contract curriculum speaks quite loudly about the atmosphere of a school. As part of its humanistic thrust, Springs, on the other hand, adds the dimension of cultural orientation to its courses. Courses in the humanities, such as American Culture, Anthropology, Media, and French conversation not only impart knowledge, but place it in the context of how people have used and will use this knowledge. Courses in the sciences try to make their body of knowledge as relevant as possible; their rationales are predicated on their being important for people. Where thematic presentation is appropriate, the themes are aimed at investigating problems that exist for people. One English theme dealt with the Negro and prejudice; another in history dealt with freedom and responsibility; still another in home economics dealt with sex, individual freedom, and social responsibility. These examples demonstrate the breadth curricular offerings can attain in the flexible atmosphere of a nongraded school.

A third way in which Miami Springs creates its humanistic aura is through its constant search for better ways to educate youngsters. Even the most stable practice is subjected to questioning, modification, or even replacement, if a better way can be developed. Just as each curriculum phase is a temporary plateau of student achievement, the programs and practices at Miami Springs are temporary plateaus, which serve as springboards towards new directions and dimensions of education. Students know that the school itself enters into a search for its own kind of truth, a search that means taking risks. They also know that the school is dedicated to finding more effective educational developments to enhance the opportunities for learning within the school. This continuous search and implementation brings with it an ever-spiraling Hawthorne Effect.[2] Each step becomes a means rather than an end, and a prelude to the next step. The move, initiated in 1968, from the phasing system to a program of continuous progress materials is just such an example. The validity of phasing is not being questioned; what is important is that an effective program of continuous progress education may go even further than phasing in truly individualizing instruction, increasing options for students, and achieving student success in learning factors that breed greater success in future learning.

By way of summary, the somewhat stylized model of a nongraded school in Figure One gives a graphic representation of the dimensions that change a traditional program to a nongraded one. This reorganization adds and modifies the standard dimensions in at least three significant directions. This is what Miami Springs looked like in the first major phase of its growth. The solid lines represent a traditional curriculum. The broken lines represent the changes to a nongraded curriculum. The standard dimension of content is expanded to offer wider and more appropriate curriculum choices. The activities dimension is made more meaningful by differentiating activities according to achievement plateaus. The two-dimensional model achieves three-dimensional meaning by placing these dimensions in the cultural or humanistic milieu. How-

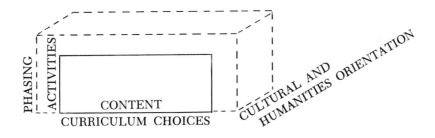

FIGURE ONE

ever, we have said that schools must search for better ways. As the program at Springs evolves, the model might well come to look like Figure Two, which keeps some programs, but ventures into new and more fruitful areas. In these ways an atmosphere is created. It is not ephemeral; it can be felt. It does not demand a great deal of sensitivity; it requires only concern about schools, students, and learning.

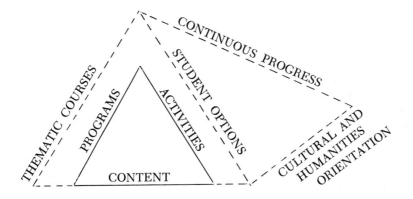

FIGURE TWO

To What End?

What difference does all this make? What are the benefits of making these changes and achieving this atmosphere? Because Springs is what it is, its students are willing to talk, get involved, and work for solutions. This quality is not universal, but neither is apathy. The students help one another, bring cultures together, strive for social integration, adopting something akin to a "There, but for the grace of God, go I" attitude. Springs has a drop-out rate of only two percent; the school feels it is too high. These students stay in school because it has meaning and relevance. They have a chance to succeed, knowing that the curriculum will adjust to them, rather than the reverse being demanded as a prerequisite for success. Above all, Spring's students trust the staff, in a time when the maxim of "Don't trust anyone over thirty" is all too prevalent. They know the school cares, and the school is people.

Teachers who are still excited about learning will find this school an appropriate place to release this excitement. Too often, it is considered gauche to be a dedicated or concerned teacher; at Miami Springs, one is expected to demonstrate these qualities. Teachers try new approaches, do some experimentation, attempt some action research, get more involved, and stimulate more inquiry. They find themselves making the move from being dispensers of knowledge to becoming guides towards learning.

Our world has not only become smaller but also more personal. Isolation of people is neither possible or even desirable. Our society needs people who are capable of liking other people. We live so close to one another that this quality is imperative. It is no longer possible to impart all or even a major part of the culture, for today's ingenuity is tomorrow's obsolescence. We are not so much in need of learned men as of men capable of learning. They are the people who can adapt, make decisions, and function effectively in a changing world. Miami Springs High School believes its program will produce men capable of learning.

Notes

1. Arthur W. Combs, "The Person in the Process," *Humanizing Education: The Person in the Process* (Washington, D.C.: The Association for Supervision and Curriculum Development, 1967), p. 74.

2. "Hawthorne Effect" is the term used to reflect the results of a now classic research study. The study was conducted by Westinghouse, and was designed to determine the effect of a changed environment on productivity. It was found that changing the environment in which a worker was asked to work generally resulted in increased productivity whether or not the change itself was positive or negative.

Selected Bibliography

Compiled by Jan Smith and Marilyn Beebe
University School, Indiana University
Revised by Neal K. Winkler
School of Education, Indiana University

Anderson, Richard C. "The Case for Non-graded Homogeneous Grouping,"
Elementary School Journal 62:193–97, January, 1962.
The author discusses, in progress report fashion, changes in school organization of the New Brunswick, N.J., schools. In this, the first of two
articles, nongraded homogeneous grouping is explained as the design
used. Also included is a frank appraisal of the number and quality of
research reports available to determine the effectiveness of nongraded
homogeneous grouping.
Anderson, Robert H. "Ungraded Primary Classes: An Administrative Contribution to Mental Health," *Understanding the Child* 24:66–72, June, 1955.
Anderson feels that the ungraded program gives better opportunity for
good mental adjustment among pupils, especially for both extremes of a
class. He presents his reasons with some practical examples from the
Milwaukee, Wis., and Park Forest, Ill., programs.
———. *Teaching in a World of Change.* New York: Harcourt, Brace and
World, 1966.
Team teaching and nongraded schools are discussed as two of the major
innovations and changes characteristic of our times.
———, and John I. Goodlad. "Self Appraisal in Non-graded Schools: A
Survey of Findings and Perceptions." *Elementary School Journal* 62:261–
69, February, 1962.
A summary report received from 89 communities which have nongraded
schools is the mainstay of this article. Included in the report are subjective
assessments of strengths and weaknesses of the programs in the following
areas: pupil achievement, pupil adjustment, pupil progress, classroom
atmosphere, impact on teachers and curriculum development, and parent
attitudes.
Asbell, Bernard. "High School for Sky High Learning," *Education Digest*
29:26–28, March, 1964.
A stimulating report of a nongraded plan at Melbourne High near Cape
Kennedy. Specific examples are cited of procedures used in such classes
as English and the sciences.

Austin, Kent C. "The Ungraded Primary School," *Childhood Education* 33:260–63, February, 1957.

This article has outstanding sections on new teacher orientation and public relations for the ungraded program. All the examples are taken from the Park Forest program.

————. "The Ungraded Primary Unit in Public Elementary Schools of the United States," *Dissertation Abstracts* 19:73–74, January, 1958.

Austin traces the development of the nongraded school and reports on his recent survey of nongraded schools.

Backroth, Sister M. Bernaedo, C.P.P.S. "An Evaluation of Ungraded Primary as an Organizational Device for Improving Learning in St. Louis Archdiocesan Schools," *Dissertation Abstracts* 19:2819–20, May, 1959.

This study represents one of the early attempts at evaluating the nongraded organization of elementary schools.

Bair, Medill, and Richard G. Woodward. *Team Teaching in Action.* Boston, Mass.: Houghton Mifflin, 1964.

Team teaching and its relationship to nongrading is explored and investigated. In many respects, team teaching and nongradedness go hand in hand. The book for the most part deals with the development of team teaching.

Ballew, Sheri, "Melbourne High School," *National Association of Secondary School Principals* 47:67–68, May, 1963.

Still more about the nongraded Melbourne High School.

Beggs, David W., III (ed.) *Team Teaching: Bold New Venture.* Bloomington: Indiana University Press, 1964.

In this volume, the possibilities of utilizing team teaching at all levels is explored and some considerations for inaugurating and evaluating team teaching programs are provided.

————, and Edward G. Buffie (eds.). *Independent Study: Bold New Venture.* Bloomington: Indiana University Press, 1965.

In addition to theory, practical suggestions for developing independent study programs in both elementary and secondary schools are discussed.

Berman, L. M. "New School Organization: Same Old Curriculum?" *National Elementary Principal* 47:16–20, November, 1967.

Aspects suggested for reconsideration are: phases of curriculum development, personalized assignments, hypothesis testing and evaluation, and emphasis on the child as an integrated being. If children are to possess the competence necessary for successful living, nongraded schools must give careful attention to developing new curriculums rather than merely reshuffling elements of the old.

Blake, Roy F. "Small Group Research and Cooperative Teaching Problems," *National Elementary Principal* 43:31–36, February, 1964.

A lucid article which summarizes research on small groups and implications for team cooperation and leadership problems. Possible structural and operational solutions are given.

Brinkman, Albert R. "Now It's the Ungraded School," *Education Digest* 27:5–7, October, 1961.

A pep talk on the virtues of an "ungraded" or "primary" school is emphasized throughout.

Brown, B. Frank. "A New Design for Individual Learning." *Journal of Secondary Education* 37:368–75, October, 1962.

Mr. Brown exposits ways in which the present educational system must readjust the content blocks and organization of students and faculties to meet the challenge in this new educational era. The author is principal of the nongraded high school at Melbourne, Fla.

————. *The Nongraded High School.* Englewood Cliffs, N.J.: Prentice-Hall, 1963.

The complete story of one of the nation's first nongraded high schools—Melbourne High School—is described in detail.

————. *The Appropriate Placement School: A Sophisticated Nongraded Curriculum.* West Nyack, N.Y.: Parker Publishing Co., 1965.

The multiphased curriculum is discussed in detail as it relates to the nongraded curriculum in primary, intermediate, and junior and senior high schools.

————. "The Non-graded High School," *Phi Delta Kappan* 44:206–209, February, 1963.

This article deals primarily with nongraded innovations in the secondary schools, with a brief discussion of the implications for colleges. The grouping procedure plus curriculum phases are described briefly. A summation of the changes in physical environment and teacher-student attitudes after three years of ungradedness is included.

————. "The Non-Graded School," *National Association of Secondary School Principals* 47:64–72, May, 1963.

The author discusses the components he sees necessary for a promising and productive nongraded secondary school. Most important among these is the element of independent study. Included in the article are reports from Melbourne, Fla., Middletown, R.I., and Setauket, N.Y.

————. "An Ungraded Secondary School," *National Association of Secondary School Principals* 45:349–52, April, 1961.

An assessment of high school programs of the past and present, and suggestions of new approaches.

————. "The Ungraded High School," *Overview* 2:61, May, 1961.

A positive statement of the advantages of ungradedness at the secondary level, which are explored in detail. One drawback is noted.

Buffie, Edward George. "A Comparison of Mental Health and Academic Achievement: The Nongraded School vs. the Graded School." Unpublished Ed. D. dissertation, School of Education, Indiana University, Bloomington, 1962.

Another of the early attempts to evaluate nongraded and graded schools. This study favors the nongraded form of elementary school organization.

Carbone, Robert F. "Comparison of Graded and Non-Graded Elementary Schools," *Elementary School Journal* 62:82–88, November, 1961.

The basis for this article is the author's doctoral research. Carbone tested three hypotheses: Is there a difference in achievement, mental health, or teacher instruction methods between the graded and nongraded approach? He discovered a significant difference in favor of graded schools in terms of achievement and mental health.

————."Non-graded School: Myth or Miracle?" *Montana Education* 39:17–18, November, 1962.

The author bases this article on the results of his research. A very basic question is raised regarding the nongraded school.

Dean, Stuart E. *Elementary School Administration and Organization.* Bulletin No. 11. Washington, D.C.: U.S. Department of Health, Education, and Welfare, 1960.

A survey regarding the growth and future of nongraded schools.

Doll, Edgar A. "The Four I.Q.'s," *Exceptional Children* 24:56–58, October, 1957.

Criteria for grouping practices could be based on the "Four I.Q.'s"—the intelligence quotient, the inner quest, the ideal qualities, and the innate quirks. Each is explored in depth.

Drake, J. C. "Everything's New But the Walls," *National Education Association Journal* 57:14–16, February, 1968.

Describes a sixty-year-old Kansas City elementary school that attempts to test several ideas of interested educators and laity. The school was chosen because it was not different and selected no special children.

Dufay, Frank R. *Ungrading the Elementary School.* Englewood Cliffs, N.J.: Prentice-Hall, 1966.

Using the Parkway Elementary School on Long Island as his major focal point, the author describes an ungraded elementary school as well as the processes for bringing about such change.

Duval, Frank H., Elizabeth Theiss, Sylvia Stryker, and Edith McKinnon. "Three Heads are Better Than One," *Grade Teacher* 81:61 ff., May, 1964.

An excellent overview of practical problems such as ungraded terminology, organization of student groups, and teacher responsibilities at the intermediate level. Some of the activities are illustrated with pictures.

Eisman, Edward. "What's Brewing in Bassett?" *Audiovisual Instruction* 8:136–37, March, 1963.

A preview of the continuous education program that was to be introduced at Bassett High in California. The program is implemented through extensive testing and sustained by the assistance of many technological devices.

Eldred, Donald M., and Maurie Hillson. "The Non-Graded School and Mental Health," *Elementary School Journal* 63:218–22, January, 1963.

Emlaw, Rita, "Organizing Schools for the Future," *Educational Leadership* 14:288–92, February, 1957.

A very interesting article describing significant movements which have begun in the schools today and will play an important role in the schools of the future.

Fallon, Berlie J. *Educational Innovation in the United States*. Bloomington, Ind.: Phi Delta Kappa, 1966.

The editor provides abstracts of over 600 best school practices initiated between 1957 and 1964.

Filbin, Robert L. "Continuous Progress for All: Implications for the High School," *American School Board Journal* 143:11–14, October, 1961.

Mr. Filbin attempts to present the need for an ungraded approach on the secondary level. He gives some excellent examples of experiments which help his ideas to be more convincing.

Flanagan, J. C. "Functional Education for the Seventies: Project PLAN," *Phi Delta Kappan* 49:27–33, September, 1967.

We already have the beginnings, in 14 schools across the nation, of a functioning model for the educational system demanded by our times. It is the offspring of CREATE, a California center dedicated to actualizing the revolution educators hear about but seldom see. The article describes what CREATE proposes to do and how it will be accomplished.

Forbes, Mary M. "So How Is A.V. Different in a Non-graded Program?" *Audiovisual Instruction* 8:578–79, October, 1963.

A short but enthusiastic affirmation that A.V. material may be used to advantage more freely under a nongraded system.

Gaudet, Joseph H. "Middletown High School," *National Association of Secondary School Principals* 47:70–72, May, 1963.

One of the nation's first nongraded high schools is described.

Gilbert, Jerome H. "Multigraded Development Plan Focuses on Pupil Achievement: Telsa School Breaks through Traditional Graded Structure," *Chicago School Journal* 43:209–14, February, 1962.

The Telsa School is described in some detail. It was one of the first Chicago schools to move in the direction of nongradedness (referred to as continuous education).

————. "Telsa School Broke the Lock Steps," *Elementary School Journal* 64:306–309, March, 1964.

A discussion of steps taken in the Woodlawn community school of Chicago to lessen early school failures. The author discusses the socioeconomic factors behind failure, philosophic reasons for moving into a program of continuous education, and specific methods utilized to implement the program.

Goodlad, John I. "Classroom Organization," in *Encyclopedia of Educational Research*, ed. by Walter Scott Monroe, pp. 221–26. New York: Macmillan, 1960.

The author provides a historical overview of both vertical and horizontal school organization practices. He traces trends in graded vs. nongraded approaches through the recent decades. He raises pertinent questions concerning class size, large group in structure, child security, and use of electronic media.

————. "Inadequacy of Graded Organization—What Then?" *Childhood Education* 39:274–77, February, 1963.

Mr. Goodlad points out several principles of child development which have been ignored by present school organization and suggests solutions for them. He illustrates graphically the overlapping approach of ungraded placement.

————. "More about the Ungraded Unit Plan," *National Education Association Journal* 44:295–97, May, 1955. (This publication will hereafter be referred to as the *N.E.A. Journal.*)

A general appraisal of how the ungraded program works in actual practice, and a compact discussion of the emphases and outcomes of 16 programs.

————. "News and Comment," *Elementary School Journal* 59:1–17, October, 1958.

A comprehensive report on action to improve schools in the communities of Englewood, Fla., Flint, Mich., Fort Wayne, Ind., and University City, Mo.

————. "Promising Practices in Non-graded Schools," *Education Digest* 27:8–10, October, 1961.

An optimistic view of nongraded elementary schools as a much needed and rapidly emerging concept. Two variations of the concept are discussed. The first view identified is one that seeks to encourage learners of varying abilities to move at differentiated rates of progress, while the second is described as one that emerges out of a complex philosophical background, which bears the slogan "teach the whole child."

————. "Ungrading the Elementary Grades," *N.E.A. Journal* 44:170–71, March, 1955.

An artful presentation of the rightful place of organization as it relates to good instruction.

————. "What about Non-grading Our Schools?" *Instructor* 70:6, May, 1961.

A summary of basic factors that point to the need for a nongraded organization are treated in limited detail.

————, and Robert H. Anderson. "Educational Practices in Non-graded Schools: A Survey of Perceptions," *Elementary School Journal* 63:33–40, October, 1962.

Many different concepts of nongradedness are explored in depth.

————, and Robert H. Anderson. *The Nongraded Elementary School.* New York: Harcourt, Brace and World, 1959.

This book represents the first authoritative work regarding the development of the nongraded school. The Park Forest, Ill., schools are featured. A 1963 revision is now available.

————, and Robert H. Anderson. "The Nongraded Elementary School," *N.E.A. Journal* 47:642–43, December, 1958.

An interesting survey involving 150 communities which were experimenting with some form of the ungraded program is described. A very helpful compilation of reasons for successful and unsuccessful experiences is included, as well as a listing of all the schools using an ungraded approach through 1958.

————, and others. "Readiness Levels Replace Grades in the Non-graded Plan," *Elementary School Journal* 57:253–56, February, 1957.
An excellent discussion of how a nongraded primary may be organized according to readiness levels. The authors close with pertinent suggestions for initiating structural changes.

Gore, Lillian. "The Non-graded Primary Unit," *School Life* 44:9–12, March, 1962.
Dr. Gore reports on 10 ungraded schools out of the 28 she had visited and studied. She cites six features basic to all nongraded programs. Test results from Flint, Mich., Milwaukee, and Appleton, Wis., show children's achievements favoring the nongraded school. Author warns against level standards that become more rigid than those of grades. Important questions are raised relative to (1) effect on curriculums, (2) effect on teachers, (3) effect on children.

Gorman, C. J. "Annual Reassignment of Teachers: An Important Ingredient of Nongrading," *Elementary School Journal* 69:192–97, January 1969.
Only when teachers see themselves as leaders can the problems related to individualization, team teaching, and independent study be dealt with effectively. Annual assignment demands that teachers see themselves as learners. When they do, children are likely to find school a more suitable place for learning.

Gran, Eldon E. "Why Not an Ungraded Intermediate Program?" *Instructor* 72:48 ff., January, 1963.
The Douglas School at Ellsworth Air Force Base is described.

Halliwell, Joseph W. "A Comparison of Pupil Achievement in Graded and Non-Graded Primary Classrooms," *The Journal of Experimental Education* 32:59–63, Fall 1963.

Hart, Richard H. "The Non-graded Primary School and Arithmetic," *Arithmetic Teacher* 9:130–33, March, 1962.
A detailed outline of the steps necessary for developing an ungraded arithmetic program, including selection of materials to be used and a testing program.

Heathers, Glen. "Field Research on Elementary School Organization and Instruction," *Journal of Educational Sociology* 34:338–43, April, 1961.
A discussion of the increasing role educational research plays in the improvement of educational practices. Included are suggested ways that applied research may or may not operate. One significant statement is that pilot studies usually are needed to prepare the way for controlled studies.

————. *Organizing Schools Through the Dual Progress Plan.* Danville, Ill.: Interstate, 1967.

————. "Grouping," *Encyclopedia of Educational Research*, fourth edition. New York: Macmillan, 1970.

Hessler, F. W. "Curriculum for Children in the Moon Port Schools," *Educational Leadership* 25:694, October, 1967.

Explains the SPACE curriculum in Brevard County, Florida where the horizontal organization is called phasing. The three phases are basic, regular, and advanced. Staging is the vertical sequence.

Hillson, Maurie. *Change and Innovation in Elementary School Organization.* New York: Holt, Rinehart and Winston, 1966.

This is a book of selected readings in which various grouping plans, departmentalization, team teaching, and nongradedness are featured.

Imhoff, Myrtle, and Wayne Young. "School Organization," *Review of Educational Research* 29:155–64, April, 1959.

An overview of the research in the areas of enrollment, size of classes and its effect, reorganization and grouping trends, promotion practices, length of the school day, and the control of the federal, state, and local governments. A very brief history background is given for each area.

Ingram, Vivian. "Flint Evaluates Its Primary Cycle," *Elementary School Journal* 61:76–80, November, 1960.

An appraisal of Flint's initial work in nongrading. The author notes that both objective data and subjective responses helped substantiate the positive aspects of the evaluation.

Josephine, Sister, C.S.J. "Student Reaction to the Ungraded Primary," *Peabody Journal of Education* 40:291–95, March, 1963.

A summary review of organizational patterns for the elementary schools in the United States is broken down by regions. It is followed by a teacher poll citing reasons why a larger percentage of those primary teachers who responded preferred the ungraded primary unit.

Kauth, Priscilla, and B. Frank Brown. "The Non-graded High School in Melbourne, Fla.," *National Association of Secondary School Principals* 46:127–34, January, 1962.

A report on nongrading procedures at the secondary level. Included are the philosophic presuppositions and implementation methods used to "provide educational experiences for a variety of talents." The authors also touch on the need for a willing faculty as well as student transfer and a guidance program.

Kaya, Esin. "Problems in Evaluating Educational Plans in the School Setting," *Journal of Elementary Sociology* 34:355–59, April, 1961.

A discussion of some of the fundamental problems in evaluating educational plans, with suggested ways for solving these problems. Kaya cites three areas which need closer scrutiny. They are establishing an operational definition of goals, establishing an effective research design, and using valid evaluation instruments.

Kelly, Florence C. "The Primary School in Milwaukee," *Childhood Education* 24:236–38, January, 1948.

An overview of the program of the children through the ungraded program as practiced at Milwaukee.

————. "Ungraded Primary Schools Make the Grade." *N.E.A. Journal* 40:645–46, December, 1951.

An evaluation of the success of the ungraded elementary program in Milwaukee.

Lamers, William M. "Milwaukee's Ungraded Primary Plan," *American School Board Journal* 145:11–18, November, 1962.

A thorough discussion of the ungraded primary plan in Milwaukee. The goals, levels of learning, process of "promotion" or "retention," parent orientation program, and reporting techniques are outlined. Lamers gives many practical hints for a more successful program.

Langer, Howard. "Melbourne Ungraded High," *Senior Scholastic* 83:18-T–19-T, October 4, 1963.

A report of nongrading procedures used in the "first nongraded high school in the U.S." Included are detailed explanations of the "quest" and "remedial" phases of the Melbourne plan and programs as they functioned for two of Melbourne's students.

Manlove, Donald C., and David W. Beggs, III. *Flexible Scheduling: Bold New Venture*. Bloomington: Indiana University Press, 1965.

Complete details for utilizing flexible scheduling at the high school level. Also included are the results of a survey of 33 schools using some form of flexible scheduling.

Mary Alice, Sister, R.S.M. "Administration of the Non-graded School," *Elementary School Journal* 61:148–52, December, 1960.

The author discusses the role of the administrator in initiating a nongraded primary.

————. "New Ventures in School Organization: The Ungraded School and Use of Teacher Aids," *Elementary School Journal* 57:268–71, February, 1957.

A brief comparison of different organizational structures, with special emphasis on the nongraded organization. Emphasized also are those factors necessary to ease transition from a graded to a nongraded organization. The use of teacher aids, as a solution to clerical, lunchroom and playground supervision, housekeeping, and other miscellaneous duties, is proposed.

Mercille, Margaret G. "The Primary School Unit," *Indiana University School of Education Bulletin*, No. 25, January, 1949, pp. 13–19.

A review of all of the more popular promotion and grouping practices used during the past fifty years, with an evaluation of their effectiveness and some of their drawbacks.

Morse, Arthur D. *Schools of Tomorrow—Today*. New York: Doubleday, 1960.

The author describes many new educational innovations. Included are descriptions of nongraded schools.

National Council of Teachers of English Conference. "Topics of Current Interest," *Education* 84:313, January, 1964.

A report of the 1964 activities of the N.C.T.E. and a brief description of a progressive learning program initiated in the Philadelphia Public Schools.

National Education Association Research Division. "Some Organizational Characteristics of Elementary Schools," *National Elementary Principal* 38:52–62, September, 1958.

A discussion of patterns and trends in school organization and supervision.

Norin, W. W. "Some Practices in Grouping," *Childhood Education* 45:189–96, December, 1968.

Lists grouping practices, such as traditional grouping plans, chronological age grading, achievement grouping patterns, ability grouping, newer grouping plans, team teaching, flexible scheduling, middle schools, nongrading, multi-age grouping, and programmed sequence or contract plan.

O'Beirne, Gladys. "An Ungraded Early Elementary School Program," *Educational Method* 21:178–80, January, 1948.

The author describes an adaptation of ungradedness to the community's needs. She describes methods of evaluation, adaptations to individual differences, grouping, and records.

Patterson, G. J. "The Unit Promotion System in the Hamilton Public Schools," *Canadian Education and Research Digest* 3:48–53, March, 1963.

A clear description of nongraded grouping practices (unit system). Considerable attention is devoted to promotion policies.

Peterson, D. L. "Non-graded High School," *School and Community* 49:20–21, September, 1962.

Here is more about the Melbourne High School. Peterson describes the concept of open-ended learning and some of its applications to curricular activities.

Polkinghorne, Ada R. "Parents and Teachers Appraise Primary-Grade Grouping," *Elementary School Journal* 51:271–79, January 1951.

Here is an interesting survey conducted by a primary teacher in the University of Chicago Laboratory School. It describes their ungraded program and gives tabulated responses from parents and intermediate grade teachers.

Prince, Thomas C. "Trends in Types of Elementary School Organization," *American School Board Journal* 106:37–38, June, 1963.

This report on trends in elementary school organization was derived through 200 questionnaires. Analysis of practices and opinions about practice are included. Departmentalization also receives specific attention in the artcle.

Retson, J. M. "Are We Back to the Little Red Schoolhouse?" *Grade Teacher* 83:108–11, February, 1966.

Appleton, Wis., installs a new system of multi-age classes. Advantages are listed. Especially relevant as Appleton was among the nongraded pioneers.

Rogers, V. R. "Nongraded Social Studies," *Instructor* 78:73–74+, May, 1969.

Among the most significant changes are: (1) The curriculum is viewed as a jumping-off place; (2) the teacher becomes an academic consultant, guide, and stimulator; (3) time is provided for free and unguided exploratory work; and (4) teachers keep better records.

Rollins, Sidney P. "High School Where No One Fails," *School Management* 5:77–79, May, 1962.

A description of Middletown, R.I., High School, a six-year secondary school with no grade designations. It has a flexible-time schedule, achievement grouping, team teaching, and a unique pattern of curriculum organization.

Ryan, W. Carson. "The Ungraded Primary Schools," *Understanding the Child* 24:65, June, 1955.

The ungraded program is viewed as an answer to many of the mental health problems among pupils.

Shaplin, Judson T., and Henry F. Olds, eds. *Team Teaching*. New York: Harper and Row, 1964.

Team teaching and nongraded schools have many characteristics in common. These common elements are described and discussed.

Skapski, Mary King. "Ungraded Primary Reading Program: An Objective Evaluation," *Elementary School Journal* 61:41–45, October, 1960.

An excellent presentation of four objective comparisons between graded and nongraded achievement on the primary level. The results favor the ungraded.

Smith, Lois. "Continuous Progress Plan," *Childhood Education* 37:320–23, March, 1961.

The language arts consultant at Appleton, Wis., explains how the ungraded approach is better suited to the growth patterns of individual children's minds.

Snyder, Edith R. "A Community School Looks at Guidance," *Education* 74:483–87, April, 1954.

A description of a school guidance program in a community where the schools had flexible organization.

Stoddard, George B. *The Dual Progress Plan*. New York: Harper and Row, 1961.

A program which is both graded and nongraded in organization is described in detail. In the latter, the following subjects are included: mathematics, science, physical education, and the creative arts. The public school programs in Long Beach and Ossining, New York, are described.

Story, M. L. "Let's Give Winnetka Another Chance," *Educational Forum* 27:99–102, November, 1962.

A description of the Winnetka Plan—an ungraded program of the 1920's which failed—and the reasons why it would be successful today. The author feels the theory followed by Winnetka is excellent and, with proper implementation, could be used very well in programs today.

Thies, H. S. "Who's Ready to Try a Birthday School?" *Nations Schools* 80:76–77, September, 1967.

Ungraded from the start! Start the girls at 4 and the boys at 5. Currently operating in theory only, but the intellectual validity and promise of the approach are great enough to warrant a careful trial and analysis.

Thompson, Ethel. "The Ungraded Plan," *N.E.A. Journal* 47:16–18, January, 1958.

A presentation of many of the problems involved in a graded approach led to acceptance and recognition of the ungraded concept. The author gives some insightful interpretations of pupil movement through an ungraded program.

Wagner, Guy. "What Schools Are Doing in Developing the Continuous Growth Program," Education 79:595–96 May, 1959.

A brief overview of the variety of names and approaches which have been used in developing the ungraded concept. Several recommended readings for further study in the area are also provided.

Washburne, Carleton, and Louis Edward Roths. "The High School Achievement of Children Trained under the Individual Technique," *Elementary School Journal* 28:214–24, November, 1957.

A careful study of the achievement attained in high school by pupils who progressed through elementary school under the "individual technique" of instruction as opposed to those who received traditional class instruction and mass promotions.

———, and Sidney P. Marland, Jr. *Winnetka: The History and Significance of an Educational Experiment.* Englewood Cliffs, N.J.: Prentice-Hall, 1963.

A complete account of the famous Winnetka school system, with its great emphasis on individualized instruction, by the two educators who know it best.

Watson, Robert A. "People Not Projects Will Improve Education," *American School Board Journal* 147:9–11, November, 1963.

A critical look at the team teaching and dual-progress approaches to teaching, as well as some thought-provoking suggestions for improving the quality of teachers' education and pupil products.

Weaver, Fred J. "A Non-Grade-Level Sequence in Elementary Mathematics," *Arithmetic Teacher* 7:431, December, 1960.

The author describes the organization of a mathematics program for a nongraded school.

Wilhour, J. and O. R. Kiehne, "Workshop Produces Continuous Progress Plans," *School and Community* 53:26–27, May, 1967.

Reports on the Benton Plan and the Harris Plan with flexibility the main ingredient within a continuous progress framework.

An Addendum

Compiled by Neal K. Winkler
School of Education, Indiana University
(For those readers who may wish to pursue this subject in greater depth)

Anastasiow, N. J. "Comparison of Two Approaches in Ungraded Reading Instruction," *Elementary English* 45:495–99, April, 1968.

Anderson, R. H. "Nongraded School: An Overview," *National Elementary Principal,* 47:4–10, November, 1967.

———. *Bibliography on Organizational Trends in Schools,* Washington, D.C.: National Educational Association, 1968.

Anthonita, Sister Mary. "Ungraded Primary: An Adventure in Achievement," *Catholic School Journal* 67:68–70, March, 1967.

Barnes, F. P. "Symptoms of Wheelphilia: A Diagnosis," *National Elementary Principal* 47:31–38, November, 1967.

Barnickle, D. W., and R. T. Lindberg. "Unwilling Accelerate: A Problem of the Nongraded School," *Elementary School Journal* 67:84–87, November, 1966.

Barone, F. J. "The Answer Is 'A Performance Curriculum'," *English Journal* 56:227–28+, February, 1967.

Beggs, David, III, and Edward G. Buffie. *Nongraded Schools in Action,* Bloomington: Indiana University Press, 1967.

Behrendt, D. "Away with Tradition: Multiunit Schools in Wisconsin," *American Education* 6:18–22, January, 1970.

Bernarda, Sister Mary. "Ungraded Pattern," *National Catholic Education Association Bulletin* 63:420–25, August, 1966.

Besvinick, S. L., and J. Crittendon. "Effectiveness of a Nongraded School," *School and Society* 96:181–84, March 16, 1968.

Bethune, P. "Nova Plan for Individualized Learning," *Science Teacher* 3:55–57, November, 1966.

Blake, H. E., and A. W. McPherson. "Individualized Instruction: Where Are We? A Guide for Teachers," *Educational Techniques* 9:63–65, December, 1969.

Boston, R. E., and M. S. Wendt. "Non-grading an Entire System," *Michigan Education Journal* 43:21–22, January, 1966.

Brandt, R. S. "Middle School in a Non-Graded System," *Secondary Education* 43:165–70, April, 1968.

Brody, E. B. "Achievement of First and Second Year Pupils in Graded and Nongraded Classrooms," *Elementary School Journal* 70:391–94, April, 1970.

Brossard, C. "School for the Future: Garden Springs Elementary School, Lexington, Kentucky," *Look* 29:55–56+, March 9, 1965.

Budde, R. "Jump on the Nongraded Bandwagon? Stop! Think!" *National Elementary Principal* 47:21–23, November, 1967.

Carswell, E. M. "Nongraded School: Planning for It, Establishing It, Maintaining It," *National Elementary Principal* 47:11–15, November, 1967.

Casavis, J. N. "Non-gradedness: A Formula for Change," *New York State Education* 57:22–23, December, 1969.

Chadwick, R. E., and others. "Report Card in a Nongraded School," *National Elementary Principal* 47:22–28, January, 1968.

Chittister, M. P. "Non-graded Educational System: An Analysis," *Catholic Education Research* 65:582–89, December, 1967.

Champlin, J. R. "Spirit in Search of Substance: Another View of Nongradedness," *New York State Education* 56, May, 1969.

Cirone, C., and P. Emerson. "Slow Learner in a New Setting: A Continuous Program," *New York State Education* 53:19, January, 1966.

Cole, C. A. "Viewing the Nongraded Intermediate School," *Pennsylvania School Journal* 118:263+, May, 1970.

Collier, C. C. "Nongraded School," *School and Society* 94:32+, January 22, 1966.

Cunningham, R. "Implementing Nongraded Advancement with Laboratory Activities as a Vehicle: An Experiment in Elementary School Science," *School Science and Math* 67:175–81, February, 1967.

Dagne, F. A. "Personalized Instruction," *Illinois Education* 56:68–70+, October, 1967.

————. "Nongraded School," *Educational Leadership* 25:122–23, November, 1967.

————, and D. W. Barnickle. "Two Schools that are Nongraded: How, What, Why," *Instructor* 78:63–70, March, 1969.

Dean, S. E. "Nongraded Schools," *School Life* 47:19–23, December, 1964.

Dobbs, V., and D. Neville. "Effect of Nonpromotion on the Achievement of Groups Matched from Retained First Graders and Promoted Second Graders," *Journal of Educational Research* 60:472–75, July, 1967.

Douglass, M. P. "Does Nongrading Improve Reading Behavior?" *Claremont Reading Conference Yearbook* 31:178–90, 1967.

Dufay, F. R. "When Nongrading Fails," *School Management* 11:110–13, February, 1967.

————, *Ungrading the Elementary School*, West Nyack, N.Y.: Parker Publishing Company, 1966.

Dyer, P. "Language Arts in the Nongraded School: Symposium," *Elementary English* 46:110–46, February, 1969.

Eddinger, J. "Report Cards, Who Needs Them?" *Grade Teacher* 86:68–70, January, 1969.

Education Digest, "Ways to Build Mistakes Out of Your Middle School," 36:11–14, November, 1970.

Ellison, M. "Let's Ungrade and Upgrade the English Curriculum," *English Journal* 56:211–15+, February, 1967.

Figurel, J. A. "Organizing to Provide for Individual Differences," *Conference on Reading University of Pittsburgh Report* 20:117–22, 1964.

Fleck, H. "Implications of the Nongraded School," *Forecast for Home Economics* 15, February, 1969; 17, November, 1969.

Ford, J. E. "Cassville Individualized Teaching," *School and Community* 55:15, May, 1969.

Franklin, M. P. "Multigrading in Elementary Education," *Childhood Education* 43:513–15, May, 1967.

————. "Nongraded Schools," *Education Forum* 30:331–34, March, 1966.

Fulford, I. "Unhurried, Unharried Climate Accommodates Continuous Learning," *Minnesota Journal of Education* 47:18–20, November, 1966.

Garth, W. D. "Marks: How Much Do They Mean?" *PTA Magazine* 63, April, 1969.

Gaskell, W., and J. Sheridan. "Team Teaching and the Social Studies in the Elementary School," *Elementary School Journal* 68:246–50, February, 1968.

Glougau, Lillian, and Murray Fessel. *The Nongraded Primary School,* West Nyack, N.Y.: Parker Publishing Company, 1967, 294 pp.

Glougau, L. "Make Me a Nongraded," *National Elementary Principal* 44:51–54, May, 1965.

Goldman, B. A. "War Is On: Graded vs. Nongraded: A Parody," *Peabody Journal of Education* 45:9–10, July, 1967.

Goodlad, J. I. "Diagnosis and Prescription in Educational Practice," *Education Digest* 31:8–11, May, 1966.

————. "Meeting Children Where They Are: Nongraded Classes at University Elementary School, University of California, Los Angeles," *Saturday Review* 48:57–9+, March 20, 1965.

————. "Toward 2000 A.D. in Education," *N.C.E.A. Bulletin* 65:16–22, August, 1968.

Goodson, R. A. "Success in the City," *Virginia Journal of Education* 61:9–10, October, 1967.

Gordon, W. M., and others. "Im Palle: A New Approach to Secondary School Language Arts," *English Journal* 59:534–39, April, 1970.

Grade Teacher, "No Child is Failing in this School," 86:70–71, January, 1969.

————. "Here's What Individualized Instruction Would Mean to You," 87:82–86, October, 1969.

Graves, W. H., Jr. "Nongraded Plan in Texas," *Texas Outlook* 50:10–11+, June, 1966.

Grooms, M. Ann. *Perspectives on the Middle School,* Columbus, Ohio: Charles E. Merrill, Inc., 1967.

Haas, A. "First-Year Organization of Elmcrest Elementary School: A Nongraded Team-Teaching School," *American School Board Journal* 151:22+, October, 1965.

Haddock, T. T. "Individualized Instruction Through Student Contacts," *Arizona Teacher* 55:10–11+, May, 1967.

Hart, H. C. "Classroom Structures Rapidly Changing: Nongraded Instruction," *Education* 86:200–201, December, 1965.

Heathers, G. "School Organization: Nongrading Dual Progress and Team Teaching," *National Social Study Education Yearbook* 65 pt. 2:110–34, 1966.

Hoban, P. F., and B. J. McManus. "How to Nongrade a Small High School: Cycling Courses in Social Studies and English," *School Management* 9:79–81, September, 1965.

Hoffman, J. P. "Reading Group Distribution Board," *National Elementary Principal* 47:42–43, January, 1968.

Hoover, W. F. "Patterns of Organization for Learning," *Audio Visual Instructor* 13:588–90, June, 1968.

Horowitz, M., and H. Smithman. "MacDonald College Dual Progress Plan: A Study in Curriculum Development and School Reorganization," *Canadian Education Research Digest* 8:60–67, March, 1968.

Honsego, B. E. J. "Nongraded Elementary School: Selected Problems," *Canadian Education Research Digest* 8:245–56, September, 1968.

Houts, P. L., "Profile of the Nongraded Child," *National Elementary Principal* 47:4–9, January, 1968.

Hogles, E. M. "Non-Streaming Benefits," *Times Education Supplement* 2756:871, March 15, 1968.

Hunter, M. C. "Home-School Communication," *National Elementary Principal* 47:24–30, November, 1967.

———. "Teachers in the Nongraded School," *National Education Association Journal* 55:12–15, February, 1966.

Instructor, "Flexible School: Meadow Moor School, Salt Lake City," 79:36–38, January, 1970.

———, "Kaleidoscope School: Ossington Public School (Junior) Toronto, Ontario," 78:46–48, November, 1968.

Irving, R. "Industrial Arts in the Ungraded Continuous-Learning School," *School Shop* 29:33–35, January, 1970.

Jackson, J. W. "Individualized School," *Journal of Secondary Education* 41:195–200, May, 1966.

Johnson, J. H. "New Appraisal of Semi-Departmentalization in the Elementary School," *Canadian Education Research Digest* 6:65–73, March, 1966.

Jones, J. C., and others. "Comparison of Pupil Achievement After One and One-Half and Three Years in a Nongraded Program," *Journal of Educational Research* 61:75–77, October, 1967.

Lachelt, M. R. "Nongrading: Encouraging Flexibility to Meet Individual Differences," *Minnesota Journal of Education* 49:12, December, 1968.

Lee, B. "Not a Solitary Seeking for Individual Glory: Touring the Non-Graded Schools of Dade County Florida," *Kentucky School Journal* 46:27–28, March, 1968.

Lewin, D. "Go Slow on Non-Grading," *Elementary School Journal* 67:131–34, December, 1966.

Lewis, James. *A Contemporary Approach to Nongraded Education*, West Nyack, N.Y.: Parker Publishing Company, 1969.

Lieberth, M. L. "Case for Nongraded Schools," *Catholic School Journal* 70:38+, March, 1970.

Lindsey, J. F. "Non-Graded Programs: Which One?" *Elementary School Journal* 68:61–62, November, 1967.

Lindvall, C. M., and J. O. Bolvin. "Programmed Instruction in the Schools: An Application of Programming Principles in Individually Prescribed Instruction," *National Social Study Education Yearbook* 66 pt. 2:217–54, 1967.

Macbeath, I. "Grade System Abolished in Wealthy Westchester," *Times Education Supplement* 2710:1405, April 28, 1967.

McCarthy, R. J. "Nongraded Middle School," *National Elementary Principal* 47:15–21, January, 1968.

McGuire, Brian P. "The Grading Game," *Today's Education* 18:32–34, March, 1969.

Mitzel, M. A. "Why Keep Cumulative Records," *Elementary School Journal* 66:195–99, January, 1966.

McLeod, D. M. "What Is a Nongraded School?" *Canadian Education Research Digest* 8:38–45, March, 1968.

McLaughlin, W. P. "Phantom Nongraded School," *Phi Delta Kappan* 19:248–50, January, 1968.

Miller, Richard I., ed. *The Nongraded School*, New York: Harper and Row, 1969, 289 pp.

Montean, J. J. "Dual Progress Plan in the West Irondiquoit Central School District," *Science Education* 50:39–43, February, 1966.

Moore, D. W. "Individualized Instruction: Achievement Levels Program," *Texas Outlook* 50:36–37, April, 1966.

National Education Association. *The Nongraded School*, Washington: Department of Elementary School Principals, 1968.

National Education Association Research Division. "Grade Organization and Nongrading Programs," *National Education Association Research Bulletin* 45:118–20, December, 1967.

———. "Middle Schools in Theory and in Fact," *The Education Digest* 35:26–28, September, 1969.

———. "Middle School Action," *Elementary Education* 15:5+, Fall, 1969.

———. "Nongraded Schools: Summary of Nongraded Schools," *National Education Association Research Bulletin* 43:93–95, October, 1965.

Neubauer, D. "Nongraded School: Some Current Questions," *National Elementary Principal* 47:2–3, January, 1968.

Niess, C. "Nongraded Program for the Small High School," *National Association of Secondary School Principals' Bulletin* 50:19–27, February, 1966.

O'Leary, H. F., and R. F. Murphy. "One Ounce of Prevention: Consider Continuous Progress Program," *Minnesota Journal of Education* 49:10–11, December, 1968.

Otto, Henry J. *Nongradedness: An Elementary School Evaluation,* Austin, Tex.: Bureau of Laboratory School Monograph no. 21 (University of Texas), 1969.

Paul, Sister Mary. "Administration Problems of the Nongraded School," *NCEA Bulletin* 64:144–47, August, 1967.

Pratt, H. M. "Space a Plan to Meet Children's Needs," *Instructor* 76:19, January 1967.

Read, E. A. "Educational Practice and the Theory of Continuous Pupil Progress," *Audio Visual Instructor* 15:33–40, February, 1970.

Reed, W. "Maxi Learning From Mini Courses: Wilson High School, Portland, Oregon," *Senior Scholastic* 94:10+, March 7, 1969.

Resnik, H. S. "High School With No Walls: Philadelphia's Parkway Program," *Education Digest* 35:16–19, March, 1970.

Rita, Sister. "Ungrading The Primary School," *Catholic School Journal* 69:23–27, May, 1969.

Rhoades, W. M. "Erasing Grade Lines," *Elementary School Journal* 67:140–45, December, 1966.

Rollins, Sidney P. *Developing Nongraded Schools,* Itasca, Ill.: F. E. Peacock Publishers, Inc., 1968.

Ryan, B. "Last Look at the Little Red Schoolhouse: Callaboose, Kentucky," *Parents Magazine* 44:54–56, February, 1969.

Sartain, H. W. "Application of Research to the Problem of Instructional Flexibility," *Conference on Reading, University of Pittsburgh Report,* 22:97–113, 1966.

Saylor, J. Galen, and William M. Alexander. *Curriculum Planning for Modern Schools,* New York: Holt, Rinehart and Winston, 1966.

School Management, "Anywhere School: One City District's Break With the Past: Parkway Program," 13:46–48+, December, 1969.

School and Society, "Nongraded School," 94:32+, January 22, 1966.

Senior Scholastic, "School of Tomorrow, Today: P.S. 219, Flushing, New York," 89: (sup. 2), October 28, 1966.

Shearron, G. F., and H. Wait. "Nongraded Elementary Schools: A Survey of Practices," *National Elementary Principal* 47:39–42, November, 1967.

Shields, M. "Reading and Transition to Junior School," *Educational Research* 11:143–47, February, 1969.

Simon, Sidney B. "Down With Grades," *Today's Education* 58:24, April, 1969.

Sloan, F. A., Jr. "Nongraded Social Studies Program for Grades Four, Five, and Six," *National Elementary Principal* 45:25–29, January, 1966.

Smith, Lee L. *Teaching in a Nongraded School,* West Nyack, N.Y.: Parker Publishing Company, 1970.

Splawn, R. E. "Nongraded Enterprise at Seminole High," *Texas Outlook* 52:36–37, January, 1968.

Sponberg, R. A. "Teacher-Written TLU's: Teacher Learning Units are Unique to Project Plan," *Instructor* 77:101, May, 1968.

Stauffer, R. G., and A. J. Harris. "Is Cross-Class Grouping Effective? Joplin Plan," *Instructor* 77:25+, April, 1968.

Stephens, E. "Ding Dong, the Bells are Gone: Chippewa Valley High School, Mount Clemens, Michigan," *Seventeen,* 25:410–11, August, 1966.

Stevens, W. K. "School Without Walls: Philadelphia's Parkway Program," *Times Education Supplement* 2858:4, February 27, 1970.

Tewksbury, John L. *Nongrading in the Elementary School.* Columbus, Ohio: Charles E. Merrill, Inc., 1967.

Thomas, J. I. "Reconciling Theory and Practice in the Elementary School," *Elementary School Journal* 68, April, 1968.

————. "Critique: The Appropriate Placement School," *Educational Leadership* 26:355–58, January, 1969.

Turner, W. E. "Ungraded Social Studies Through a Library Approach," *Elementary School Journal* 68:26–30, October, 1967.

————. "Plan to Appraise Individual Progress for Continuous Learning," *Elementary School Journal* 69:426–30, May, 1969.

————. "Ungraded Primary Room at Kremlin," *Montana Education* 42:19, April, 1966.

Ubben, G. C. "Look at Nongradedness and Self-Paced Learning," *Audio Visual Instructor* 15:31, February, 1970.

Ward, D. N. "Continuous Progress," *Texas Outlook* 52:65–67, October, 1968.

Warren, J. W. "Tour of Nongraded Schools," *National Elementary Principal* 47:29–33, January, 1968.

Watson, C. "Learning and Liking It: Lincoln School, Staples, Minnesota," *American Education* 6:18–22, May, 1970.

Webb, C., and J. H. Baird. "Learning Differences Resulting from Teacher and Student-Centered Teaching Methods," *Higher Education* 39:456–60, November, 1968.

Weise, D. F. "Nongrading Electing and Phasing: Basics of Revolution for Relevance," *English Journal* 59:122–30, January, 1970.

Wendt, M., and R. E. Boston. "Continuous Progress from K to 12," *Michigan Education Journal* 46:26–29, January, 1969.

Williams, W. "Academic Achievement in a Graded School and in a Nongraded School," *Elementary School Journal* 67:135–39, December, 1966.

Wilson, R. R. "We Formed a Vertical Team," *Instructor* 79:129, April, 1970.

Wolfson, B. J. "Promise of Multiage Grouping for Individualizing Instruction," *Elementary School Journal* 67:354–62, April, 1967.

Wood, F. H. "McClever Plan: An Innovative Non-graded Foreign Language Program," *Modern Language Journal* 54:184–87, March 1970.

Wormley, G. W. "Non-graded Classes: A Better Start for Your Kids?" *Farm Journal* 90:74, February, 1966.

Index

ability grouping. *See* grouping students

academic house plan, 253–56, 261–62

achievement: compared to competence, 123

achievement tests, 40, 67, 140–41, 200, 277–80

administration, school: decentralized, 126–27

administrator, school: in educational change, 126–29, 144–46, 147–48, 191–92, 194, 195, 198–99

age-grading, 31, 40

Alexander, William A., 18

American Association for the Advancement of Science, 89

anarchy: need for, in high school, 165–66

Andersen, G. I., 211

Anderson, Robert H.: 5, 19: quoted, 6, 16–17, 29, 33

Anthonita, Sister Mary, 19

anxiety, student, 35, 174–75, 211

"appointment learning," 298

Archbishop Ryan Memorial High School, Omaha, Neb., 296–99

arithmetic. *See* mathematics

audio-visual aids, 109–10, 255–56, 291, 292

Austin, Kent C., 17

Baltimore, Md.: nongraded program in, 38

basal readers. *See* readers

Batavia, N. Y.: program for slow learners in, 9

Baynham, Dorsey, 285

Beatty, Willard W., 11

Binford Junior High School, Bloomington, Ind., 268–83

Biological Sciences Curriculum Study, 159

Bloom, *Taxonomy of Education Objectives*, 159

Bloomington, Ind.: results of diagnostic tests in, 24

Bluffton, Ind.: platoon system in, 12

board of education: role in planning nongraded schools, 194–95

Brandwein, Paul, 131

Brickell, Henry M.: quoted, 191

Brigham Young University Laboratory Schools, 213

British primary schools, 20

Bronxville, N. Y.: Winnetka Plan in, 11

Brossard, C., 19

Broward County, Fla., School District, Developmental Research Center, 243–51

Brown, B. Frank, 19, 49

Bruner, Jerome S.: quoted, 31, 128, 152, 212

buildings, school. *See* school buildings

Burk, Frederick, 9, 10, 11

Burton, William H., 30

California Statewide Social Sciences Study Committee, 105–107

Cambridge, Mass.: modification of graded schools in, 8

Carter, James G., 5

Casavis, J. N., 20

Casis Elementary School, Austin, Tex., 175–79, 180, 181, 182

change: in education, 20, 26, 126–27, 144–46, 147–48, 188–91

Chase, Francis, 192

Chicago, Ill.: individualized instruction in high schools in, 10–11

327

children, disadvantaged, 111–12
children, gifted, 8–9, 23
children, slow-learning. *See* slow-learning students
children's rights, 118
classroom seating plan, 70
Cleveland, Ohio,: nongraded schools in, 16
Cole, Luella, 32
Coleman, James, 123
Coleman Report, 114, 116, 142
collective bargaining by teachers, 192
college, 4, 120
College Avenue School, Athens, Ga., 16
Combs, Arthur.: quoted, 300
Commission on the Experimental Study of the Utilization of the Staff in the Secondary School, 19, 284
Committee on Economic Development: quoted, 216
communism; course in, 151nl
community and school relations, 125–26, 128, 148, 194–95, 201, 203
computers: and social science program, 110; and student records, 30–36
conferences, parent-teacher, 176, 260
conferences, student-teacher, 247, 248
Continuous Progress Plan, 16
continuous progress program in high school, 136–39, 155, 158–62
continuous progress schools. *See* nongraded schools
continuous progress theory, 208–13
contracts, educational, 11, 64, 67, 255, 264, 298
Cook, Walter W.: quoted, 210
Cooperative Group Plan, 13
cooperative teaching. *See* team teaching
counselors, guidance, 141
Cronbach, Lee J.: quoted, 31, 32, 211
Culkin, John: quoted, 146

Dalton Plan, 10–11
dame school, 4
data retrieval bank, 109–10
Dean, Stuart quoted, 17–18
departmentalization, 12, 15

district school, 4–5
Doll, Edgar A.: quoted, 30
Drake, J. C., 20
dropouts, school, 6, 153
Dual Progress Plan, 13–14, 187–88
education, public support of, 4
Dwight D. Eisenhower Elementary School, Fort Lauderdale, Fla., 243–44

Elizabeth, N. J.: more frequent promotion in, 7
Enders, Mary, 60
English influence on schools in U. S., 4
European influence on schools in U. S., 4, 5
evaluation of students: 164, 215, 248; basic tenets, 31–32, 87; method of, 67–69, 96–97; use of computers in, 229–36; at Meadowbrook, 266–67; at Binford, 282
evaluation, self, 68, 222–24, 247

Fairview School District #72, Skokie, Ill.: nongraded science program at, 87–99
field trips, 112
Flexible Progress Plan, 15
Fond du Lac, Wis.: nongraded schools in, 16
Fort Worth, Tex.: evaluation of schools in, 174–75
Fox Lane Middle School, Bedford, N. Y., 115, 252–56
Frazier, Alexander, 28
Fresno, Cal.: nongraded schools in, 38

Gardner, John W.: quoted, 189, 209
Gary, Ind.: platoon system in, 12
Gillen, Sister Alice, 38
Glencoe, Ill. nongraded schools in, 16
Goff, Charles E., 267
Golding, William, *Lord of the Flies*, 118
Goodlad, John I.: 5, 16, 17, 208, 238–39: quoted, 6, 31, 33
Goodrich, Lowell P., 16
Gordon, Edmund, 142

grade reports, 10, 97, 130, 131, 138, 176, 181
Grade-Standard Theory, 209, 210
graded schools: historical background, 3, 5–6; early modifications, 7–15; criticism of, 7, 10, 14, 23–24, 84–86; problems, 189–90
Grambs, Jean D., 49
Grant, Nigil, 122
Gray, William S.: quoted, 32
grouping students: 8–9, 22, 181; by age, 31, 40; in elementary school, 38–42; in mathematics, 46–49; in science, 94–95; in high school, 136–39, 162; at Meadowbrook, 265; at Binford, 277–82; by compatibility, 296

Hall, Samuel, 5
Hawthorne Effect, 314
Head Start project, 21
Heathers, Glen, 88
"high-agency" students, 267
high schools, nongraded: 10–12, 19, 49–50, 135–51; phasing program in, 136–39, 156–58; continuous progress program in, 136–39, 155, 158–62; atmosphere, 142–44; principal and staff, 144–48, 163; teachers, 144–47, 150–51, 155, 163–65; physical plant, 148–49; evaluation, 149–51, 162–64; curriculum, 152–67
houses, academic, 253–56, 261–62

Immaculate Conception School, Dayton, Ohio: ungraded reading program at, 59
independent study, 149, 276–77, 285, 287, 290–92
Indiana University Evaluation Center in Reading Education, 60
individual differences: 7, 8, 13, 23, 28, 30, 32, 49, 99, 124, 135, 255; tested, 24–25; variety of, 119–21; briefing parents on, 201–202; theory of, 209–13, 258
individualized teaching: xi, xii, 110–12, 20; in reading, 70–72, 227–28; in science, 95, 220–25; in social studies, 104, 106, 108–10; in high

school, 140–42; varies, 173–74; in theory of continuous pupil progress, 208–13, 214; based on learner's need, 215–16; in spelling, 217–18; in mathematics, 218–19, 225–26; organization for, 236–40; at Nova Schools, 243, 245, 247–49; at Fox Lane, 255; at Meadowbrook, 264; at Ridgewood, 292–93; at Ryan, 296, 298
in-service training for teachers, 56, 145, 164, 197
instructional materials: 20; for reading, 63–64; for social sciences, 109–10
instructional materials center: 64; for social sciences, 109–10; at Fox Lane, 255–56; at Meadowbrook, 263; at Ridgewood, 291, 292
intelligence quotient, 30, 39–40, 118
intelligence tests, 40, 67, 278
interest inventory, 65

Johnson, Glenn R., 172–74
Jones, Maureen, 220
junior high schools: criticized, 18, 115; nongraded, 49; Meadowbrook, 257–67; Binford, 268–83

kindergarten, 21
King, Bettina, 266

laboratory activities, 89, 92, 95, 159
laboratory phase of instruction at Ridgewood, 290–92
Lamb, Pose, 60
language arts, nongraded, 34, 54, 59, 268–83
Latin grammar school, 4
laws, school, 5
Lazarus, Arnold, 60
learning activities packages (LAPS), 137–38, 161–62, 245–48, 255, 292–93, 298, 299
learning center, See instructional materials center
learning, individualized. See individualized teaching
learning process: in science, 78–84; varies, 128
learning team, 39, 124, 125

libraries: classroom, 9; school, 50, 64, 149, 175, 176, 276–77, 291
Lieberman, Myron, 192
Long Beach, Cal.: Dual Progress Plan in, 10
Los Angeles, Cal.: individualized learning in, 10

McDade, James E., 11
McDonough, Ernestine, 267
McGuffey Eclectic Reader, 5
McLoughlin, William R., 171–72
Mann, Horace, 5
mathematics; in nongraded education, 34; nongraded elementary program in, 45–49; individualized instruction in, 218–19; continuous progress in, 225–26
Mead, Margaret, 115, 121
Meadowbrook Junior High School, Newton, Mass., 147, 257–66
Melbourne High School, Melbourne, Fla., 49–50
Miami Springs Senior High School, Miami Springs, Fla., 156–58
middle schools: 18, 20, 64, 113–33; Fox Lane, 252–56
Middlesex County, Conn., and student classification, 5
Middletown, R. I.: nongraded school at, 50
Milwaukee, Wis.: oldest nongraded school plan in, 16
monitorial system, 6
MODU-BUILDING, 148
Mort, Paul R., 208
Moskow, Michael H., 192
Mountain Lakes, N. J.: nongraded schools in, 38

National Education Association Project on Instruction, 19
National Education Association Research Division, 17, 18
National Elementary Principals Department, 19
National Science Foundation, 200
New York City Bureau of Curriculum Development, 57
nongraded high schools. *See* high schools, nongraded

nongraded schools: benefits, xii–xiii, 44–45, 50–51; growth, xii, 15–20; basic goals, xii, 23, 29–32, 34–38, 78, 86–87, 102–103, 136, 152–54, 208–13, 216, 285–87, 296, 301–304; costs, 7, 64, 98; defined, 17, 21–23, 44–45; justification, 23–26; bibliographies, 51, 184–87; analysis of scholastic achievement of, 171–72, 266–67; evaluation, 150–51, 162–64, 179–81, 199–201; suggestions for research, 182–84; planning for, 189–91
non-promotion, 10, 30, 32, 35
normal curve, 118
normal school: first, 5
North Denver, Col.: enriched program for bright students, 9
Nova High School, Fort Lauderdale, Fla., 158–62, 243–51
Nystrand, Raphael O., 192

one-room school, 5
Orange, Vt.: learning center at middle school in, 64
Ossining, N. Y.: Dual Progress Plan in, 13

parent-teacher conferences, 176, 260
Parent-Teacher Association, 195, 202, 298
parents: reports to, 36, 54, 57, 68–69, 97, 176, 248, 265–66; orientation of, for nongrading, 194, 195, 196, 201–13
Parkhurst, Helen, 11
Patterson, Franklin, 49
Petoski, Mich.: nongraded schools in, 16
Petty, Mary Clare, 176
phasing, in nongraded high school, 136–39, 155–58
Phillips, Beeman N., 175
Piaget, Jean, 80–81, 98–99
Plato: quoted, 163
platoon system, 12
Pope, Alexander, 3
Portland, Ore.: modification of graded schools in, 8–9
Portsmouth, Va.: nongraded classes in, 54–55

pre-primary school, 21
President's Commission on National Goals, 209
primary unit, 17–18
principal: role in nongraded high school, 144–46, 147–48
promotion of students, 7–8, 35
Providence, R. I.: and student classification, 5
Prussia: graded schools in, 5
public support of education, 4
Pueblo, Col.: modified graded schools in, 9–10
pupil. *See* student

Quincy Grammar School, 5

readers, 36–38, 59–60
reading: remedial, 9, 72–73; nongraded program in, 36–38, 54–74; ability and student grouping, 34–36, 38–44; readiness, 41; skills, 57–58, 60–63, 73–74, 227–28
records of student progress, 36, 54, 57, 71, 215, 229–36
Red Guard Movement in China, 118
reports to parents, 36, 54, 57, 68–69, 97, 176, 248, 265–66
research suggestions, 182–84
Richmond, Cal.: nongraded reading land language arts program in, 59
Richmond, Va.: nongraded schools in, 16
Ridgewood High School, Norridge, Ill., 50, 284–94
relevance in high school curriculum, 139–140, 155
Rogers, Will: quoted, 165
Russian education, 122–23
Ryan Memorial High School, Omaha, Neb., 295–99

St. Louis, Mo.: modification of graded school in, 8
Santa Barbara, Cal.: Concentric Plan in, 9
school administration. *See* administration, school
school buildings, 148–49, 197–98
school finances, 126

school spirit, 142–44
science: definition, 78; how children learn, 78–84; basic processes of, 89–90
science education, nongraded: need for, 34, 84–87; difficulties in starting, 76–77; summer program in, 98–99; philosophy, 86–87; at Fairview School District, 87–88; in primary grades, 98–99, 220–25; in high school, 158–62
Search, Preston W., 10
seating arrangements, 70
Secondary Continuous Advancement Program at Binford Junior High School, 268–83
self-evaluation, 68, 222–24, 247
shorthand: individualized teaching of, 293
Slater, Eva M., 16
slow-learning students, 9, 22, 30, 42, 54–55, 72–73, 96, 147, 153, 162
social maturity: a factor in grouping students, 40
social studies: purpose of, 102–103; nongraded primary program in, 105–107; nongraded intermediate program in, 107–11; at Binford, 268–71, 273, 275, 281–82
Soviet schools, 122–23
spelling: individualized teaching of, 217–18
Staff Utilization Studies, 19, 284
Steffenson, Robert, 230
Stein, Gertrude, 295
Stensrud, Raymond D., 225
Stoddard, George D., 13, 87–88
student-centered curriculum, 215–16, 297
student decisions, 260, 265, 296, 301
student diaries: evaluate nongraded schools, 172–73
student failure, 6–8
student performance information management, 229–36
student placement. *See* grouping students
student role in educational change, 192
students, evaluation of. *See* evaluation of students

teacher aides, 141, 236, 254

teacher-counselor, 132, 141, 259

teacher-training schools, 5

teachers: role in nongraded education, 25, 64–67, 95–96, 165, 214–15, 286–87; "ungrading" of, 56; meetings, 145, 147–48, 176, 193; selection and deployment in high school, 146–47; vary in teaching methods, 174–75; role in educational change, 191–92, 193, 196

teaching, individualized. See individualized teaching

team teaching: 13, 19, 21, 25, 33, 39, 46, 146–47, 158, 162, 208, 237, 238; at Fox Lane, 253, 254, 256; at Binford, 273–74, 282; at Ridgewood, 285, 288–90, 292

testing: in reading, 58; to learn student deficiencies, 132; for comparison with traditional programs, 200; at Binford, 277–80

tests: achievement, 40, 67, 140–41, 200, 277–80; intelligence, 40, 67, 278

textbooks: graded, 5; reading, 36–38, 55, 59–60; mathematics, 45; reliance on, criticized, 85–86; limitations of, in social science, 112; eliminated in nongraded high school, 140; not used at Binford, 180

Thornton, Mildred A., 221

Toklas, Alice, 295

Trump, J. Lloyd, 19, 284–85

tutorial groups, 162

UCLA Center for the Evaluation of Instruction, 60

unified arts program at Fox Lane, 256

University of Chicago High School, 10

U. S. Office of Education, 17–18

Utah: nongraded schools in, 207–208

variability. See individual differences

Ward, Dayton N., 174–75

Washburne, Carleton, 10, 11

Weaver, Fred, 34

Weise, D. F., 20

Weiser, Robert, 267

Western Springs, Ill.: first nongraded school in, 15

Wiles, Kimball, 49

Wilhelms, Fred T.: quoted, 220

Williams, Emmett, 124

Williams, Roger, 119

Winnetka Plan, 11–12

Wirt, William A., 12

Woodring, Paul, 18

writing school, 4

Zimmerman, Isa, 267